SACRED
SPACE

SACRED SPACE

The Prayer Book 2023

from the website www.sacredspace.ie

Prayer from the Irish Jesuits

LOYOLA PRESS.
A JESUIT MINISTRY
Chicago

LOYOLA PRESS.
A JESUIT MINISTRY
www.loyolapress.com

Copyright © by The Irish Jesuits 2022

This edition of *Sacred Space Prayer Book* is published by arrangement with Messenger
Publications, 37 Lower Leeson Street, Dublin D02 W938, Ireland.

Scripture quotations are from the *New Revised Standard Version Bible: Anglicised Catholic
Edition*, copyright © 1989, 1993 National Council of the Churches of Christ in the
United States of America. Used by permission. All rights reserved.

Loyola Press in Chicago thanks the Irish Jesuits and Messenger Press for preparing this
book for publication.

Cover art credit: beastfromeast/Digital Vision/Getty Images

ISBN-13: 978-0-8294-5533-5

Printed in the United States of America.
22 23 24 25 26 27 28 29 30 Lake Book 10 9 8 7 6 5 4 3 2 1

Contents

Sacred Space Prayer

Bless all who worship you, almighty God,
from the rising of the sun to its setting:
from your goodness enrich us,
by your love inspire us,
by your Spirit guide us,
by your power protect us,
in your mercy receive us,
now and always.

Preface

In 1999 an Irish Jesuit named Alan McGuckian had the simple – but at the time radical – idea of bringing daily prayer to the Internet. No one imagined that his experimental project would grow into a global community with volunteers translating the prayer experience into seventeen different languages.

Millions of people, from numerous Christian traditions, visit www .sacredspace.ie each year, and what they find is an invitation to step away from their busy routines for a few minutes a day to concentrate on what is really important in their lives. Sacred Space offers its visitors the opportunity to grow in prayerful awareness of their friendship with God.

Besides the daily prayer experience, Sacred Space also offers Living Space, with commentaries on the Scripture readings for each day's Catholic Mass. The Chapel of Intentions allows people to add their own prayers, while Pray with the Pope joins the community to the international Apostleship of Prayer. In addition, Sacred Space provides Lenten and Advent retreats, often in partnership with Pray as You Go, an audio prayer service from the British Jesuits.

The contents of this printed edition, first produced in 2004, are taken directly from our Internet site. Despite the increased use of Sacred Space on mobile devices, many people want a book they can hold and carry, and this book has proven especially helpful for prayer groups.

In 2014 the Irish Jesuits entered into an apostolic agreement with the Chicago-Detroit Jesuits, and Sacred Space now operates in partnership with Loyola Press.

I am delighted to bring you the *Sacred Space Prayer Book 2023*, and I pray that your prayer life will flourish with its help.

Yours in Christ
Paul Campbell SJ

Introduction to *Sacred Space: The Prayer Book 2023*

There would be no point learning from the greatest football coach in the world if you thought you already knew everything there is to know about football. In a similar way, we cannot learn how to pray unless we admit how little we actually know about praying. But if we are humble enough to acknowledge that 'we do not know how to pray as we ought' (Romans 8:26), the Spirit will help us in our weakness.

The Holy Spirit unites us with the prayer of Jesus, enabling us to cry out 'Abba, Father'. It is the Holy Spirit who helps us to see that all of Scripture speaks of Christ. The Bible is the book of the Holy Spirit, and *Sacred Space* is one way of opening this treasured text. Through our prayerful reflection upon the material of Sacred Space, the Holy Spirit who is in our hearts helps us to recognise the Holy Spirit who is speaking through the pages of the Bible. In fact, if we open ourselves to the Holy Spirit, he will make each of our lives into a marvellously creative book, for the glory of God the Father.

The Bible is an *inspiring* book. Because of the Holy Spirit, it is even more: it is an *inspired* book. This inspired and inspiring book did not fall down ready-made from heaven; it was not dictated by God to writers who copied everything they heard like robots. The marvel of the Bible is that there are two freedoms at work in it: the freedom of the human authors with all their individuality and idiosyncrasies, and the sovereign freedom of the divine author, God himself, working through the power of the Holy Spirit.

Sacred Space helps us to read the Bible in a deeper way so that we can receive it as the Word of God. To receive it in this profound way, it makes sense to read Scripture with both the help of the Holy Spirit who is its divine author, and the help of short commentaries, prayers and meditations, which open up its deeper layers of meaning.

Although people sometimes describe Christianity as a religion of the Book, in a deeper way it is a religion of the Word, a word that speaks to the core of our being. 'Indeed, the word of God is living and active, sharper than any two-edged sword, piercing until it divides soul from spirit, joints from marrow; it is able to judge the thoughts and intentions of the heart.' (Hebrews 4:12).

Sacred Space helps us to pray. But what is prayer? It is a cry of the heart and oxygen for the soul; it is a loving encounter with God. Fundamentally, prayer is our response to someone who has always desired us with an infinite love. *Sacred Space* opens up something of the beauty of this God of infinite love.

Prayer is at once simple and complicated. It is simple, because prayer is a matter of thinking of God while loving him. The simple truth is that God creates us and gives us life, a life we receive every morning when we wake up, a life we return to his hands on going to sleep each evening. Through prayer, we humbly enter into a relationship with this God who is already present within us, and who is always yearning for us.

But prayer is also complicated, and that's because we're complex. It takes a real effort to be simple, because we are weighed down by everything from anxiety about the future to worry about what others think of us. We have lost touch with immediacy and spontaneity. We need to become childlike once again: 'Truly I tell you, unless you change and become like children, you will never enter the kingdom of heaven' (Matthew 18:3).

Recognising that prayer is a gift will help us enter into its simplicity. Prayer is a gift because God is within us, and not in any old way, but as the Trinity. When we pray, we tune in to the infinitely loving relationship of the Father with the Son, an infinite love that is the Holy Spirit in person. Prayer is the powerful means God gives us to be present to his presence within. Moreover, with the help of prayer we come to realise that this God to whom we pray is also hidden in the hearts of our neighbours.

Sometimes it feels as though nothing is happening during prayer. But even if our time of prayer seems dry and empty, we often discover afterwards that we are more patient and loving as a result. Our experience is like that of Jacob in the Book of Genesis: 'Surely the Lord is in this place—and I did not know it!' (Genesis 28:16). Even though we won't always feel emotion when we pray, the Holy Spirit is in motion in all genuine prayer, making it bear fruit.

Lord, we praise you, because you speak to us and reveal yourself in our lives. May your Holy Spirit help us to hear your voice in the Bible, and guide us towards you, who are Lord for ever and ever. Amen.

Thomas G. Casey SJ

How to Use This Book

During each week of the liturgical year, begin by reading the section entitled 'Something to think and pray about each day this week'. Then proceed through 'The Presence of God', 'Freedom' and 'Consciousness' steps to prepare yourself to hear the word of God in your heart. In the next step, 'The Word', turn to the Scripture reading for each day of the week. Inspiration points are provided in case you need them. Then return to the 'Conversation' and 'Conclusion' steps. Use this process every day of the year.

The First Week of Advent
27 November–3 December 2022

Something to think and pray about each day this week:

Advent is a time when, as a Church, we journey together and realise our need for the Lord to save us. It is the same plea of the disciples to a sleeping Jesus on the storm-torn Sea of Galilee: 'Save us, Lord, we are going down' (Matthew 8:25). We all have our personal storms, where we tend to feel God is asleep in the middle of the messiness and mayhem of our lives. Our Church has been navigating a seemingly endless journey through choppy waters.

Advent enables us to see the present world as a signpost to a larger reality. Advent gives us a glimpse of hope amidst the ruins in our lives. Advent anticipates and waits for Christ's return, who pledges a solemn promise to free us from all that corrupts and defaces our personal and collective lives.

John Cullen,
Alert, Aware, Attentive: Advent Reflections

The Presence of God

'Be still, and know that I am God!' (Psalm 46:10) Lord, your words lead us to the calmness and greatness of your presence.

Freedom

I am free. When I look at these words in writing, they seem to create in me a feeling of awe. Yes, a wonderful feeling of freedom. Thank you, God.

Consciousness

At this moment, Lord, I turn my thoughts to you.
I will leave aside my chores and preoccupations.
I will take rest and refreshment in your presence, Lord.

The Word

The word of God comes down to us through the Scriptures. May the Holy Spirit enlighten my mind and my heart to respond to the gospel teachings.

(Please turn to the Scripture on the following pages. Inspiration points are there, should you need them. When you are ready, return here to continue.)

Conversation

Begin to talk with Jesus about the Scripture you have just read. What part of it strikes a chord in you? Perhaps the words of a friend – or some story you have heard recently – will slowly rise to the surface of your consciousness. If so, does the story throw light on what the Scripture passage may be trying to say to you?

Conclusion

Glory be to the Father, and to the Son, and to the Holy Spirit,
As it was in the beginning, is now and ever shall be,
World without end. Amen.

Sunday 27 November
First Sunday of Advent
Matthew 24:37–44

Jesus said, 'For as the days of Noah were, so will be the coming of the Son of Man. For as in those days before the flood they were eating and drinking, marrying and giving in marriage, until the day Noah entered the ark, and they knew nothing until the flood came and swept them all away, so too will be the coming of the Son of Man. Then two will be in the field; one will be taken and one will be left. Two women will be grinding meal together; one will be taken and one will be left. Keep awake therefore, for you do not know on what day your Lord is coming. But understand this: if the owner of the house had known in what part of the night the thief was coming, he would have stayed awake and would not have let his house be broken into. Therefore you also must be ready, for the Son of Man is coming at an unexpected hour.'

• Jesus is not asking us to stay awake all night, but to live in the present, so that we can recognise the Lord when he appears in our lives. He shows himself in the unrehearsed moments, the interruptions and accidents that can throw us off balance.

• Teach me, Lord, to recognise your face wherever I encounter you.

Monday 28 November
Matthew 8:5–11

When he entered Capernaum, a centurion came to him, appealing to him and saying, 'Lord, my servant is lying at home paralysed, in terrible distress.' And he said to him, 'I will come and cure him.' The centurion answered, 'Lord, I am not worthy to have you come under my roof; but only speak the word, and my servant will be healed. For I also am a man under authority, with soldiers under me; and I say to one, "Go", and he goes, and to another, "Come", and he comes, and to my slave, "Do this", and the slave does it.' When Jesus heard him, he was amazed and said to those who followed him, 'Truly I tell you, in no one in Israel have I found such faith. I tell you, many will come from east and west and will eat with Abraham and Isaac and Jacob in the kingdom of heaven.'

- The centurion interceded with Jesus on behalf of his servant, not himself. Who do I want to intercede for today?
- 'Lord, I am not worthy.' Do I ever feel that way? Do I ever feel I am getting more than I deserve? We live in a culture of entitlement, thinking we deserve to get everything on offer. How about me?

Tuesday 29 November
Luke 10:21–24

At that same hour Jesus rejoiced in the Holy Spirit and said, 'I thank you, Father, Lord of heaven and earth, because you have hidden these things from the wise and the intelligent and have revealed them to infants; yes, Father, for such was your gracious will. All things have been handed over to me by my Father; and no one knows who the Son is except the Father, or who the Father is except the Son and anyone to whom the Son chooses to reveal him.'

Then, turning to the disciples, Jesus said to them privately, 'Blessed are the eyes that see what you see! For I tell you that many prophets and kings desired to see what you see, but did not see it, and to hear what you hear, but did not hear it.'

- Gratitude was important in Jesus' life as he rejoiced in the Holy Spirit and gave thanks to the Father. Giving thanks is important in the lives of all who follow Jesus for all we have is gift (1 Corinthians 4:7). It is the humble who can receive and acknowledge gifts and be grateful. The self-sufficient are not open to it, as they do not experience the need of what Jesus offers.
- We need freedom to receive gifts as we often think we have to earn them or justify them. The invitation is to live the truth of who we are and who God is for us. During this time of prayer, what am I grateful for?

Wednesday 30 November
St Andrew, Apostle
Matthew 4:18–22

As he walked by the Sea of Galilee, he saw two brothers, Simon, who is called Peter, and Andrew his brother, casting a net into the lake – for they were fishermen. And he said to them, 'Follow me, and I will make you fish for people.' Immediately they left their nets and followed him. As he went from there, he saw two other brothers, James son of Zebedee and his brother John, in the boat with their father Zebedee, mending their nets, and he called them. Immediately they left the boat and their father, and followed him.

- 'Immediately they left their nets and followed him.' What an example is set for us by Peter, Andrew, James and John! There is no 'shortly', 'maybe tomorrow', 'I'm busy just now'.

- What nets do I need to leave in order to follow Jesus wholeheartedly? What obstacles, what material attachments, what comfort zones have wound themselves so tightly around me that I cannot get up and follow him?

Thursday 1 December
Matthew 7:21, 24–27

Jesus said, 'Not everyone who says to me, "Lord, Lord", will enter the kingdom of heaven, but only one who does the will of my Father in heaven.

'Everyone then who hears these words of mine and acts on them will be like a wise man who built his house on rock. The rain fell, the floods came, and the winds blew and beat on that house, but it did not fall, because it had been founded on rock. And everyone who hears these words of mine and does not act on them will be like a foolish man who built his house on sand. The rain fell, and the floods came, and the winds blew and beat against that house, and it fell – and great was its fall!'

- We all know that actions speak louder than words. We are told here that our eternal life depends upon our ability to act according to God's will. It is a stark message, but it is reassuring to know that our true efforts will reap their own rewards.

- I am challenged by Jesus to take time daily to reflect and discern the Father's will. Otherwise I will live a shallow life that will not survive the floods and storms of life.

Friday 2 December
Matthew 9:27–31

As Jesus went on from there, two blind men followed him, crying loudly, 'Have mercy on us, Son of David!' When he entered the house, the blind men came to him; and Jesus said to them, 'Do you believe that I am able to do this?' They said to him, 'Yes, Lord.' Then he touched their eyes and said, 'According to your faith let it be done to you.' And their eyes were opened. Then Jesus sternly ordered them, 'See that no one knows of this.' But they went away and spread the news about him throughout that district.

- Desire is important in life. I am guided by knowing what I want, and having energy to pursue it. The Lord has desires for me too. These desires can meet, as happened for the blind men. Their faith and their need brought them to Jesus. I am invited to do the same, recognising that Jesus can transform my desires to bring them into harmony with his own.

- What are my deepest desires and how influential are they in living as a follower of Jesus? I pray to be in touch with Jesus' desire for me, knowing that my blindness can get in the way.

Saturday 3 December
Matthew 9:35; 10:1, 5–8

Then Jesus went about all the cities and villages, teaching in their synagogues, and proclaiming the good news of the kingdom, and curing every disease and every sickness.

Then Jesus summoned his twelve disciples and gave them authority over unclean spirits, to cast them out, and to cure every disease and every sickness.

These twelve Jesus sent out with the following instructions: 'Go nowhere among the Gentiles, and enter no town of the Samaritans, but go rather to the lost sheep of the house of Israel. As you go, proclaim the good news, "The kingdom of heaven has come near." Cure the sick, raise the dead, cleanse the lepers, cast out demons. You received without payment; give without payment.'

- Do I know any people who are harassed and helpless like sheep without a shepherd? Let me hold them before my mind's eye for a moment. Can I now imagine Jesus looking at them? How does he see them?

- If I feel harassed and helpless, how does he see me? I ask for the grace to look on the world around me with the compassionate eyes of Jesus.

The Second Week of Advent
4–10 December 2022

Something to think and pray about each day this week:

It is possible to live a merely sentient existence, paying attention only to the immediate and being satisfied once the urgent, obvious appetites are met. It is hard to say how many manage to sustain this form of sleepwalking! In our better moments, we all know that this is wholly inadequate, even on a merely human level. We are all of us called to rise above mere existence and to live life abundantly (cf. John 10:10). In the faith, the Advent call is to wake up from our slumbers. *Metanoia* (conversion or repentance) means a whole change of mindset, going right down to the roots of our being. It's the only game in town. Of course it takes time, but the time is *now*.

Kieran J. O'Mahony OSA,
Hearers of the Word: Praying and Exploring the
Readings for Advent and Christmas

The Presence of God

'Come to me, all you that are weary and are carrying heavy burdens, and I will give you rest' (Matthew 11:28). Here I am, Lord. I come to seek your presence. I long for your healing power.

Freedom

'In these days, God taught me as a schoolteacher teaches a pupil' (St Ignatius).

I remind myself that there are things God has to teach me yet, and I ask for the grace to hear those things and let them change me.

Consciousness

Help me, Lord, to be more conscious of your presence. Teach me to recognise your presence in others.

Fill my heart with gratitude for the times your love has been shown to me through the care of others.

The Word

God speaks to each of us individually. I listen attentively to hear what he is saying to me. Read the text a few times, then listen.

(Please turn to the Scripture on the following pages. Inspiration points are there, should you need them. When you are ready, return here to continue.)

Conversation

Conversation requires talking and listening.

As I talk to Jesus, may I also learn to be still and listen.

I picture the gentleness in his eyes and the smile full of love as he gazes on me.

I can be totally honest with Jesus as I tell him of my worries and my cares.

I will open my heart to him as I tell him of my fears and my doubts.

I will ask him to help me place myself fully in his care and to abandon myself to him, knowing that he always wants what is best for me.

Conclusion

I thank God for these moments we have spent together and for any insights I have been given concerning the text.

Sunday 4 December
Second Sunday of Advent
Matthew 3:1–12

In those days John the Baptist appeared in the wilderness of Judea, proclaiming, 'Repent, for the kingdom of heaven has come near.' This is the one of whom the prophet Isaiah spoke when he said,

'The voice of one crying out in the wilderness:
"Prepare the way of the Lord,
make his paths straight."'

Now John wore clothing of camel's hair with a leather belt around his waist, and his food was locusts and wild honey. Then the people of Jerusalem and all Judea were going out to him, and all the region along the Jordan, and they were baptised by him in the river Jordan, confessing their sins.

But when he saw many Pharisees and Sadducees coming for baptism, he said to them, 'You brood of vipers! Who warned you to flee from the wrath to come? Bear fruit worthy of repentance. Do not presume to say to yourselves, "We have Abraham as our ancestor"; for I tell you, God is able from these stones to raise up children to Abraham. Even now the axe is lying at the root of the trees; every tree therefore that does not bear good fruit is cut down and thrown into the fire.

'I baptise you with water for repentance, but one who is more powerful than I is coming after me; I am not worthy to carry his sandals. He will baptise you with the Holy Spirit and fire. His winnowing-fork is in his hand, and he will clear his threshing-floor and will gather his wheat into the granary; but the chaff he will burn with unquenchable fire.'

- I may feel uncomfortable when confronted with John's call to repentance, but I let myself listen, acknowledging that I am a sinner in need of God's mercy. If I cannot admit this, Advent is not for me.

Monday 5 December
Luke 5:17–26

One day, while he was teaching, Pharisees and teachers of the law were sitting nearby (they had come from every village of Galilee and Judea and from Jerusalem); and the power of the Lord was with him to heal.

Just then some men came, carrying a paralysed man on a bed. They were trying to bring him in and lay him before Jesus; but finding no way to bring him in because of the crowd, they went up on the roof and let him down with his bed through the tiles into the middle of the crowd in front of Jesus. When he saw their faith, he said, 'Friend, your sins are forgiven you.' Then the scribes and the Pharisees began to question, 'Who is this who is speaking blasphemies? Who can forgive sins but God alone?' When Jesus perceived their questionings, he answered them, 'Why do you raise such questions in your hearts? Which is easier, to say, "Your sins are forgiven you", or to say, "Stand up and walk"? But so that you may know that the Son of Man has authority on earth to forgive sins' – he said to the one who was paralysed – 'I say to you, stand up and take your bed and go to your home.' Immediately he stood up before them, took what he had been lying on, and went to his home, glorifying God. Amazement seized all of them, and they glorified God and were filled with awe, saying, 'We have seen strange things today.'

- The paralysed man would not have been able to get to Jesus without the help of his friends. We need help also. Can I think of anyone who needs a helping hand from me?

Tuesday 6 December
Matthew 18:12–14

Jesus said, 'What do you think? If a shepherd has a hundred sheep, and one of them has gone astray, does he not leave the ninety-nine on the mountains and go in search of the one that went astray? And if he finds it, truly I tell you, he rejoices over it more than over the ninety-nine that never went astray. So it is not the will of your Father in heaven that one of these little ones should be lost.'

- Do I believe in the value of one? If each Christian helped even one person at a time, the world would be changed. But do I sometimes ignore both the ninety-nine – and also the one?

- If it is God's desire that none of the 'little ones' should be lost, that must be the desire of my heart also. To what 'little one' can I reach out today?

Wednesday 7 December
Matthew 11:28–30

Jesus said, 'Come to me, all you that are weary and are carrying heavy burdens, and I will give you rest. Take my yoke upon you, and learn from me; for I am gentle and humble in heart, and you will find rest for your souls. For my yoke is easy, and my burden is light.'

• This simple invitation goes straight to the heart. I spend time letting it echo within me, as I bring to Jesus all my weariness and heavy burdens, one by one.

• 'Learn from me; for I am gentle and humble in heart.' One of the most popular titles for Jesus in the Gospels was that of Rabbi, teacher. Here he invites us to learn from him: he describes himself as gentle and humble. Were these the two qualities he liked most about himself, where he wants us to be most like him? I pray to be a good student of this unique teacher.

Thursday 8 December
The Immaculate Conception of the Blessed Virgin Mary
Luke 1:26–38

In the sixth month the angel Gabriel was sent by God to a town in Galilee called Nazareth, to a virgin engaged to a man whose name was Joseph, of the house of David. The virgin's name was Mary. And he came to her and said, 'Greetings, favoured one! The Lord is with you.' But she was much perplexed by his words and pondered what sort of greeting this might be. The angel said to her, 'Do not be afraid, Mary, for you have found favour with God. And now, you will conceive in your womb and bear a son, and you will name him Jesus. He will be great, and will be called the Son of the Most High, and the Lord God will give to him the throne of his ancestor David. He will reign over the house of Jacob for ever, and of his kingdom there will be no end.' Mary said to the angel, 'How can this be, since I am a virgin?' The angel said to her, 'The Holy Spirit will come upon you, and the power of the Most High will overshadow you; therefore the child to be born will be holy; he will be called Son of God. And now, your relative Elizabeth in her old age has also conceived a son; and this is the sixth month for her who was said to be barren. For nothing will be impossible with God.' Then Mary said, 'Here am I, the servant of the Lord; let it be with me according to your word.' Then the angel departed from her.

- Let us consider today that, long before we were born, we are called by God to know, love and serve him. We have been the constant recipients of his blessings. Do we notice these in our daily lives? Do we take time to listen to the still small voice of God in our day?

Friday 9 December
Matthew 11:16–19

Jesus said, 'But to what will I compare this generation? It is like children sitting in the market-places and calling to one another,
  "We played the flute for you, and you did not dance;
  we wailed, and you did not mourn."
'For John came neither eating nor drinking, and they say, "He has a demon"; the Son of Man came eating and drinking, and they say, "Look, a glutton and a drunkard, a friend of tax-collectors and sinners!" Yet wisdom is vindicated by her deeds.'

- We live in a world with many prejudices. The person who says something can be taken as more important than what was said. There can be failure to acknowledge the context. While Jesus' life-style was very different from that of John, both were rejected. The hearers saw the difficulty as outside themselves, not within. They needed wisdom to be able to interpret the truth of the call to change.

- The Lord desires me to be free. I have my own prejudices. Where am I called to be more free of them? Who are the tax collectors and sinners that I am called to befriend? I ask the Lord for the freedom that opens me more fully to follow him more closely.

Saturday 10 December
Matthew 17:9–13

As they were coming down the mountain, Jesus ordered them, 'Tell no one about the vision until after the Son of Man has been raised from the dead.' And the disciples asked him, 'Why, then, do the scribes say that Elijah must come first?' He replied, 'Elijah is indeed coming and will restore all things; but I tell you that Elijah has already come, and they did not recognise him, but they did to him whatever they pleased. So also the Son of Man is about to suffer at their hands.' Then the disciples understood that he was speaking to them about John the Baptist.

- The desire for signs is a common experience. Elijah had been taken up in a whirlwind, so there was a belief that he would come again. John the Baptist was similar to Elijah in many ways – another fiery prophet. John was carrying the role of Elijah. Both suffered because of their teaching. Jesus as a prophet would face the same reality.

- There is a call to recognise who is truly prophetic and have the courage and conviction to follow that. How do I recognise false prophets at this time? I pray to be prophetic in living and sharing the Good News of Jesus' coming in our midst.

The Third Week of Advent
11–17 December 2022

Something to think and pray about each day this week:

Pope Francis says: 'There is no prayer in which Jesus does not inspire us to do something.' Our faith in Jesus is seen in strong action. The poor are helped at our pre-Christmas collections. We might ask not what we might get for Christmas, but how our Christmas might help others. We might ask that Christmas will be happy for others because of us – happy in body, with enough food for every family, happy in mind that we know the truth of God's coming into the world, and happy in forgiveness, as that is one of God's biggest gifts.

Donal Neary SJ,
Gospel Reflections for Sundays of Year A

The Presence of God

'I am standing at the door, knocking' (Revelation 3:20), says the Lord. What a wonderful privilege that the Lord of all creation desires to come to me. I welcome his presence.

Freedom

Leave me here freely all alone. / In cell where never sunlight shone. / Should no one ever speak to me. / This golden silence makes me free!
– Part of a poem written by a prisoner at Dachau concentration camp

Consciousness

How am I really feeling? Lighthearted? Heavy-hearted? I may be very much at peace, happy to be here. Equally, I may be frustrated, worried or angry.
I acknowledge how I really am. It is the real me whom the Lord loves.

The Word

I take my time to read the word of God slowly, a few times, allowing myself to dwell on anything that strikes me.
(Please turn to the Scripture on the following pages. Inspiration points are there, should you need them. When you are ready, return here to continue.)

Conversation

Do I notice myself reacting as I pray with the word of God? Do I feel challenged, comforted, angry? Imagining Jesus sitting or standing by me, I speak out my feelings, as one trusted friend to another.

Conclusion

Glory be to the Father, and to the Son, and to the Holy Spirit,
As it was in the beginning, is now and ever shall be,
World without end. Amen.

Sunday 11 December
Third Sunday of Advent
Matthew 11:2–11

When John heard in prison what the Messiah was doing, he sent word by his disciples and said to him, 'Are you the one who is to come, or are we to wait for another?' Jesus answered them, 'Go and tell John what you hear and see: the blind receive their sight, the lame walk, the lepers are cleansed, the deaf hear, the dead are raised, and the poor have good news brought to them. And blessed is anyone who takes no offence at me.'

As they went away, Jesus began to speak to the crowds about John: 'What did you go out into the wilderness to look at? A reed shaken by the wind? What then did you go out to see? Someone dressed in soft robes? Look, those who wear soft robes are in royal palaces. What then did you go out to see? A prophet? Yes, I tell you, and more than a prophet. This is the one about whom it is written,

"See, I am sending my messenger ahead of you,
who will prepare your way before you."

'Truly I tell you, among those born of women no one has arisen greater than John the Baptist; yet the least in the kingdom of heaven is greater than he.'

- God's ways are not our ways. God is not predictable. We must be alert to 'the signs of the times' and accept the fact that God seems to live easily with change, and enjoys doing 'new things' (Isaiah 48:6).

Monday 12 December
Luke 1:26–38

In the sixth month the angel Gabriel was sent by God to a town in Galilee called Nazareth, to a virgin engaged to a man whose name was Joseph, of the house of David. The virgin's name was Mary. And he came to her and said, 'Greetings, favoured one! The Lord is with you.' But she was much perplexed by his words and pondered what sort of greeting this might be. The angel said to her, 'Do not be afraid, Mary, for you have found favour with God. And now, you will conceive in your womb and bear a son, and you will name him Jesus. He will be great, and will be called the Son of the Most High, and the Lord God will give to him the throne of his ancestor David. He will reign over the house of Jacob for ever, and of his kingdom there will be no end.' Mary said to the angel, 'How can this be, since I am a virgin?' The angel said to her, 'The Holy Spirit will come upon you, and the power of the Most High will overshadow you; therefore the child to be born will be holy; he will be called Son of God. And now, your relative Elizabeth in her old age has also conceived a son; and this is the sixth month for her who was said to be barren. For nothing will be impossible with God.' Then Mary said, 'Here am I, the servant of the Lord; let it be with me according to your word.' Then the angel departed from her.

- Lord, when the silence seems heavy and impenetrable, I recall how it can be broken at the most unexpected times and in the most unexpected circumstances. Like Mary, I must be still enough to hear the voice and courageous enough to act on it.

Tuesday 13 December
Matthew 21:28–32

Jesus said to them, 'What do you think? A man had two sons; he went to the first and said, "Son, go and work in the vineyard today." He answered, "I will not"; but later he changed his mind and went. The father went to the second and said the same; and he answered, "I go, sir"; but he did not go. Which of the two did the will of his father?' They said, 'The first.' Jesus said to them, 'Truly I tell you, the tax-collectors and the prostitutes are going into the kingdom of God ahead of you. For John came to you in the way of righteousness and you did not believe him, but the tax-collectors and the prostitutes believed him; and even after you saw it, you did not change your minds and believe him.'

- This simple parable is turned into a fierce polemic against the chief priests and elders. This is understandable given their role in the Passion. Only in Luke's Gospel do we have the words of Jesus from the cross, 'Father, forgive them, they know not what they do.' How would that fit into Matthew's Gospel?

Wednesday 14 December
Luke 7:18–23

The disciples of John reported all these things to him. So John summoned two of his disciples and sent them to the Lord to ask, 'Are you the one who is to come, or are we to wait for another?' When the men had come to him, they said, 'John the Baptist has sent us to you to ask, "Are you the one who is to come, or are we to wait for another?"' Jesus had just then cured many people of diseases, plagues and evil spirits, and had given sight to many who were blind. And he answered them, 'Go and tell John what you have seen and heard: the blind receive their sight, the lame walk, the lepers are cleansed, the deaf hear, the dead are raised, the poor have good news brought to them. And blessed is anyone who takes no offence at me.'

- Lord, I can identify with John. I too find the wick of my lamp can quiver and splutter when things don't go my way. My desire for a world of peace and justice is met by a world of violence and injustice. This Advent day refill my inner lamp and let me walk in faith and trust.

Thursday 15 December
Luke 7:24–30

When John's messengers had gone, Jesus began to speak to the crowds about John: 'What did you go out into the wilderness to look at? A reed shaken by the wind? What then did you go out to see? Someone dressed in soft robes? Look, those who put on fine clothing and live in luxury are in royal palaces. What then did you go out to see? A prophet? Yes, I tell you, and more than a prophet. This is the one about whom it is written,

"See, I am sending my messenger ahead of you,

who will prepare your way before you."

'I tell you, among those born of women no one is greater than John; yet the least in the kingdom of God is greater than he.' (And all the people who heard this, including the tax-collectors, acknowledged the justice of God, because they had been baptised with John's baptism. But by refusing to be baptised by him, the Pharisees and the lawyers rejected God's purpose for themselves.)

- Jesus reminds the people of what they sought and found in John the Baptist: they did not search for some trivial reed or elegant courtesan but encountered a sign of God's presence. I take some time to recall and savour again the people who have helped me to discover God's ways.

Friday 16 December
John 5:33–36

Jesus said, 'You sent messengers to John, and he testified to the truth. Not that I accept such human testimony, but I say these things so that you may be saved. He was a burning and shining lamp, and you were willing to rejoice for a while in his light. But I have a testimony greater than John's. The works that the Father has given me to complete, the very works that I am doing, testify on my behalf that the Father has sent me.'

- Jesus is clear about his mission – it comes from the Father. My mission is clear too: God wants me to live out of unconditional love. But do I want this mission? I talk with Jesus about this.

Saturday 17 December
Matthew 1:1–17

An account of the genealogy of Jesus the Messiah, the son of David, the son of Abraham.

Abraham was the father of Isaac, and Isaac the father of Jacob, and Jacob the father of Judah and his brothers, and Judah the father of Perez and Zerah by Tamar, and Perez the father of Hezron, and Hezron the father of Aram, and Aram the father of Aminadab, and Aminadab the father of Nahshon, and Nahshon the father of Salmon, and Salmon the father of Boaz by Rahab, and Boaz the father of Obed by Ruth, and Obed the father of Jesse, and Jesse the father of King David.

And David was the father of Solomon by the wife of Uriah, and Solomon the father of Rehoboam, and Rehoboam the father of Abijah, and Abijah the father of Asaph, and Asaph the father of Jehoshaphat, and Jehoshaphat the father of Joram, and Joram the father of Uzziah, and Uzziah the father of Jotham, and Jotham the father of Ahaz, and Ahaz the father of Hezekiah, and Hezekiah the father of Manasseh, and Manasseh the father of Amos, and Amos the father of Josiah, and Josiah the father of Jechoniah and his brothers, at the time of the deportation to Babylon.

And after the deportation to Babylon: Jechoniah was the father of Salathiel, and Salathiel the father of Zerubbabel, and Zerubbabel the father of Abiud, and Abiud the father of Eliakim, and Eliakim the father of Azor, and Azor the father of Zadok, and Zadok the father of Achim, and

Achim the father of Eliud, and Eliud the father of Eleazar, and Eleazar the father of Matthan, and Matthan the father of Jacob, and Jacob the father of Joseph the husband of Mary, of whom Jesus was born, who is called the Messiah.

So all the generations from Abraham to David are fourteen generations; and from David to the deportation to Babylon, fourteen generations; and from the deportation to Babylon to the Messiah, fourteen generations.

- There are surprises in this list of Jesus' ancestors. Matthew's genealogy is revolutionary for his time, in that it features five women. In addition, four of the women were Gentiles. Add to that the presence of some notable sinners, like Judah and King David, and the intention is clear. It is to highlight the inclusivity of Jesus' mission.

The Fourth Week of Advent
18–24 December 2022

Something to think and pray about each day this week:

The text from a friend said that he wasn't sending Christmas cards but wanted to wish me peace and blessings at this special time. I called him back and asked if he was getting mean in his old age. I continued to joke with him for a little while and then he said, 'You mustn't have heard that my mother died.' I hadn't. He told me his mother had been diagnosed with cancer and died shortly after the diagnosis was given. I told him I'd not heard and of course he knew that because, had I heard, I'd have been there for him over those December days.

As we enter the final days of Advent, maybe we could remember him and how easy it is not to hear news. Gossip is all around us and seems to blow easily on the wind – easily and dangerously – but often the news we need to hear passes by unheard or untold. I wondered does God feel that way sometimes, not least around Christmas, and wondered how it is that this story, this very sacred story, can remain unheard and untold.

Vincent Sherlock,
Let Advent be Advent

The Presence of God

'Be still, and know that I am God!' (Psalm 46:10) Lord, may your spirit guide me to seek your loving presence more and more for it is there I find rest and refreshment from this busy world.

Freedom

By God's grace I was born to live in freedom. Free to enjoy the pleasures he created for me. Dear Lord, grant that I may live as you intended, with complete confidence in your loving care.

Consciousness

How am I today?
Where am I with God? With others?
Do I have something to be grateful for? Then I give thanks.
Is there something I am sorry for? Then I ask forgiveness.

The Word

God speaks to each of us individually. I need to listen, to hear what he is saying to me. Read the text a few times, then listen.
(Please turn to the Scripture on the following pages. Inspiration points are there, should you need them. When you are ready, return here to continue.)

Conversation

How has God's word moved me? Has it left me cold?
Has it consoled me or moved me to act in a new way?
I imagine Jesus standing or sitting beside me.
I turn and share my feelings with him.

Conclusion

I thank God for these moments we have spent together and for any insights I have been given concerning the text.

Sunday 18 December
Fourth Sunday of Advent
Matthew 1:18–24

Now the birth of Jesus the Messiah took place in this way. When his mother Mary had been engaged to Joseph, but before they lived together, she was found to be with child from the Holy Spirit. Her husband Joseph, being a righteous man and unwilling to expose her to public disgrace, planned to dismiss her quietly. But just when he had resolved to do this, an angel of the Lord appeared to him in a dream and said, 'Joseph, son of David, do not be afraid to take Mary as your wife, for the child conceived in her is from the Holy Spirit. She will bear a son, and you are to name him Jesus, for he will save his people from their sins.' All this took place to fulfil what had been spoken by the Lord through the prophet:

> 'Look, the virgin shall conceive and bear a son,
>   and they shall name him Emmanuel',

which means, 'God is with us.' When Joseph awoke from sleep, he did as the angel of the Lord commanded him; he took her as his wife.

• We are invited to take our challenging situations to the Lord in trust. God's surprising ways are revealed to Mary and to Joseph. Joseph, the righteous man, gives me a message on how to accept Jesus as Saviour. Lord, help me see the surprising ways in which you reveal yourself to me now.

Monday 19 December
Luke 1:5–25

In the days of King Herod of Judea, there was a priest named Zechariah, who belonged to the priestly order of Abijah. His wife was a descendant of Aaron, and her name was Elizabeth. Both of them were righteous before God, living blamelessly according to all the commandments and regulations of the Lord. But they had no children, because Elizabeth was barren, and both were getting on in years.

Once when he was serving as priest before God and his section was on duty, he was chosen by lot, according to the custom of the priesthood, to enter the sanctuary of the Lord and offer incense. Now at the time of the incense-offering, the whole assembly of the people was praying outside.

Then there appeared to him an angel of the Lord, standing at the right side of the altar of incense. When Zechariah saw him, he was terrified; and fear overwhelmed him. But the angel said to him, 'Do not be afraid, Zechariah, for your prayer has been heard. Your wife Elizabeth will bear you a son, and you will name him John. You will have joy and gladness, and many will rejoice at his birth, for he will be great in the sight of the Lord. He must never drink wine or strong drink; even before his birth he will be filled with the Holy Spirit. He will turn many of the people of Israel to the Lord their God. With the spirit and power of Elijah he will go before him, to turn the hearts of parents to their children, and the disobedient to the wisdom of the righteous, to make ready a people prepared for the Lord.' Zechariah said to the angel, 'How will I know that this is so? For I am an old man, and my wife is getting on in years.' The angel replied, 'I am Gabriel. I stand in the presence of God, and I have been sent to speak to you and to bring you this good news. But now, because you did not believe my words, which will be fulfilled in their time, you will become mute, unable to speak, until the day these things occur.'

Meanwhile, the people were waiting for Zechariah, and wondered at his delay in the sanctuary. When he did come out, he could not speak to them, and they realised that he had seen a vision in the sanctuary. He kept motioning to them and remained unable to speak. When his time of service was ended, he went to his home.

After those days his wife Elizabeth conceived, and for five months she remained in seclusion. She said, 'This is what the Lord has done for me when he looked favourably on me and took away the disgrace I have endured among my people.'

• Zechariah and Elizabeth were not expecting these amazing things to happen to them; they were simply ordinary pious Jews living according to the Law. The things that happen in our lives are normally undramatic but just as much a part of God's plan.

Tuesday 20 December
Luke 1:26–38

In the sixth month the angel Gabriel was sent by God to a town in Galilee called Nazareth, to a virgin engaged to a man whose name was Joseph, of the house of David. The virgin's name was Mary. And he came to her and said, 'Greetings, favoured one! The Lord is with you.' But she was much perplexed by his words and pondered what sort of greeting this might be. The angel said to her, 'Do not be afraid, Mary, for you have found favour with God. And now, you will conceive in your womb and bear a son, and you will name him Jesus. He will be great, and will be called the Son of the Most High, and the Lord God will give to him the throne of his ancestor David. He will reign over the house of Jacob for ever, and of his kingdom there will be no end.' Mary said to the angel, 'How can this be, since I am a virgin?' The angel said to her, 'The Holy Spirit will come upon you, and the power of the Most High will overshadow you; therefore the child to be born will be holy; he will be called Son of God. And now, your relative Elizabeth in her old age has also conceived a son; and this is the sixth month for her who was said to be barren. For nothing will be impossible with God.' Then Mary said, 'Here am I, the servant of the Lord; let it be with me according to your word.' Then the angel departed from her.

- Nothing is impossible to God! In difficult times, it is good to remember that God is fully in charge of our world. Everything happens according to his plan. There is always hope.

Wednesday 21 December
Luke 1:39–45

In those days Mary set out and went with haste to a Judean town in the hill country, where she entered the house of Zechariah and greeted Elizabeth. When Elizabeth heard Mary's greeting, the child leapt in her womb. And Elizabeth was filled with the Holy Spirit and exclaimed with a loud cry, 'Blessed are you among women, and blessed is the fruit of your womb. And why has this happened to me, that the mother of my Lord comes to me? For as soon as I heard the sound of your greeting, the child in my womb leapt for joy. And blessed is she who believed that there would be a fulfilment of what was spoken to her by the Lord.'

- Mary brought God to Elizabeth in her heart and in her womb. We bring God to everyone we meet, and everyone we meet brings God to us.

Thursday 22 December

Luke 1:46–56

And Mary said,

'My soul magnifies the Lord,
   and my spirit rejoices in God my Saviour,
for he has looked with favour on the lowliness of his servant.
   Surely, from now on all generations will call me blessed;
for the Mighty One has done great things for me,
   and holy is his name.
His mercy is for those who fear him
   from generation to generation.
He has shown strength with his arm;
   he has scattered the proud in the thoughts of their hearts.
He has brought down the powerful from their thrones,
   and lifted up the lowly;
he has filled the hungry with good things,
   and sent the rich away empty.
He has helped his servant Israel,
   in remembrance of his mercy,
according to the promise he made to our ancestors,
   to Abraham and to his descendants for ever.'

And Mary remained with her for about three months and then returned to her home.

- Mary prayed her own Magnificat. She is full of praise. Her grateful heart overflows with thanksgiving. God is the great one in her life, working marvels beyond all imagining.

- Can I write my own Magnificat today? For what do I want to give thanks? Meister Eckhart wrote, 'If the only prayer we ever say is thanks, that will suffice.'

Friday 23 December

Luke 1:57–66

Now the time came for Elizabeth to give birth, and she bore a son. Her neighbours and relatives heard that the Lord had shown his great mercy to her, and they rejoiced with her.

On the eighth day they came to circumcise the child, and they were going to name him Zechariah after his father. But his mother said, 'No; he is to be called John.' They said to her, 'None of your relatives has this name.' Then they began motioning to his father to find out what name he wanted to give him. He asked for a writing-tablet and wrote, 'His name is John.' And all of them were amazed. Immediately his mouth was opened and his tongue freed, and he began to speak, praising God. Fear came over all their neighbours, and all these things were talked about throughout the entire hill country of Judea. All who heard them pondered them and said, 'What then will this child become?' For, indeed, the hand of the Lord was with him.

- Lord, praise, amazement and joy are hallmarks of a life rooted in you. Fill me with these gifts. Enable me to be a tracer of your grace in my life and to lift up my voice in joyful thanksgiving.

Saturday 24 December
Luke 1:67–79

Then his father Zechariah was filled with the Holy Spirit and spoke this prophecy:

'Blessed be the Lord God of Israel,
> for he has looked favourably on his people and redeemed them.
He has raised up a mighty saviour for us
> in the house of his servant David,
as he spoke through the mouth of his holy prophets from of old,
> that we would be saved from our enemies and from the hand of
> all who hate us.
Thus he has shown the mercy promised to our ancestors,
> and has remembered his holy covenant,
the oath that he swore to our ancestor Abraham,
> to grant us that we, being rescued from the hands of our
> enemies,
might serve him without fear, in holiness and righteousness
> before him all our days.
And you, child, will be called the prophet of the Most High;
> for you will go before the Lord to prepare his ways,
to give knowledge of salvation to his people

by the forgiveness of their sins.
By the tender mercy of our God,
 the dawn from on high will break upon us,
to give light to those who sit in darkness and in the shadow of
 death,
 to guide our feet into the way of peace.'

- God has come to rescue his people as he promised long ago. The promise still holds for us. Whatever trouble we may be in, God is coming to save us and we can be at peace.

The First Week of Christmas
25–31 December 2022

Something to think and pray about each day this week:

Most homes have a crib of some sort; it is part of our Christmas. It brings the mystery of the birth of Jesus into our homes. Some church cribs have an open front – a sign that all are welcome. Many people feel unwelcome in the Church – people in second and other relationships that cause questions, people who have been through crime or in prison, people in addiction, families who feel the worse for what some family members have done, people of homosexual orientation, former priests and religious. Like the shepherds at the first crib, all are welcome. The Church welcomes all at this time of the year and, indeed, always. May we welcome all as God does, with the compassion and love of God?

Christmas reminds us to deal with each other in love and compassion. Someone was very harsh on someone when speaking to me recently. I just said, 'God loves him, and I would prefer to be with God on this one'. Just as we take a while to know the full story of Jesus, we take a while to know the full story of everyone.

Donal Neary SJ,
Gospel Reflections for Sundays of Year A

The Presence of God

As I sit here, the beating of my heart,
the ebb and flow of my breathing, the movements of my mind
are all signs of God's ongoing creation of me.
I pause for a moment and become aware
of this presence of God within me.

Freedom

Everything has the potential to draw from me a fuller love and life.
Yet my desires are often fixed, caught, on illusions of fulfilment.
I ask that God, through my freedom, may orchestrate my desires in a vibrant loving melody rich in harmony.

Consciousness

I ask, how am I within myself today? Am I particularly tired, stressed or off-form? If any of these characteristics apply, can I try to let go of the concerns that disturb me?

The Word

I read the word of God slowly, a few times over, and I listen to what God is saying to me.

(Please turn to the Scripture on the following pages. Inspiration points are there, should you need them. When you are ready, return here to continue.)

Conversation

I begin to talk with Jesus about the Scripture I have just read. What part of it strikes a chord in me? Perhaps the words of a friend or a story I have heard recently will slowly rise to the surface of my consciousness. If so, does the story throw light on what the Scripture passage may be trying to say to me?

Conclusion

Glory be to the Father, and to the Son, and to the Holy Spirit,
As it was in the beginning, is now and ever shall be,
World without end. Amen.

Sunday 25 December
The Nativity of the Lord
John 1:1–18

In the beginning was the Word, and the Word was with God, and the Word was God. He was in the beginning with God. All things came into being through him, and without him not one thing came into being. What has come into being in him was life, and the life was the light of all people. The light shines in the darkness, and the darkness did not overcome it.

There was a man sent from God, whose name was John. He came as a witness to testify to the light, so that all might believe through him. He himself was not the light, but he came to testify to the light. The true light, which enlightens everyone, was coming into the world.

He was in the world, and the world came into being through him; yet the world did not know him. He came to what was his own, and his own people did not accept him. But to all who received him, who believed in his name, he gave power to become children of God, who were born, not of blood or of the will of the flesh or of the will of man, but of God.

And the Word became flesh and lived among us, and we have seen his glory, the glory as of a father's only son, full of grace and truth. (John testified to him and cried out, 'This was he of whom I said, "He who comes after me ranks ahead of me because he was before me."') From his fullness we have all received, grace upon grace. The law indeed was given through Moses; grace and truth came through Jesus Christ. No one has ever seen God. It is God the only Son, who is close to the Father's heart, who has made him known.

- Jesus is God's greatest gift to us. Prayer today can rest in the mystery of God, who is revealed to us in the coming of Jesus. From the beginning he was a sign to be rejected. Jesus desires to be at home with us and desires us to be at home with him. We pray to have room in our hearts and lives for him.

Monday 26 December
St Stephen, the First Martyr
Matthew 10:17–22

Jesus said to his disciples, 'Beware of them, for they will hand you over to councils and flog you in their synagogues; and you will be dragged before governors and kings because of me, as a testimony to them and the Gentiles. When they hand you over, do not worry about how you are to speak or what you are to say; for what you are to say will be given to you at that time; for it is not you who speak, but the Spirit of your Father speaking through you. Brother will betray brother to death, and a father his child, and children will rise against parents and have them put to death; and you will be hated by all because of my name. But the one who endures to the end will be saved.'

* It can seem strange to celebrate St Stephen, who was martyred, right after Christmas Day when our dominant emotion is joy in the birth of Christ. The point, however, is that this is why Christ came on earth, to save us from our sins by his death on the Cross.

Tuesday 27 December
St John, Apostle and Evangelist
John 20:1–8

Early on the first day of the week, while it was still dark, Mary Magdalene came to the tomb and saw that the stone had been removed from the tomb. So she ran and went to Simon Peter and the other disciple, the one whom Jesus loved, and said to them, 'They have taken the Lord out of the tomb, and we do not know where they have laid him.' Then Peter and the other disciple set out and went towards the tomb. The two were running together, but the other disciple outran Peter and reached the tomb first. He bent down to look in and saw the linen wrappings lying there, but he did not go in. Then Simon Peter came, following him, and went into the tomb. He saw the linen wrappings lying there, and the cloth that had been on Jesus' head, not lying with the linen wrappings but rolled up in a place by itself. Then the other disciple, who reached the tomb first, also went in, and he saw and believed.

* John saw and he believed. Blessed are those who have not seen and yet believe. That's us. Lord, help my unbelief.

Wednesday 28 December
Matthew 2:13–18

Now after they had left, an angel of the Lord appeared to Joseph in a dream and said, 'Get up, take the child and his mother, and flee to Egypt, and remain there until I tell you; for Herod is about to search for the child, to destroy him.' Then Joseph got up, took the child and his mother by night, and went to Egypt, and remained there until the death of Herod. This was to fulfil what had been spoken by the Lord through the prophet, 'Out of Egypt I have called my son.'

When Herod saw that he had been tricked by the wise men, he was infuriated, and he sent and killed all the children in and around Bethlehem who were two years old or under, according to the time that he had learned from the wise men. Then was fulfilled what had been spoken through the prophet Jeremiah:

> 'A voice was heard in Ramah,
>> wailing and loud lamentation,
> Rachel weeping for her children;
>> she refused to be consoled, because they are no more.'

- The persecution of Christians for their faith continues in our world today. Let us remember our brothers and sisters who are suffering and pray for them.

Thursday 29 December
Luke 2:22–35

When the time came for their purification according to the law of Moses, they brought him up to Jerusalem to present him to the Lord (as it is written in the law of the Lord, 'Every firstborn male shall be designated as holy to the Lord'), and they offered a sacrifice according to what is stated in the law of the Lord, 'a pair of turtle-doves or two young pigeons.'

Now there was a man in Jerusalem whose name was Simeon; this man was righteous and devout, looking forward to the consolation of Israel, and the Holy Spirit rested on him. It had been revealed to him by the Holy Spirit that he would not see death before he had seen the Lord's Messiah. Guided by the Spirit, Simeon came into the temple; and when the parents brought in the child Jesus, to do for him what was customary under the law, Simeon took him in his arms and praised God, saying,

> 'Master, now you are dismissing your servant in peace,
>> according to your word;
> for my eyes have seen your salvation,

which you have prepared in the presence of all peoples,
  a light for revelation to the Gentiles
    and for glory to your people Israel.'

And the child's father and mother were amazed at what was being said about him. Then Simeon blessed them and said to his mother Mary, 'This child is destined for the falling and the rising of many in Israel, and to be a sign that will be opposed so that the inner thoughts of many will be revealed – and a sword will pierce your own soul too.'

- Simeon recognised Jesus as 'a light for revelation to the Gentiles', and so for us. We in turn are to be a light for revelation to all those who have not yet accepted Jesus as the light of their lives.

Friday 30 December
The Holy Family of Jesus, Mary and Joseph
Matthew 2:13–15, 19–23

Now after they had left, an angel of the Lord appeared to Joseph in a dream and said, 'Get up, take the child and his mother, and flee to Egypt, and remain there until I tell you; for Herod is about to search for the child, to destroy him.' Then Joseph got up, took the child and his mother by night, and went to Egypt, and remained there until the death of Herod. This was to fulfil what had been spoken by the Lord through the prophet, 'Out of Egypt I have called my son.'

When Herod died, an angel of the Lord suddenly appeared in a dream to Joseph in Egypt and said, 'Get up, take the child and his mother, and go to the land of Israel, for those who were seeking the child's life are dead.' Then Joseph got up, took the child and his mother, and went to the land of Israel. But when he heard that Archelaus was ruling over Judea in place of his father Herod, he was afraid to go there. And after being warned in a dream, he went away to the district of Galilee. There he made his home in a town called Nazareth, so that what had been spoken through the prophets might be fulfilled, 'He will be called a Nazorean.'

- The angels are delivering messages from God throughout the infancy narratives. We might think of our own guardian angel, whose role is 'to light, to guard, to rule and to guide' us.

Saturday 31 December
John 1:1–18

In the beginning was the Word, and the Word was with God, and the Word was God. He was in the beginning with God. All things came into being through him, and without him not one thing came into being. What has come into being in him was life, and the life was the light of all people. The light shines in the darkness, and the darkness did not overcome it.

There was a man sent from God, whose name was John. He came as a witness to testify to the light, so that all might believe through him. He himself was not the light, but he came to testify to the light. The true light, which enlightens everyone, was coming into the world.

He was in the world, and the world came into being through him; yet the world did not know him. He came to what was his own, and his own people did not accept him. But to all who received him, who believed in his name, he gave power to become children of God, who were born, not of blood or of the will of the flesh or of the will of man, but of God.

And the Word became flesh and lived among us, and we have seen his glory, the glory as of a father's only son, full of grace and truth. (John testified to him and cried out, 'This was he of whom I said, "He who comes after me ranks ahead of me because he was before me."') From his fullness we have all received, grace upon grace. The law indeed was given through Moses; grace and truth came through Jesus Christ. No one has ever seen God. It is God the only Son, who is close to the Father's heart, who has made him known.

- As our year draws to a close, today's scripture brings us back to the beginning of all time. As we stand on the threshold of another year, we take time to recall the greatest event of all: God has entered our world, not just for a day's visit, but has made it his permanent dwelling.

The Second Week of Christmas
1–7 January 2023

Something to think and pray about each day this week:

The beginning of a new year is an especially appropriate time to hear Jesus' question, 'What do you want?' as a question that is addressed to each of us personally. Jesus' second set of words in John's Gospel, again addressed to the disciples of John the Baptist, takes the form of an invitation, 'Come and see'. The question and the invitation very much go together. As we become aware of what it is we really want, we sense a call to set out on a journey towards the Lord as the one who alone can fully satisfy those deep hungers and thirsts in our hearts. The beginning of a new year is a good moment for us to get in touch with our deepest desire to see the Lord, and then to move closer to him, to grow in our relationship with him, so that we come to see and know him as he sees and knows us. We might allow both the question and the invitation of Jesus to resonate within us as we set out into the year that beckons.

Martin Hogan,
The Word of God Is Living and Active

The Presence of God
Dear Jesus, I come to you today longing for your presence. I desire to love you as you love me. May nothing ever separate me from you.

Freedom
Lord, grant me the grace to be free from the excesses of this life. Let me not get caught up with the desire for wealth. Keep my heart and mind free to love and serve you.

Consciousness
Where do I sense hope, encouragement and growth in my life? By looking back over the past few months, I may be able to see which activities and occasions have produced rich fruit. If I do notice such areas, I will determine to give those areas both time and space in the future.

The Word
God speaks to each of us individually. I listen attentively to hear what he is saying to me. Read the text a few times, then listen.
(Please turn to the Scripture on the following pages. Inspiration points are there, should you need them. When you are ready, return here to continue.)

Conversation
What is stirring in me as I pray? Am I consoled, troubled, left cold? I imagine Jesus standing or sitting at my side, and I share my feelings with him.

Conclusion
Glory be to the Father, and to the Son, and to the Holy Spirit,
As it was in the beginning, is now and ever shall be,
World without end. Amen.

Sunday 1 January
Mary, The Mother of God
Luke 2:16–21

So they went with haste and found Mary and Joseph, and the child lying in the manger. When they saw this, they made known what had been told them about this child; and all who heard it were amazed at what the shepherds told them. But Mary treasured all these words and pondered them in her heart. The shepherds returned, glorifying and praising God for all they had heard and seen, as it had been told them.

After eight days had passed, it was time to circumcise the child; and he was called Jesus, the name given by the angel before he was conceived in the womb.

• Mary had a unique relationship with the Blessed Trinity as daughter of the Father, mother of the Son, and spouse of the Holy Spirit. She was 'full of grace', not only for being chosen to be God's mother but in her total openness to be filled with that love of God.

• We too are constantly 'graced' and can live out of this grace more fully by opening to the call of God as it unfolds in the unique circumstances of our own lives each day.

Monday 2 January
John 1:19–28

This is the testimony given by John when the Jews sent priests and Levites from Jerusalem to ask him, 'Who are you?' He confessed and did not deny it, but confessed, 'I am not the Messiah.' And they asked him, 'What then? Are you Elijah?' He said, 'I am not.' 'Are you the prophet?' He answered, 'No.' Then they said to him, 'Who are you? Let us have an answer for those who sent us. What do you say about yourself?' He said,

> 'I am the voice of one crying out in the wilderness,
> "Make straight the way of the Lord",'
> as the prophet Isaiah said.

Now they had been sent from the Pharisees. They asked him, 'Why then are you baptising if you are neither the Messiah, nor Elijah, nor the prophet?' John answered them, 'I baptise with water. Among you stands one whom you do not know, the one who is coming after me; I am not worthy to untie the thong of his sandal.' This took place in Bethany across the Jordan where John was baptising.

• In the gospel John the Baptist deflects attention from himself onto Christ. John's role is to 'make straight the way of the Lord' and then to step aside. John represents what all Christians are called to be: witnesses to Christ, heralds of the Good News. Do you see yourself as a witness and a herald?

Tuesday 3 January
John 1:29–34

The next day he saw Jesus coming towards him and declared, 'Here is the Lamb of God who takes away the sin of the world! This is he of whom I said, "After me comes a man who ranks ahead of me because he was before me." I myself did not know him; but I came baptising with water for this reason, that he might be revealed to Israel.' And John testified, 'I saw the Spirit descending from heaven like a dove, and it remained on him. I myself did not know him, but the one who sent me to baptise with water said to me, "He on whom you see the Spirit descend and remain is the one who baptises with the Holy Spirit." And I myself have seen and have testified that this is the Son of God.'

• 'I saw the spirit descending from heaven.' Each one of us has also received the same Spirit in our baptism. It was that Spirit which inspired Jesus in all his work. May the same Spirit inspire us to follow in Jesus' footsteps and join with him in his work to build the kingdom.

Wednesday 4 January
John 1:35–42

The next day John again was standing with two of his disciples, and as he watched Jesus walk by, he exclaimed, 'Look, here is the Lamb of God!' The two disciples heard him say this, and they followed Jesus. When Jesus turned and saw them following, he said to them, 'What are you looking for?' They said to him, 'Rabbi' (which translated means Teacher), 'where are you staying?' He said to them, 'Come and see.' They came and saw where he was staying, and they remained with him that day. It was about four o'clock in the afternoon. One of the two who heard John speak and followed him was Andrew, Simon Peter's brother. He first found his brother Simon and said to him, 'We have found the Messiah' (which is translated Anointed). He brought Simon to Jesus, who looked at him and said, 'You are Simon son of John. You are to be called Cephas' (which is translated Peter).

• The author of a play takes great care with the first words spoken by the main protagonist. These words must grab our attention and they usually reveal something of that person's character. Here we read the first words spoken by Jesus in the Gospel of John. They are not a teaching, a precept or a challenge (as we might expect), but a simple question: 'What are you looking for?', or 'What do you want?' Jesus asks about our desires so that he can respond to them.

Thursday 5 January
John 1:43–51

The next day Jesus decided to go to Galilee. He found Philip and said to him, 'Follow me.' Now Philip was from Bethsaida, the city of Andrew and Peter. Philip found Nathanael and said to him, 'We have found him about whom Moses in the law and also the prophets wrote, Jesus son of Joseph from Nazareth.' Nathanael said to him, 'Can anything good come out of Nazareth?' Philip said to him, 'Come and see.' When Jesus saw Nathanael coming towards him, he said of him, 'Here is truly an Israelite in whom there is no deceit!' Nathanael asked him, 'Where did you come to know me?' Jesus answered, 'I saw you under the fig tree before Philip called you.' Nathanael replied, 'Rabbi, you are the Son of God! You are the King of Israel!' Jesus answered, 'Do you believe because I told you that I saw you under the fig tree? You will see greater things than these.' And he said to him, 'Very truly, I tell you, you will see heaven opened and the angels of God ascending and descending upon the Son of Man.'

• The Lord communicates with us in many ways. Sometimes it may seem direct and unambiguous, at other times more indirect, as when the call is mediated by other people. Can you name men and women in your life who brought you to Jesus (as Philip brought Nathanael), or who made you aware of what Jesus was asking of you? Have you been grateful for these mediators?

Friday 6 January
The Epiphany of the Lord (Ireland) – see entry for
Sunday 8 January
Mark 1:7–11

John proclaimed, 'The one who is more powerful than I is coming after me; I am not worthy to stoop down and untie the thong of his sandals. I have baptised you with water; but he will baptise you with the Holy Spirit.'

In those days Jesus came from Nazareth of Galilee and was baptised by John in the Jordan. And just as he was coming up out of the water, he saw the heavens torn apart and the Spirit descending like a dove on him. And a voice came from heaven, 'You are my Son, the Beloved; with you I am well pleased.'

- Imagine yourself witnessing the scene, perhaps standing in the shallows, the water flowing around your ankles. Picture the scene and allow it to unfold. What is it like? The young man from Nazareth joins the queue waiting for John's baptism: a symbol of purifying but also of birth – coming up out of the waters of the womb into a new life as God's beloved child.

- Lord, when I realise that you love me, and are well pleased with me, it is like the start of a new life. As I hear your voice, I know that I have a purpose and a destiny.

Saturday 7 January
John 2:1–11

On the third day there was a wedding in Cana of Galilee, and the mother of Jesus was there. Jesus and his disciples had also been invited to the wedding. When the wine gave out, the mother of Jesus said to him, 'They have no wine.' And Jesus said to her, 'Woman, what concern is that to you and to me? My hour has not yet come.' His mother said to the servants, 'Do whatever he tells you.' Now standing there were six stone water-jars for the Jewish rites of purification, each holding twenty or thirty gallons. Jesus said to them, 'Fill the jars with water.' And they filled them up to the brim. He said to them, 'Now draw some out, and take it to the chief steward.' So they took it. When the steward tasted the water that had become wine, and did not know where it came from (though the servants who had drawn the water knew), the steward called the bridegroom and said to him, 'Everyone serves the good wine first, and then the inferior wine after the guests have become drunk. But you have kept the good wine until now.' Jesus did this, the first of his signs, in Cana of Galilee, and revealed his glory; and his disciples believed in him.

- It is through the Christian community that Jesus comes to us. It is through the Church, through our brothers and sisters in the community, that we learn about the life that God in Jesus wants us to enjoy and share with him and others we meet.

The First Week in Ordinary Time
8–14 January 2023

Something to think and pray about each day this week:

Recently an American writer and some old college friends were having their annual get-together, catching up on how life was treating them. They also exchanged news, of course, about absent friends. One of those had been flying very high indeed. He was a banker on Wall Street and they reckoned he was now earning more in a day than any of the rest of them would earn, if they were lucky, in a month.

'And yet,' said the writer, 'I have something that he will never have.'
'What's that?' he was asked.

'Enough.'

What the writer is saying is that becoming rich has compelled the man on Wall Street to become richer and that becoming richer will compel him to become richer still. Now there's a sense in which that doesn't make him all that different from many of the rest of us. Ambition, the urge to do better, to aim for higher goals, is part of our make-up as human beings. It's a common characteristic which hasn't just created individual fortunes, it has made possible all kinds of advances in society.

However, in personal terms, a drive towards getting more and always more is a drive that can never be satisfied. The driven person will never be able to say 'this is enough'. When the writer says that he himself has enough, I don't think he's just talking about money. I think he's echoing a line from the poet R. S. Thomas, 'Life is not hurrying on to a receding future'. Now and then, we need to stop hurrying. We need to become aware of ourselves as we are.

Denis Tuohy,
Streets and Secret Places: Reflections of a News Reporter

The Presence of God

'I am standing at the door, knocking' (Revelation 3:20), says the Lord. What a wonderful privilege that the Lord of all creation desires to come to me. I welcome his presence.

Freedom

I will ask God's help
to be free from my own preoccupations,
to be open to God in this time of prayer,
to come to know, love and serve God more.

Consciousness

In God's loving presence I unwind the past day,
starting from now and looking back, moment by moment.
I gather in all the goodness and light, in gratitude.
I attend to the shadows and what they say to me,
seeking healing, courage, forgiveness.

The Word

Now I turn to the Scripture set out for me this day. I read slowly over the words and see if any sentence or sentiment appeals to me.
(Please turn to the Scripture on the following pages. Inspiration points are there, should you need them. When you are ready, return here to continue.)

Conversation

Sometimes I wonder what I might say if I were to meet you in person, Lord. I think I might say, 'Thank you' because you are always there for me.

Conclusion

I thank God for these moments we have spent together and for any insights I have been given concerning the text.

Sunday 8 January
The Epiphany of the Lord (USA)
Matthew 2:1–12

In the time of King Herod, after Jesus was born in Bethlehem of Judea, wise men from the East came to Jerusalem, asking, 'Where is the child who has been born king of the Jews? For we observed his star at its rising, and have come to pay him homage.' When King Herod heard this, he was frightened, and all Jerusalem with him; and calling together all the chief priests and scribes of the people, he inquired of them where the Messiah was to be born. They told him, 'In Bethlehem of Judea; for so it has been written by the prophet:

> "And you, Bethlehem, in the land of Judah,
>   are by no means least among the rulers of Judah;
> for from you shall come a ruler
>   who is to shepherd my people Israel."'

Then Herod secretly called for the wise men and learned from them the exact time when the star had appeared. Then he sent them to Bethlehem, saying, 'Go and search diligently for the child; and when you have found him, bring me word so that I may also go and pay him homage.' When they had heard the king, they set out; and there, ahead of them, went the star that they had seen at its rising, until it stopped over the place where the child was. When they saw that the star had stopped, they were overwhelmed with joy. On entering the house, they saw the child with Mary his mother; and they knelt down and paid him homage. Then, opening their treasure-chests, they offered him gifts of gold, frankincense and myrrh. And having been warned in a dream not to return to Herod, they left for their own country by another road.

- Jesus may be an infant but we learn from Matthew that God is very much in charge. He guides the wise men by a star and warns them later in a dream. They are from the East, a sign that the Messiah is for all peoples, not just the Jews. They bring highly symbolic gifts, gold for a king, frankincense for a priest and myrrh for anointing the dead – prophetic insights regarding Jesus for Mary to ponder in her heart.

Monday 9 January
The Baptism of the Lord
Matthew 3:13–17

Then Jesus came from Galilee to John at the Jordan, to be baptised by him. John would have prevented him, saying, 'I need to be baptised by you, and do you come to me?' But Jesus answered him, 'Let it be so now; for it is proper for us in this way to fulfil all righteousness.' Then he consented. And when Jesus had been baptised, just as he came up from the water, suddenly the heavens were opened to him and he saw the Spirit of God descending like a dove and alighting on him. And a voice from heaven said, 'This is my Son, the Beloved, with whom I am well pleased.'

- I hear the voice from heaven identifying Jesus, son of Mary, as the Beloved of God the Father; the Holy Spirit too alighting on him. The salvation of humankind is under way in the person of Jesus. At my baptism I was called to 'receive the light of Christ' and keep it 'burning brightly' in my world of family, work and leisure.

Tuesday 10 January
Mark 1:14–28

Now after John was arrested, Jesus came to Galilee, proclaiming the good news of God, and saying, 'The time is fulfilled, and the kingdom of God has come near; repent, and believe in the good news.'

As Jesus passed along the Sea of Galilee, he saw Simon and his brother Andrew casting a net into the lake – for they were fishermen. And Jesus said to them, 'Follow me and I will make you fish for people.' And immediately they left their nets and followed him. As he went a little farther, he saw James son of Zebedee and his brother John, who were in their boat mending the nets. Immediately he called them; and they left their father Zebedee in the boat with the hired men, and followed him.

They went to Capernaum; and when the sabbath came, he entered the synagogue and taught. They were astounded at his teaching, for he taught them as one having authority, and not as the scribes. Just then there was in their synagogue a man with an unclean spirit, and he cried out, 'What have you to do with us, Jesus of Nazareth? Have you come to destroy us? I know who you are, the Holy One of God.' But Jesus rebuked him, saying, 'Be silent, and come out of him!' And the unclean spirit, throwing him into convulsions and crying with a loud voice, came out of him. They were all amazed, and they kept on asking one another, 'What is this? A new teaching – with authority! He commands even the unclean spirits, and they obey him.' At once his fame began to spread throughout the surrounding region of Galilee.

- In this gospel we see metanoia, that radical change of life, taking place. These men follow Jesus with total trust. They have no idea where they are going but they believe and trust Jesus. We may not be called to the same journey, but are invited to trust in Jesus a little more in our daily work.

Wednesday 11 January
Mark 1:29–39

As soon as they left the synagogue, they entered the house of Simon and Andrew, with James and John. Now Simon's mother-in-law was in bed with a fever, and they told him about her at once. He came and took her by the hand and lifted her up. Then the fever left her, and she began to serve them.

That evening, at sunset, they brought to him all who were sick or possessed with demons. And the whole city was gathered around the door. And he cured many who were sick with various diseases, and cast out many demons; and he would not permit the demons to speak, because they knew him.

In the morning, while it was still very dark, he got up and went out to a deserted place, and there he prayed. And Simon and his companions hunted for him. When they found him, they said to him, 'Everyone is searching for you.' He answered, 'Let us go on to the neighbouring towns, so that I may proclaim the message there also; for that is what I came out to do.' And he went throughout Galilee, proclaiming the message in their synagogues and casting out demons.

- Having 'quality time' with God, to pray, reflect and renew our energy is central. Jesus gives us an excellent example here by going away to a deserted place to pray. Let us remember to stay close to the source of all love.

Thursday 12 January
Mark 1:40–45

A leper came to him begging him, and kneeling he said to him, 'If you choose, you can make me clean.' Moved with pity, Jesus stretched out his hand and touched him, and said to him, 'I do choose. Be made clean!' Immediately the leprosy left him, and he was made clean. After sternly warning him he sent him away at once, saying to him, 'See that you say nothing to anyone; but go, show yourself to the priest, and offer for your cleansing what Moses commanded, as a testimony to them.' But he went out and began to proclaim it freely, and to spread the word, so that Jesus could no longer go into a town openly, but stayed out in the country; and people came to him from every quarter.

• In your prayer today tell Jesus of some way you were hurt or wounded by something people said or did to you. Listen to how sensitive and responsive he is when he is 'moved with pity' or compassion for you. Tell him how you feel about him being like this.

Friday 13 January
Mark 2:1–12

When he returned to Capernaum after some days, it was reported that he was at home. So many gathered around that there was no longer room for them, not even in front of the door; and he was speaking the word to them. Then some people came, bringing to him a paralysed man, carried by four of them. And when they could not bring him to Jesus because of the crowd, they removed the roof above him; and after having dug through it, they let down the mat on which the paralytic lay. When Jesus saw their faith, he said to the paralytic, 'Son, your sins are forgiven.' Now some of the scribes were sitting there, questioning in their hearts, 'Why does this fellow speak in this way? It is blasphemy! Who can forgive sins but God alone?' At once Jesus perceived in his spirit that they were discussing these questions among themselves; and he said to them, 'Why do you raise such questions in your hearts? Which is easier, to say to the paralytic, "Your sins are forgiven", or to say, "Stand up and take your mat and walk"? But so that you may know that the Son of Man has authority on earth to forgive sins' – he said to the paralytic – 'I say to you, stand up, take your mat and go to your home.' And he stood up, and immediately took the mat and went out before all of them; so that they were all amazed and glorified God, saying, 'We have never seen anything like this!'

- I meet up with Jesus when the house is quiet and ask him to explain to me what was really going on. He talks with me about the opposition I may face as a true disciple of his.

Saturday 14 January
Mark 2:13–17

Jesus went out again beside the lake; the whole crowd gathered around him, and he taught them. As he was walking along, he saw Levi son of Alphaeus sitting at the tax booth, and he said to him, 'Follow me.' And he got up and followed him.

And as he sat at dinner in Levi's house, many tax-collectors and sinners were also sitting with Jesus and his disciples – for there were many who followed him. When the scribes of the Pharisees saw that he was eating with sinners and tax-collectors, they said to his disciples, 'Why does he eat with tax-collectors and sinners?' When Jesus heard this, he said to them, 'Those who are well have no need of a physician, but those who are sick; I have come to call not the righteous but sinners.'

- By being with sinners, Jesus is not approving or turning a blind eye to their behaviour. He says the 'sick' are in need of healing. This can only be done by reaching out to them. Where can I reach out and bring healing and restoration to the people with whom I am in direct contact?

The Second Week in Ordinary Time
15–21 January 2023

Something to think and pray about each day this wesek:

The Irish countryside is blessed with a variety of pilgrim paths. Each pilgrimage has its own rituals and customs. Many pilgrims set off with a clear purpose in mind, while others are not sure why they have set out, much like the pilgrims who take on the challenge of the Camino to Santiago de Compostela in Spain. In his 'Principle and Foundation' Ignatius challenges us to get in touch with our core values, what we really desire in our heart of hearts, as we make our personal life pilgrimage. What happens between womb and tomb is of utmost significance as we get only one shot at life – one opportunity to leave our mark, to add to the store of the world's goodness, like the way we pile one stone upon another.

Of course, there will be obstacles along the path. If we're lucky we'll have only a few scrapes and bruises, the odd insect bite and a bit of sunburn. But if we're unlucky we may lose our way when the sea mist comes rolling in from the Atlantic and obscures our navigation aids, such as a forest here and a stone wall there. Ignatius knew human life inside out. He was only too familiar with the inner landscape of the soul. He knew all about moods and feelings. He knew only too well what it was like to go around in circles in unfamiliar territory when the storm clouds gathered and when the thick fog descended. He had to spend long hours and days living in his own dark and desolate psychological deserts, bearing the brunt of the assaults of his own terrifying demons. He descended metaphorically into hell, especially when he wanted to take his own life due to the awful intensity of his darkest feelings which had got the better of him.

Jim Maher,
Pathways to a Decision with Ignatius of Loyola

The Presence of God

At any time of the day or night we can call on Jesus.
He is always waiting, listening for our call.
What a wonderful blessing.
No phone needed, no e-mails, just a whisper.

Freedom

If God were trying to tell me something, would I know?
If God were reassuring me or challenging me, would I notice?
I ask for the grace to be free of my own preoccupations
and open to what God may be saying to me.

Consciousness

Help me, Lord, become more conscious of your presence. Teach me to
recognise your presence in others. Fill my heart with gratitude for the
times your love has been shown to me through the care of others.

The Word

In this expectant state of mind, please turn to the text for the day with
confidence. Believe that the Holy Spirit is present and may reveal whatever the passage has to say to you. Read reflectively, listening with a third
ear to what may be going on in your heart.

(Please turn to the Scripture on the following pages. Inspiration points are there, should you need them. When you are ready, return here to continue.)

Conversation

Conversation requires talking and listening.
As I talk to Jesus, may I also learn to pause and listen.
I picture the gentleness in his eyes and the love in his smile.
I can be totally honest with Jesus as I tell him my worries and cares.
I will open my heart to Jesus as I tell him my fears and doubts.
I will ask him to help me place myself fully in his care, knowing that he
always desires good for me.

Conclusion

I thank God for these moments we have spent together and for any insights I have been given concerning the text.

Sunday 15 January
Second Sunday in Ordinary Time
John 1:29–34

The next day he saw Jesus coming towards him and declared, 'Here is the Lamb of God who takes away the sin of the world! This is he of whom I said, "After me comes a man who ranks ahead of me because he was before me." I myself did not know him; but I came baptising with water for this reason, that he might be revealed to Israel.' And John testified, 'I saw the Spirit descending from heaven like a dove, and it remained on him. I myself did not know him, but the one who sent me to baptise with water said to me, "He on whom you see the Spirit descend and remain is the one who baptises with the Holy Spirit." And I myself have seen and have testified that this is the Son of God.'

- Reflecting on this scripture passage, you might hear Jesus say to you the words he says to every disciple, 'And you, who do you say that I am?' Tell him how you see and feel about him, and then listen to how much he appreciates you for remaining with him as his companion.

Monday 16 January
Mark 2:18–22

Now John's disciples and the Pharisees were fasting; and people came and said to him, 'Why do John's disciples and the disciples of the Pharisees fast, but your disciples do not fast?' Jesus said to them, 'The wedding-guests cannot fast while the bridegroom is with them, can they? As long as they have the bridegroom with them, they cannot fast. The days will come when the bridegroom is taken away from them, and then they will fast on that day.

'No one sews a piece of unshrunk cloth on an old cloak; otherwise, the patch pulls away from it, the new from the old, and a worse tear is made. And no one puts new wine into old wineskins; otherwise, the wine will burst the skins, and the wine is lost, and so are the skins; but one puts new wine into fresh wineskins.'

- The life of religious people is always open to scrutiny and examination from outside. I pray that my way of living communicates gospel values. I take care not to come to uncharitable judgements about the way others live.

Tuesday 17 January
Mark 2:23–28

One sabbath he was going through the cornfields; and as they made their way his disciples began to pluck heads of grain. The Pharisees said to him, 'Look, why are they doing what is not lawful on the sabbath?' And he said to them, 'Have you never read what David did when he and his companions were hungry and in need of food? He entered the house of God, when Abiathar was high priest, and ate the bread of the Presence, which it is not lawful for any but the priests to eat, and he gave some to his companions.' Then he said to them, 'The sabbath was made for humankind, and not humankind for the sabbath; so the Son of Man is lord even of the sabbath.'

• Lord, when human need was crying out to you, the law took second place. It seems so obvious that the sabbath, and law, are made for humankind, not vice versa. But it took courage as well as clarity of mind to state the obvious.

Wednesday 18 January
Mark 3:1–6

Again he entered the synagogue, and a man was there who had a withered hand. They watched him to see whether he would cure him on the sabbath, so that they might accuse him. And he said to the man who had the withered hand, 'Come forward.' Then he said to them, 'Is it lawful to do good or to do harm on the sabbath, to save life or to kill?' But they were silent. He looked around at them with anger; he was grieved at their hardness of heart and said to the man, 'Stretch out your hand.' He stretched it out, and his hand was restored. The Pharisees went out and immediately conspired with the Herodians against him, how to destroy him.

• Perhaps when I'm in difficulty and looking for help people sometimes might not always go out of their way for me; they can hide behind 'red tape' and regulations. But Jesus cuts through the 'red tape' – like he did here in the synagogue – and is always ready to help me.

Thursday 19 January
Mark 3:7–12

Jesus departed with his disciples to the lake, and a great multitude from Galilee followed him; hearing all that he was doing, they came to him in great numbers from Judea, Jerusalem, Idumea, beyond the Jordan, and the region around Tyre and Sidon. He told his disciples to have a boat ready for him because of the crowd, so that they would not crush him; for he had cured many, so that all who had diseases pressed upon him to touch him. Whenever the unclean spirits saw him, they fell down before him and shouted, 'You are the Son of God!' But he sternly ordered them not to make him known.

- This move to the lakeside is away from the synagogues where he was meeting the passive resistance of the scribes. Jesus is at his ease in open spaces, near lakeside, hills and sky, unprotected by institutional walls. People converge on him from unexpected places, seeking healing and good news.

- Lord, I come to you seeking to be healed and to hear good news. No place is too far that we cannot come to you.

Friday 20 January
Mark 3:13–19

He went up the mountain and called to him those whom he wanted, and they came to him. And he appointed twelve, whom he also named apostles, to be with him, and to be sent out to proclaim the message, and to have authority to cast out demons. So he appointed the twelve: Simon (to whom he gave the name Peter); James son of Zebedee and John the brother of James (to whom he gave the name Boanerges, that is, Sons of Thunder); and Andrew, and Philip, and Bartholomew, and Matthew, and Thomas, and James son of Alphaeus, and Thaddaeus, and Simon the Cananaean, and Judas Iscariot, who betrayed him.

- As I read this list of names I consider how my name, too, is called by Jesus. He knows who I am, loves me and believes that I am ready to work by his side.

- I pray for my friends and acquaintances. We are, each of us, called by God. I pray that I may cherish each of them as God does.

Saturday 21 January
Mark 3:20–21

The Jesus went home; and the crowd came together again, so that they could not even eat. When his family heard it, they went out to restrain him, for people were saying, 'He has gone out of his mind.'

- Why did people think Jesus was out of his mind? Because he had abandoned a secure trade as a carpenter for a wandering life; he had run into trouble with the authorities in what seemed like a deliberate way; he had gathered an odd group of disciples around him. He seemed indifferent to financial and social security and the opinion of others.

- Lord, you ask me to take risks as you did. This is not a comfortable prayer, as I think about what you have in store for me. Give me courage.

The Third Week in Ordinary Time
22–28 January 2023

Something to think and pray about each day this week:

Jesus' disciples were experienced fishermen who knew exactly how to rec-ognise a bad storm, yet they were still afraid when the storm rose and their boat was threatening to sink. The fears that beat us do not come from lack of knowledge or experience; they come from a lack of faith. Look how Jesus responds to their fears: 'Why are you afraid? Have you still no faith?' (Mark 4:40). Faith is the ability to know, not just in the head but in the heart, that even if the very worst happens, Jesus is still with us in the boat, and he loves us and saves us.

Paul O'Reilly SJ,
Hope in All Things

The Presence of God

'Come to me, all you who are weary and are carrying heavy burdens, and I will give you rest' (Matthew 11:28). Here I am, Lord. I come to seek your presence. I long for your healing power.

Freedom

God is not foreign to my freedom. The Spirit breathes life into my most intimate desires, gently nudging me towards all that is good. I ask for the grace to let myself be enfolded by the Spirit.

Consciousness

I remind myself that I am in the presence of the Lord. I will take refuge in his loving heart. He is my strength in times of weakness. He is my comforter in times of sorrow.

The Word

I take my time to read the word of God slowly, a few times, allowing myself to dwell on anything that strikes me.

(Please turn to the Scripture on the following pages. Inspiration points are there, should you need them. When you are ready, return here to continue.)

Conversation

Jesus, you always welcomed little children when you walked on this earth. Teach me to have a childlike trust in you. Teach me to live in the knowledge that you will never abandon me.

Conclusion

Glory be to the Father, and to the Son, and to the Holy Spirit,
As it was in the beginning, is now and ever shall be,
World without end. Amen.

Sunday 22 January
Third Sunday in Ordinary Time
Matthew 4:12–23

Now when Jesus heard that John had been arrested, he withdrew to Galilee. He left Nazareth and made his home in Capernaum by the lake, in the territory of Zebulun and Naphtali, so that what had been spoken through the prophet Isaiah might be fulfilled:

'Land of Zebulun, land of Naphtali,
on the road by the sea, across the Jordan, Galilee of the Gentiles –
the people who sat in darkness
have seen a great light,
and for those who sat in the region and shadow of death
light has dawned.'

From that time Jesus began to proclaim, 'Repent, for the kingdom of heaven has come near.'

As he walked by the Sea of Galilee, he saw two brothers, Simon, who is called Peter, and Andrew his brother, casting a net into the lake – for they were fishermen. And he said to them, 'Follow me, and I will make you fish for people.' Immediately they left their nets and followed him. As he went from there, he saw two other brothers, James son of Zebedee and his brother John, in the boat with their father Zebedee, mending their nets, and he called them. Immediately they left the boat and their father, and followed him.

Jesus went throughout Galilee, teaching in their synagogues and proclaiming the good news of the kingdom and curing every disease and every sickness among the people.

• I am amazed at the personal magnetism of Jesus, that these four industrious young fishermen, including the married Simon Peter, could drop everything, leave home and follow him. They go throughout Galilee, where people are oppressed, poor and hungry. The people have seen a great light. 'Light has dawned' – am I a light to my world?

Monday 23 January
Mark 3:22–30

And the scribes who came down from Jerusalem said, 'He has Beelzebul, and by the ruler of the demons he casts out demons.' And he called them to him, and spoke to them in parables, 'How can Satan cast out Satan? If a kingdom is divided against itself, that kingdom cannot stand. And if a house is divided against itself, that house will not be able to stand. And if Satan has risen up against himself and is divided, he cannot stand, but his end has come. But no one can enter a strong man's house and plunder his property without first tying up the strong man; then indeed the house can be plundered.

'Truly I tell you, people will be forgiven for their sins and whatever blasphemies they utter; but whoever blasphemes against the Holy Spirit can never have forgiveness, but is guilty of an eternal sin' – for they had said, 'He has an unclean spirit.'

- Passages such as this remind us that the world-view shared by Jesus and his critics was very different from ours in the twenty-first century. We may need to ask, even more insistently than usual, for grace to understand how the story is relevant for us today. Always remember that Mark is trying to explain (as are the other evangelists) who Jesus is and what it means to call him Saviour. That is the heart of the gospel.

Friday 24 January
Mark 3:31–35

Then his mother and his brothers came; and standing outside, they sent to him and called him. A crowd was sitting around him; and they said to him, 'Your mother and your brothers and sisters are outside, asking for you.' And he replied, 'Who are my mother and my brothers?' And looking at those who sat around him, he said, 'Here are my mother and my brothers! Whoever does the will of God is my brother and sister and mother.'

- We can picture members of the crowd, no doubt more eager to hear what he had to say, ranging themselves in a circle round Jesus.
- Jesus had already been inviting those who heard him to the totally new life of members of the kingdom of heaven. Then, born into that new

life, they would be his brothers and sisters in a new way – a bond even deeper than the normal ties of family. This is the invitation that he still extends to all of us.

Wednesday 25 January
The Conversion of St Paul, Apostle
Mark 16:15–18

And he said to them, 'Go into all the world and proclaim the good news to the whole creation. The one who believes and is baptised will be saved; but the one who does not believe will be condemned. And these signs will accompany those who believe: by using my name they will cast out demons; they will speak in new tongues; they will pick up snakes in their hands, and if they drink any deadly thing, it will not hurt them; they will lay their hands on the sick, and they will recover.'

• Do you see how appropriate this reading is on a feast of St Paul? His conversion (which is the focus of this particular feast) prepared him to become an apostle to the Gentiles (the pagans). His long journeys led him to cover much of the territory that comprised the Roman Empire. He preached and healed, founded and supported local communities. His life teaches us that mission (outreach) is not optional. The Church is missionary of its very nature.

Thursday 26 January
Mark 4:21–25

He said to them, 'Is a lamp brought in to be put under the bushel basket, or under the bed, and not on the lampstand? For there is nothing hidden, except to be disclosed; nor is anything secret, except to come to light. Let anyone with ears to hear listen!' And he said to them, 'Pay attention to what you hear; the measure you give will be the measure you get, and still more will be given you. For to those who have, more will be given; and from those who have nothing, even what they have will be taken away.'

• What we give out to others is what we will ourselves receive – and even more. 'To the one who has, more will be given; from the one who has not, even what he has will be taken away.' In the Christian life, we gain by giving, not by getting. It is only when we give that we can receive.

Friday 27 January
Mark 4:26–34

He also said, 'The kingdom of God is as if someone would scatter seed on the ground, and would sleep and rise night and day, and the seed would sprout and grow, he does not know how. The earth produces of itself, first the stalk, then the head, then the full grain in the head. But when the grain is ripe, at once he goes in with his sickle, because the harvest has come.'

He also said, 'With what can we compare the kingdom of God, or what parable will we use for it? It is like a mustard seed, which, when sown upon the ground, is the smallest of all the seeds on earth; yet when it is sown it grows up and becomes the greatest of all shrubs, and puts forth large branches, so that the birds of the air can make nests in its shade.'

With many such parables he spoke the word to them, as they were able to hear it; he did not speak to them except in parables, but he explained everything in private to his disciples.

• Lord, your images of the kingdom are alive and organic. It has its own pattern of growth, a tiny plant that grows into a massive tree with room for every creature. Let me never imagine that I am the architect or builder of your kingdom. Enough for me to be patient, a seed growing slowly, animated by your spirit.

Saturday 28 January
Mark 4:35–41

On that day, when evening had come, he said to them, 'Let us go across to the other side.' And leaving the crowd behind, they took him with them in the boat, just as he was. Other boats were with him. A great gale arose, and the waves beat into the boat, so that the boat was already being swamped. But he was in the stern, asleep on the cushion; and they woke him up and said to him, 'Teacher, do you not care that we are perishing?' He woke up and rebuked the wind, and said to the sea, 'Peace! Be still!' Then the wind ceased, and there was a dead calm. He said to them, 'Why are you afraid? Have you still no faith?' And they were filled with great awe and said to one another, 'Who then is this, that even the wind and the sea obey him?'

- Yesterday, Jesus invited me to trust, and today he shows me I can do so with confidence. He is with me throughout the storms of my life, and is able with a word to bring a great calm. But he understands my fears, and allows me to express them to him, like the disciples who cried out, 'Do you not care?'

- In the storms of my own life, I too can cry out, 'Lord, do you not care?' He will hear me, reassure me and say, 'Why are you afraid? I am here with you.'

The Fourth Week in Ordinary Time
29 January–4 February 2023

Something to think and pray about each day this week:

When I was about thirteen or fourteen, one of our group walking to school was a boy in my class called Michael. To tell you the truth I never really enjoyed it, because Michael always took us out of our way to walk through the graveyard, where he would always stop at a particular place and say a Hail Mary. When we asked him he wouldn't talk about it. He wouldn't explain why it always had to be that particular place or why it always had to be a Hail Mary.

Eventually, when we were in the sixth form, he told me. He said that when he was ten, just before his mother died from cancer, she had asked him to say one Hail Mary for her every day. He had done that faithfully, and whenever he could he went and said it at her grave.

I asked him why she had asked him to do this. He supposed that she had wanted someone to pray for her after she had gone, but he wasn't really sure. That was what she had asked of him and because he was her son and he loved her that was what he did.

I think it is that same spirit of remembrance that brings us together, every Sunday, to celebrate Our Lord's Eucharist. He could have asked us to do many different things in remembrance of him but he asked us to meet and eat and drink together his body and blood in remembrance of him and be united with him and one another as his people in this world. We do what he asked us to do because we love him. We do this in memory of him. It was his last request to us and that's good enough for us.

Paul O'Reilly SJ,
Hope in All Things

The Presence of God

What is present to me is what has a hold on my becoming.
I reflect on the presence of God always there in love,
amidst the many things that have a hold on me.
I pause and pray that I may let God
affect my becoming in this precise moment.

Freedom

By God's grace I was born to live in freedom. Free to enjoy the pleasures
he created for me. Dear Lord, grant that I may live as you intended, with
complete confidence in your loving care.

Consciousness

I exist in a web of relationships: links to nature, people, God.
I trace out these links, giving thanks for the life that flows through them.
Some links are twisted or broken; I may feel regret, anger, disappointment.
I pray for the gift of acceptance and forgiveness.

The Word

God speaks to each of us individually. I listen attentively to hear what he
is saying to me. Read the text a few times, then listen.
*(Please turn to the Scripture on the following pages. Inspiration points are there,
should you need them. When you are ready, return here to continue.)*

Conversation

I begin to talk with Jesus about the Scripture I have just read. What part
of it strikes a chord in me? Perhaps the words of a friend – or some story
I have heard recently – will rise to the surface in my consciousness. If so,
does the story throw light on what the Scripture passage may be saying
to me?

Conclusion

Glory be to the Father, and to the Son, and to the Holy Spirit,
As it was in the beginning, is now and ever shall be,
World without end. Amen.

Sunday 29 January
Fourth Sunday in Ordinary Time
Matthew 5:1–12

When Jesus saw the crowds, he went up the mountain; and after he sat down, his disciples came to him. Then he began to speak, and taught them, saying:

> 'Blessed are the poor in spirit, for theirs is the kingdom of heaven.
> 'Blessed are those who mourn, for they will be comforted.
> 'Blessed are the meek, for they will inherit the earth.
> 'Blessed are those who hunger and thirst for righteousness, for they will be filled.
> 'Blessed are the merciful, for they will receive mercy.
> 'Blessed are the pure in heart, for they will see God.
> 'Blessed are the peacemakers, for they will be called children of God.
> 'Blessed are those who are persecuted for righteousness' sake, for theirs is the kingdom of heaven.
> 'Blessed are you when people revile you and persecute you and utter all kinds of evil against you falsely on my account. Rejoice and be glad, for your reward is great in heaven, for in the same way they persecuted the prophets who were before you.'

- I allow these blessings to come home to me. I imagine Jesus carefully speaking them to me, aware of my poverty, sadness and hunger.
- I might choose two of these beatitudes to be a backdrop to my prayer and reflection today: one that affirms me and one that calls me further.

Monday 30 January
Mark 5:1–20

They came to the other side of the lake, to the country of the Gerasenes. And when he had stepped out of the boat, immediately a man out of the tombs with an unclean spirit met him. He lived among the tombs; and no one could restrain him any more, even with a chain; for he had often been restrained with shackles and chains, but the chains he wrenched apart, and the shackles he broke in pieces; and no one had the strength to subdue him. Night and day among the tombs and on the mountains he was always howling and bruising himself with stones. When he saw Jesus from a distance, he ran and bowed down before him; and he shouted at the top of his voice, 'What have you to do with me, Jesus, Son of the Most High God? I adjure you by God, do not torment me.' For he had said to him, 'Come out of the man, you unclean spirit!' Then Jesus asked him, 'What is your name?' He replied, 'My name is Legion; for we are many.' He begged him earnestly not to send them out of the country. Now there on the hillside a great herd of swine was feeding; and the unclean spirits begged him, 'Send us into the swine; let us enter them.' So he gave them permission. And the unclean spirits came out and entered the swine; and the herd, numbering about two thousand, rushed down the steep bank into the lake, and were drowned in the lake.

The swineherds ran off and told it in the city and in the country. Then people came to see what it was that had happened. They came to Jesus and saw the demoniac sitting there, clothed and in his right mind, the very man who had had the legion; and they were afraid. Those who had seen what had happened to the demoniac and to the swine reported it. Then they began to beg Jesus to leave their neighbourhood. As he was getting into the boat, the man who had been possessed by demons begged him that he might be with him. But Jesus refused, and said to him, 'Go home to your friends, and tell them how much the Lord has done for you, and what mercy he has shown you.' And he went away and began to proclaim in the Decapolis how much Jesus had done for him; and everyone was amazed.

• Perhaps we think that following Jesus means spending a lot of time 'with Jesus' in religious activities or committing to religious life. For most of us, our calling and our following of Jesus take place right where we are.

• It is there that we need to share with others our experience of knowing and being loved by Jesus. Let us go home and tell others what Jesus means in our lives and pray that, like the people in the gospel, they may be amazed.

Tuesday 31 January
Mark 5:21–43

When Jesus had crossed again in the boat to the other side, a great crowd gathered round him; and he was by the lake. Then one of the leaders of the synagogue named Jairus came and, when he saw him, fell at his feet and begged him repeatedly, 'My little daughter is at the point of death. Come and lay your hands on her, so that she may be made well, and live.' So he went with him.

And a large crowd followed him and pressed in on him. Now there was a woman who had been suffering from haemorrhages for twelve years. She had endured much under many physicians, and had spent all that she had; and she was no better, but rather grew worse. She had heard about Jesus, and came up behind him in the crowd and touched his cloak, for she said, 'If I but touch his clothes, I will be made well.' Immediately her haemorrhage stopped; and she felt in her body that she was healed of her disease. Immediately aware that power had gone forth from him, Jesus turned about in the crowd and said, 'Who touched my clothes?' And his disciples said to him, 'You see the crowd pressing in on you; how can you say, "Who touched me?"' He looked all round to see who had done it. But the woman, knowing what had happened to her, came in fear and trembling, fell down before him, and told him the whole truth. He said to her, 'Daughter, your faith has made you well; go in peace, and be healed of your disease.'

While he was still speaking, some people came from the leader's house to say, 'Your daughter is dead. Why trouble the teacher any further?' But overhearing what they said, Jesus said to the leader of the synagogue, 'Do not fear, only believe.' He allowed no one to follow him except Peter, James, and John, the brother of James. When they came to the house of the leader of the synagogue, he saw a commotion, people weeping and wailing loudly. When he had entered, he said to them, 'Why do you make a commotion and weep? The child is not dead but sleeping.' And they laughed at him. Then he put them all outside, and took the child's father and mother and those who were with him, and went in where the child was. He took her by the hand and said to her, 'Talitha cum', which means, 'Little girl, get up!' And immediately the girl got up and began to walk about (she was twelve years of age). At this they were overcome with amazement. He strictly ordered them that no one should know this, and told them to give her something to eat.

- Note the stress that Jesus places on faith in both stories. To the woman he says: 'Daughter, your faith has made you well'. And to Jairus: 'Do not fear, only believe'. What does this say to you as you live your life as a Christian today?

Wednesday 1 February
Mark 6:1–6

He left that place and came to his home town, and his disciples followed him. On the sabbath he began to teach in the synagogue, and many who heard him were astounded. They said, 'Where did this man get all this? What is this wisdom that has been given to him? What deeds of power are being done by his hands! Is not this the carpenter the son of Mary and brother of James and Joses and Judas and Simon, and are not his sisters here with us?' And they took offence at him. Then Jesus said to them, 'Prophets are not without honour, except in their home town, and among their own kin, and in their own house.' And he could do no deed of power there, except that he laid his hands on a few sick people and cured them. And he was amazed at their unbelief.

- Perhaps today's gospel invites us to be with Jesus in the profound suffering this must have caused him. You might then let Jesus be with you in the ways you suffer when people are not sensitive to, or show respect for your dignity as a human being or as a Christian.

Thursday 2 February
The Presentation of the Lord
Luke 2:22–40

When the time came for their purification according to the law of Moses, they brought him up to Jerusalem to present him to the Lord (as it is written in the law of the Lord, 'Every firstborn male shall be designated as holy to the Lord'), and they offered a sacrifice according to what is stated in the law of the Lord, 'a pair of turtle-doves or two young pigeons.'

Now there was a man in Jerusalem whose name was Simeon; this man was righteous and devout, looking forward to the consolation of Israel, and the Holy Spirit rested on him. It had been revealed to him by the

Holy Spirit that he would not see death before he had seen the Lord's Messiah. Guided by the Spirit, Simeon came into the temple; and when the parents brought in the child Jesus, to do for him what was customary under the law, Simeon took him in his arms and praised God, saying,

> 'Master, now you are dismissing your servant in peace,
>   according to your word;
> for my eyes have seen your salvation,
> which you have prepared in the presence of all peoples,
> a light for revelation to the Gentiles
> and for glory to your people Israel.'

And the child's father and mother were amazed at what was being said about him. Then Simeon blessed them and said to his mother Mary, 'This child is destined for the falling and the rising of many in Israel, and to be a sign that will be opposed so that the inner thoughts of many will be revealed – and a sword will pierce your own soul too.'

There was also a prophet, Anna the daughter of Phanuel, of the tribe of Asher. She was of a great age, having lived with her husband for seven years after her marriage, then as a widow to the age of eighty-four. She never left the temple but worshipped there with fasting and prayer night and day. At that moment she came, and began to praise God and to speak about the child to all who were looking for the redemption of Jerusalem.

When they had finished everything required by the law of the Lord, they returned to Galilee, to their own town of Nazareth. The child grew and became strong, filled with wisdom; and the favour of God was upon him.

- Jesus was destined to be a sign that would be opposed. We are his followers and can also expect opposition. Let us try to welcome it and grow through it.

Friday 3 February
Mark 6:14–29

King Herod heard of it, for Jesus' name had become known. Some were saying, 'John the baptiser has been raised from the dead; and for this reason these powers are at work in him.' But others said, 'It is Elijah.' And others said, 'It is a prophet, like one of the prophets of old.' But when Herod heard of it, he said, 'John, whom I beheaded, has been raised.'

For Herod himself had sent men who arrested John, bound him, and put him in prison on account of Herodias, his brother Philip's wife, because Herod had married her. For John had been telling Herod, 'It is not lawful for you to have your brother's wife.' And Herodias had a grudge against him, and wanted to kill him. But she could not, for Herod feared John, knowing that he was a righteous and holy man, and he protected him. When he heard him, he was greatly perplexed; and yet he liked to listen to him. But an opportunity came when Herod on his birthday gave a banquet for his courtiers and officers and for the leaders of Galilee. When his daughter Herodias came in and danced, she pleased Herod and his guests; and the king said to the girl, 'Ask me for whatever you wish, and I will give it.' And he solemnly swore to her, 'Whatever you ask me, I will give you, even half of my kingdom.' She went out and said to her mother, 'What should I ask for?' She replied, 'The head of John the baptiser.' Immediately she rushed back to the king and requested, 'I want you to give me at once the head of John the Baptist on a platter.' The king was deeply grieved; yet out of regard for his oaths and for the guests, he did not want to refuse her. Immediately the king sent a soldier of the guard with orders to bring John's head. He went and beheaded him in the prison, brought his head on a platter, and gave it to the girl. Then the girl gave it to her mother. When his disciples heard about it, they came and took his body, and laid it in a tomb.

• How might this awful story help me in my prayer? Perhaps I might think of the vulnerable, the innocent, the foolish – all those who are exploited to achieve the ends of others. I pray that I might grow in compassion for them.

Saturday 4 February
Mark 6:30–34

The apostles gathered around Jesus, and told him all that they had done and taught. He said to them, 'Come away to a deserted place all by yourselves and rest a while.' For many were coming and going, and they had no leisure even to eat. And they went away in the boat to a deserted place by themselves. Now many saw them going and recognised them, and they hurried there on foot from all the towns and arrived ahead of them. As he went ashore, he saw a great crowd; and he had compassion for them, because they were like sheep without a shepherd; and he began to teach them many things.

- Lord, there are times when I want to get away from the crowds, when I feel oppressed by company. There are other times when I just wish that somebody knew that I exist; I can have too much of aloneness. If I can reach you in prayer, and know that you are more central to me than my own thoughts, I feel at peace, as the apostles must have felt.

5–11 February 2023

Something to think and pray about each day this week:

We are all pilgrims in the world and only passing through, but it is easy to get attached to things and believe the illusion of the material world. It goes without saying that you have to let go of a lot to be a pilgrim; walking the Camino de Santiago is the modern equivalent. As on the Camino and as in life, we have to travel light and adapt to whatever comes our way, whether it is the weather, health issues, unexpected obstacles or inner wounds or blocks. The liberation involved in letting go of comfort, ease and security is hard won.

Being a pilgrim on the Camino teaches this freedom from trivial 'things' to concentrate on more important ones: walking, talking, praying, appreciating, living. You actually need very little to get by and all the things we think we need (technology, comfort, riches, style etc.) have no value on the road. A rucksack that contains everything you think you need would be impossible to carry. This is a great liberation and the recuperation of what it means to be human: a pilgrim on the road, dependent on providence and on others. The joy attached to this is palpable and infectious.

St Ignatius calls this spiritual freedom, the ability to be free of small things for greater things; things are good but only up to a point, in so far as they bring me to God. Deeper living is the desire for things that really satisfy, not empty distractions. The opposite of freedom is attachment: I can't move as I'm 'chained' to something. I have to have certain things, I impose limits. I won't accept the basic simplicity of the Camino. This is the tragedy, of course, that such great joy exists so close and yet we are kept from it by smaller things.

Brendan McManus SJ,
Contemplating the Camino: An Ignatian Guide

The Presence of God
'Be still, and know that I am God!' (Psalm 46:10) Lord, your words lead us to the calmness and greatness of your presence.

Freedom
'In these days, God taught me as a schoolteacher teaches a pupil' (St Ignatius). I remind myself that there are things God has to teach me yet, and I ask for the grace to hear them and let them change me.

Consciousness
How am I really feeling? Lighthearted? Heavyhearted? I may be very much at peace, happy to be here.
Equally, I may be frustrated, worried, or angry.
I acknowledge how I really am. It is the real me whom the Lord loves.

The Word
God speaks to each of us individually. I listen attentively to hear what he is saying to me. Read the text a few times, then listen.
(Please turn to the Scripture on the following pages. Inspiration points are there, should you need them. When you are ready, return here to continue.)

Conversation
Do I notice myself reacting as I pray with the word of God? Do I feel challenged, comforted, angry? Imagining Jesus sitting or standing by me, I speak out my feelings, as one trusted friend to another.

Conclusion
I thank God for these moments we have spent together and for any insights I have been given concerning the text.

Sunday 5 February
Fifth Sunday in Ordinary Time
Matthew 5:13–16

Jesus said, 'You are the salt of the earth; but if salt has lost its taste, how can its saltiness be restored? It is no longer good for anything, but is thrown out and trampled under foot.

'You are the light of the world. A city built on a hill cannot be hidden. No one after lighting a lamp puts it under the bushel basket, but on the lampstand, and it gives light to all in the house. In the same way, let your light shine before others, so that they may see your good works and give glory to your Father in heaven.'

• Light does not change a room: it enables us to see what is in it. It helps us appreciate what is good and beautiful, just as it facilitates avoiding pitfalls. We are children of the light: our lives are illumined by Jesus, the light of the world (John 8:12). This light helps us to see the hidden hope of glory that is in us. So we can rejoice even in the darkness of the world.

Monday 6 February
Mark 6:53–56

When they had crossed over, they came to land at Gennesaret and moored the boat. When they got out of the boat, people at once recognised him, and rushed about that whole region and began to bring the sick on mats to wherever they heard he was. And wherever he went, into villages or cities or farms, they laid the sick in the market-places, and begged him that they might touch even the fringe of his cloak; and all who touched it were healed.

• St Mark's Gospel is full of movement! Several times already we have come across the phrase 'they crossed over'. Crossing over, for us, can mean leaving something behind in order to be with Jesus. It demands a readiness to take a risk, to step away from the familiar and comfortable, and follow Jesus to some new situation. A good prayer each morning is to ask, 'Lord, where are we going today?'

Tuesday 7 February
Mark 7:1–13

Now when the Pharisees and some of the scribes who had come from Jerusalem gathered around him, they noticed that some of his disciples were eating with defiled hands, that is, without washing them. (For the Pharisees, and all the Jews, do not eat unless they thoroughly wash their hands, thus observing the tradition of the elders; and they do not eat anything from the market unless they wash it; and there are also many other traditions that they observe, the washing of cups, pots and bronze kettles.) So the Pharisees and the scribes asked him, 'Why do your disciples not live according to the tradition of the elders, but eat with defiled hands?' He said to them, 'Isaiah prophesied rightly about you hypocrites, as it is written,

"This people honours me with their lips,
     but their hearts are far from me;
in vain do they worship me,
     teaching human precepts as doctrines."

You abandon the commandment of God and hold to human tradition.'

Then he said to them, 'You have a fine way of rejecting the commandment of God in order to keep your tradition! For Moses said, "Honour your father and your mother"; and, "Whoever speaks evil of father or mother must surely die." But you say that if anyone tells father or mother, "Whatever support you might have had from me is Corban" (that is, an offering to God) – then you no longer permit doing anything for a father or mother, thus making void the word of God through your tradition that you have handed on. And you do many things like this.'

- The kingdom of God is always unexpected; it catches me by surprise and demands responses from me that jolt me out of my mediocrity. Its values are counter-cultural. There the poor come first; despised people are important; wealth is for sharing; hatred is out; forgiveness is in; love is all that matters in the end. Wow!

Wednesday 8 February
Mark 7:14–23

Then he called the crowd again and said to them, 'Listen to me, all of you, and understand: there is nothing outside a person that by going in can defile, but the things that come out are what defile.'

When he had left the crowd and entered the house, his disciples asked him about the parable. He said to them, 'Then do you also fail to understand? Do you not see that whatever goes into a person from outside cannot defile, since it enters, not the heart but the stomach, and goes out into the sewer?' (Thus he declared all foods clean.) And he said, 'It is what comes out of a person that defiles. For it is from within, from the human heart, that evil intentions come: fornication, theft, murder, adultery, avarice, wickedness, deceit, licentiousness, envy, slander, pride, folly. All these evil things come from within, and they defile a person.'

• Jesus, with his uneducated disciples, is mixing with sophisticated Pharisees from Jerusalem, men who have mastered the intricate rules about ritual purity, and look down on those who are ignorant of them. As Christians we can set up our own norms of what is god-fearing and respectable, and forget that it is the heart that matters. Jesus always sees through the externals of behaviour to the love and goodness that may lie beneath.

Thursday 9 February
Mark 7:24–30

From there he set out and went away to the region of Tyre. He entered a house and did not want anyone to know he was there. Yet he could not escape notice, but a woman whose little daughter had an unclean spirit immediately heard about him, and she came and bowed down at his feet. Now the woman was a Gentile, of Syrophoenician origin. She begged him to cast the demon out of her daughter. He said to her, 'Let the children be fed first, for it is not fair to take the children's food and throw it to the dogs.' But she answered him, 'Sir, even the dogs under the table eat the children's crumbs.' Then he said to her, 'For saying that, you may go – the demon has left your daughter.' So she went home, found the child lying on the bed, and the demon gone.

- The depth of the woman's faith is an example to us. She has not presented her daughter to Jesus, but in her eyes the prospect of long-distance healing presents no difficulties. Jesus sometimes said that he met deeper faith among foreigners than among his own people.

Friday 10 February
Mark 7:31–37

Then he returned from the region of Tyre, and went by way of Sidon towards the Sea of Galilee, in the region of the Decapolis. They brought to him a deaf man who had an impediment in his speech; and they begged him to lay his hand on him. He took him aside in private, away from the crowd, and put his fingers into his ears, and he spat and touched his tongue. Then looking up to heaven, he sighed and said to him, 'Ephphatha', that is, 'Be opened.' And immediately his ears were opened, his tongue was released, and he spoke plainly. Then Jesus ordered them to tell no one; but the more he ordered them, the more zealously they proclaimed it. They were astounded beyond measure, saying, 'He has done everything well; he even makes the deaf to hear and the mute to speak.'

- The initiative for this healing miracle did not come from the deaf man himself. It was others who brought Jesus to him. It was these people of good will who 'begged him to lay his hand on him'. Perhaps we should remember that many of the good things that happen to us come from the good will and prayers of others on our behalf.

Saturday 11 February
Mark 8:1–10

In those days when there was again a great crowd without anything to eat, he called his disciples and said to them, 'I have compassion for the crowd, because they have been with me now for three days and have nothing to eat. If I send them away hungry to their homes, they will faint on the way – and some of them have come from a great distance.' His disciples replied, 'How can one feed these people with bread here in the desert?' He asked them, 'How many loaves do you have?' They said, 'Seven.' Then he ordered the crowd to sit down on the ground; and he took the seven loaves, and after giving thanks he broke them and gave them to his disciples to distribute; and they distributed them to the crowd. They had also a few small fish; and after blessing them, he ordered that these too should be distributed. They ate and were filled; and they took up the broken pieces left over, seven baskets full. Now there were about four thousand people. And he sent them away. And immediately he got into the boat with his disciples and went to the district of Dalmanutha.

- Am I compassionate to others? Is that what I'd like to be said of me when I die? A wise man once advised me: 'Have endless compassion for those who have not yet reached their goal'. It's a life's agenda!

Something to think and pray about each day this week:

I believe in God. I believe in a force that holds me in cupped hands especially when things are against me. The world can be my enemy and God's at the same time.

The first thing that ever existed according to our Bible was not darkness or light, it was chaos and it was God who tamed it. This work continues today as it did in the beginning and yes indeed, sometimes it appears to be futile – chaos may appear to reign supreme. But in the still silence of God there is always an order. There has to be as love brings with it an order that rises above chaos. Love can be present strongly among people in the most tumbledown house and love can be present in the most tumbledown world. It holds things together even if there is a real fear that everything could fall apart in one swift moment.

The great evidence of that love for me is the gift of joy. I do not mean raucous laughter or false happiness. I mean the joy of knowing, believing and feeling that all is well. There is a joy that comes as gift when love touches us – joy is the scent of that love and it can linger long, and we can linger long in those cupped hands.

Alan Hilliard,
Dipping into Life: 40 Reflections for a Fragile Faith

The Presence of God

I remind myself that, as I sit here now,
God is gazing on me with love and holding me in being.
I pause for a moment and think of this.

Freedom

'There are very few people who realise what God would make of them if
they abandoned themselves into his hands, and let themselves be formed
by his grace' (St Ignatius). I ask for the grace to entrust myself totally to
God's love.

Consciousness

Where do I sense hope, encouragement and growth in my life? By looking
back over the past few months, I may be able to see which activities and
occasions have produced rich fruit. If I do notice such areas, I will determine to give those areas both time and space in the future.

The Word

Lord Jesus, you became human to communicate with me.
You walked and worked on this earth.
You endured the heat and struggled with the cold.
All your time on this earth was spent in caring for humanity.
You healed the sick, you raised the dead.
Most important of all, you saved me from death.
*(Please turn to the Scripture on the following pages. Inspiration points are there,
should you need them. When you are ready, return here to continue.)*

Conversation

What is stirring in me as I pray? Am I consoled, troubled, left cold? I
imagine Jesus standing or sitting at my side, and I share my feelings with
him.

Conclusion

Glory be to the Father, and to the Son, and to the Holy Spirit,
As it was in the beginning, is now and ever shall be,
World without end. Amen.

Sunday 12 February
Sixth Sunday in Ordinary Time
Matthew 5:17–37

Jesus said, 'Do not think that I have come to abolish the law or the prophets; I have come not to abolish but to fulfil. For truly I tell you, until heaven and earth pass away, not one letter, not one stroke of a letter, will pass from the law until all is accomplished. Therefore, whoever breaks one of the least of these commandments, and teaches others to do the same, will be called least in the kingdom of heaven; but whoever does them and teaches them will be called great in the kingdom of heaven. For I tell you, unless your righteousness exceeds that of the scribes and Pharisees, you will never enter the kingdom of heaven.

'You have heard that it was said to those of ancient times, "You shall not murder"; and "whoever murders shall be liable to judgement." But I say to you that if you are angry with a brother or sister, you will be liable to judgement; and if you insult a brother or sister, you will be liable to the council; and if you say, "You fool", you will be liable to the hell of fire. So when you are offering your gift at the altar, if you remember that your brother or sister has something against you, leave your gift there before the altar and go; first be reconciled to your brother or sister, and then come and offer your gift. Come to terms quickly with your accuser while you are on the way to court with him, or your accuser may hand you over to the judge, and the judge to the guard, and you will be thrown into prison. Truly I tell you, you will never get out until you have paid the last penny.

'You have heard that it was said, "You shall not commit adultery." But I say to you that everyone who looks at a woman with lust has already committed adultery with her in his heart. If your right eye causes you to sin, tear it out and throw it away; it is better for you to lose one of your members than for your whole body to be thrown into hell. And if your right hand causes you to sin, cut it off and throw it away; it is better for you to lose one of your members than for your whole body to go into hell.

'It was also said, "Whoever divorces his wife, let him give her a certificate of divorce." But I say to you that anyone who divorces his wife, except on the ground of unchastity, causes her to commit adultery; and whoever marries a divorced woman commits adultery.

'Again, you have heard that it was said to those of ancient times, "You shall not swear falsely, but carry out the vows you have made to the Lord." But I say to you, Do not swear at all, either by heaven, for it is the throne of God, or by the earth, for it is his footstool, or by Jerusalem, for it is the city of the great King. And do not swear by your head, for you cannot make one hair white or black. Let your word be "Yes, Yes" or "No, No"; anything more than this comes from the evil one.'

- The implication here is that Jesus is a more authoritative person than Moses. The influential leaders who were unsympathetic to the person of Jesus met his saving message with hostility. They were resistant to his preaching of a kingdom that demanded a higher standard of human conduct than that called for by Moses. Jesus is proclaiming a new era.

Monday 13 February
Mark 8:11–13

The Pharisees came and began to argue with him, asking him for a sign from heaven, to test him. And he sighed deeply in his spirit and said, 'Why does this generation ask for a sign? Truly I tell you, no sign will be given to this generation.' And he left them, and getting into the boat again, he went across to the other side.

- Lord, do we make you 'sigh deeply'? You do everything for us, and still we want more. Firstly, you love us limitlessly. Pope Francis reminds us of this: 'When everything is said and done, we are infinitely loved'. How about that! Secondly, each of us is a brother or sister for whom you willingly died. Thirdly, you are with us always: everything that is good in our lives comes from you. Finally, you have breathtaking and glorious plans for our future after death.

Tuesday 14 February
Mark 8:14–21

Now the disciples had forgotten to bring any bread; and they had only one loaf with them in the boat. And he cautioned them, saying, 'Watch out – beware of the yeast of the Pharisees and the yeast of Herod.' They said to one another, 'It is because we have no bread.' And becoming aware of it, Jesus said to them, 'Why are you talking about having no bread? Do you still not perceive or understand? Are your hearts hardened? Do you have eyes, and fail to see? Do you have ears, and fail to hear? And do you not remember? When I broke the five loaves for the five thousand, how many baskets full of broken pieces did you collect?' They said to him, 'Twelve.' 'And the seven for the four thousand, how many baskets full of broken pieces did you collect?' And they said to him, 'Seven.' Then he said to them, 'Do you not yet understand?'

- I think of Jesus looking at me lovingly, speaking to me gently, inviting me to understand and to receive his good news into my heart.

- The daily bread of which Jesus speaks is not for the stomach. I pray that my eyes may see, that my ears may hear and that my memory may be blessed to notice God's goodness and to receive the food God offers to me each day.

Wednesday 15 February
Mark 8:22–26

They came to Bethsaida. Some people brought a blind man to him and begged him to touch him. He took the blind man by the hand and led him out of the village; and when he had put saliva on his eyes and laid his hands on him, he asked him, 'Can you see anything?' And the man looked up and said, 'I can see people, but they look like trees, walking.' Then Jesus laid his hands on his eyes again; and he looked intently and his sight was restored, and he saw everything clearly. Then he sent him away to his home, saying, 'Do not even go into the village.'

- I put myself in the sandals of the blind man brought to Jesus, the healer everybody wanted to meet. He takes me gently by the hand, warm and reassuring. As he gives me his full attention, I grow in trust and confidence. Jesus opens my eyes and I see what a good man he is.

- I cannot thank the Lord enough for his goodness and kindness. Every moment of my life is his gift to me.

Thursday 16 February
Mark 8:27–33

Jesus went on with his disciples to the villages of Caesarea Philippi; and on the way he asked his disciples, 'Who do people say that I am?' And they answered him, 'John the Baptist; and others, Elijah; and still others, one of the prophets.' He asked them, 'But who do you say that I am?' Peter answered him, 'You are the Messiah.' And he sternly ordered them not to tell anyone about him.

Then he began to teach them that the Son of Man must undergo great suffering, and be rejected by the elders, the chief priests, and the scribes, and be killed, and after three days rise again. He said all this quite openly. And Peter took him aside and began to rebuke him. But turning and looking at his disciples, he rebuked Peter and said, 'Get behind me, Satan! For you are setting your mind not on divine things but on human things.'

- Lord, when I fail to understand your ways don't lose hope in me. May I heed your call to 'get behind you' like a good disciple following the Master. Strengthen me in times of suffering: may I patiently bear unavoidable suffering, as you did. May I believe that what I endure helps in the saving of the world.

Friday 17 February
Mark 8:34–9:1

He called the crowd with his disciples, and said to them, 'If any want to become my followers, let them deny themselves and take up their cross and follow me. For those who want to save their life will lose it, and those who lose their life for my sake, and for the sake of the gospel, will save it. For what will it profit them to gain the whole world and forfeit their life? Indeed, what can they give in return for their life? Those who are ashamed of me and of my words in this adulterous and sinful generation, of them the Son of Man will also be ashamed when he comes in the glory of his Father with the holy angels.' And he said to them, 'Truly I tell you, there are some standing here who will not taste death until they see that the kingdom of God has come with power.'

- Lord, our world is crowded with people staggering beneath their burdens of poverty, oppression, violence and hunger. Give me strong shoulders to reach out daily to shoulder some of their burdens. Help me to notice the mysterious consolation that comes when I go out of myself to help someone.

Saturday 18 February
Mark 9:2–13

Six days later, Jesus took with him Peter and James and John, and led them up a high mountain apart, by themselves. And he was transfigured before them, and his clothes became dazzling white, such as no one on earth could bleach them. And there appeared to them Elijah with Moses, who were talking with Jesus. Then Peter said to Jesus, 'Rabbi, it is good for us to be here; let us make three dwellings, one for you, one for Moses, and one for Elijah.' He did not know what to say, for they were terrified. Then a cloud overshadowed them, and from the cloud there came a voice, 'This is my Son, the Beloved; listen to him!' Suddenly when they looked around, they saw no one with them any more, but only Jesus.

As they were coming down the mountain, he ordered them to tell no one about what they had seen, until after the Son of Man had risen from the dead. So they kept the matter to themselves, questioning what this rising from the dead could mean. Then they asked him, 'Why do the scribes say that Elijah must come first?' He said to them, 'Elijah is indeed coming first to restore all things. How then is it written about the Son of Man, that he is to go through many sufferings and be treated with contempt? But I tell you that Elijah has come, and they did to him whatever they pleased, as it is written about him.'

- Prayer can often feel like a long mountain walk! You wonder if it's worth it, and you don't always have the stamina. But if you give quality time to it, as you are doing now, it is always worthwhile. Jesus 'took with him Peter, James and John' and he will take you too, if you are willing to climb. Try not to be irritable and edgy as you make your way upwards with him.

19–25 February 2023

Something to think and pray about each day this week:

The Christian centre is the person of Christ. Our work for Jesus and our love for people, no matter what our calling in life, flow from this. Mother Teresa was once asked why she did what she did, and she simply said 'for Jesus'. This centre always holds, it cannot be unhinged. It is a deeply personal relationship: we are led by Jesus 'one by one', known by name, not as one of a group. We follow him as one we know, not a stranger.

We study his life and times, getting to know the places and events of his life; we become familiar with the gospels and get to know him in the heart. Prayer is the way of keeping our centre of conviction and motivation strong. Freedom grows and we begin to find him everywhere.

Different types of people and spirituality stress different aspects of Jesus. The Eastern approach to Jesus is very much the 'way'; while the African is the 'life'. The European stress is the 'truth'. In Europe we need to rediscover also the joy and vibrancy of the African and Latin American expressions of faith, and also the presence of God in all life's moods and journeys of the Indian and Eastern traditions.

We can get so caught up in small or even big truths and doctrines that we miss other centres of faith. All faith needs the balanced approach to Jesus – way, truth and life.

Donal Neary SJ,
Gospel Reflections for Sundays of Year A

The Presence of God
I pause for a moment
and reflect on God's life-giving presence
in every part of my body,
in everything around me,
in the whole of my life.

Freedom
Many countries are at this moment suffering the agonies of war. I bow my head in thanksgiving for my freedom. I pray for all prisoners and captives.

Consciousness
Knowing that God loves me unconditionally, I look honestly over the past day, its events, and my feelings. Do I have something to be grateful for? Then I give thanks. Is there something I am sorry for? Then I ask forgiveness.

The Word
Now I turn to the Scripture set out for me this day. I read slowly over the words and see if any sentence or sentiment appeals to me.
(Please turn to the Scripture on the following pages. Inspiration points are there, should you need them. When you are ready, return here to continue.)

Conversation
I know with certainty that there were times when you carried me, Lord. There were times when it was through your strength that I got through the dark times in my life.

Conclusion
Glory be to the Father, and to the Son, and to the Holy Spirit,
As it was in the beginning, is now and ever shall be,
World without end. Amen.

Sunday 19 February
Seventh Sunday in Ordinary Time
Matthew 5:38–48

Jesus said, 'You have heard that it was said, "An eye for an eye and a tooth for a tooth." But I say to you, Do not resist an evildoer. But if anyone strikes you on the right cheek, turn the other also; and if anyone wants to sue you and take your coat, give your cloak as well; and if anyone forces you to go one mile, go also the second mile. Give to everyone who begs from you, and do not refuse anyone who wants to borrow from you.

'You have heard that it was said, "You shall love your neighbour and hate your enemy." But I say to you, Love your enemies and pray for those who persecute you, so that you may be children of your Father in heaven; for he makes his sun rise on the evil and on the good, and sends rain on the righteous and on the unrighteous. For if you love those who love you, what reward do you have? Do not even the tax-collectors do the same? And if you greet only your brothers and sisters, what more are you doing than others? Do not even the Gentiles do the same? Be perfect, therefore, as your heavenly Father is perfect.'

• Jesus portrays God as a loving and proud Father who sees himself in me and in each one of his sons and daughters. So he expects of me, as a dearly loved child of his, created in his image, that I will be good to all my brothers and sisters, even my 'enemies' and persecutors.

• I am not to retaliate, but should give, share, lend and go the extra mile.

Monday 20 February
Mark 9:14–29

When they came to the disciples, they saw a great crowd around them, and some scribes arguing with them. When the whole crowd saw him, they were immediately overcome with awe, and they ran forward to greet him. He asked them, 'What are you arguing about with them?' Someone from the crowd answered him, 'Teacher, I brought you my son; he has a spirit that makes him unable to speak; and whenever it seizes him, it dashes him down; and he foams and grinds his teeth and becomes rigid; and I asked your disciples to cast it out, but they could not do so.' He answered them, 'You faithless generation, how much longer must I be

among you? How much longer must I put up with you? Bring him to me.'
And they brought the boy to him. When the spirit saw him, immediately
it threw the boy into convulsions, and he fell on the ground and rolled
about, foaming at the mouth. Jesus asked the father, 'How long has this
been happening to him?' And he said, 'From childhood. It has often cast
him into the fire and into the water, to destroy him; but if you are able to
do anything, have pity on us and help us.' Jesus said to him, 'If you are
able! – All things can be done for the one who believes.' Immediately the
father of the child cried out, 'I believe; help my unbelief!' When Jesus saw
that a crowd came running together, he rebuked the unclean spirit, saying
to it, 'You spirit that keep this boy from speaking and hearing, I command you, come out of him, and never enter him again!' After crying out
and convulsing him terribly, it came out, and the boy was like a corpse, so
that most of them said, 'He is dead.' But Jesus took him by the hand and
lifted him up, and he was able to stand. When he had entered the house,
his disciples asked him privately, 'Why could we not cast it out?' He said
to them, 'This kind can come out only through prayer.'

• Jesus wants to expel anything that keeps me from sight or hearing, any
  spirit that threatens my peace of mind. I pray for myself and for those
  who are dear to me, that we may receive more fully the goodness of
  God as we pray for one another.

Tuesday 21 February
Mark 9:30–37

They went on from there and passed through Galilee. He did not want
anyone to know it; for he was teaching his disciples, saying to them, 'The
Son of Man is to be betrayed into human hands, and they will kill him,
and three days after being killed, he will rise again.' But they did not understand what he was saying and were afraid to ask him.

Then they came to Capernaum; and when he was in the house he
asked them, 'What were you arguing about on the way?' But they were
silent, for on the way they had argued with one another about who was
the greatest. He sat down, called the twelve, and said to them, 'Whoever
wants to be first must be last of all and servant of all.' Then he took a
little child and put it among them; and taking it in his arms, he said to

them, 'Whoever welcomes one such child in my name welcomes me, and whoever welcomes me welcomes not me but the one who sent me.'

- Jesus comes among us to show us how to love. He showed that love even to the end. Recall your experiences of loving in your own life and a time when your loving made demands on you. What kinds of feelings does this memory evoke for you? Talk to Jesus about those feelings.

Wednesday 22 February
Ash Wednesday
Matthew 6:1–6, 16–18

Jesus said to them, 'Beware of practising your piety before others in order to be seen by them; for then you have no reward from your Father in heaven.

'So whenever you give alms, do not sound a trumpet before you, as the hypocrites do in the synagogues and in the streets, so that they may be praised by others. Truly I tell you, they have received their reward. But when you give alms, do not let your left hand know what your right hand is doing, so that your alms may be done in secret; and your Father who sees in secret will reward you.

'And whenever you pray, do not be like the hypocrites; for they love to stand and pray in the synagogues and at the street corners, so that they may be seen by others. Truly I tell you, they have received their reward. But whenever you pray, go into your room and shut the door and pray to your Father who is in secret; and your Father who sees in secret will reward you.

'And whenever you fast, do not look dismal, like the hypocrites, for they disfigure their faces so as to show others that they are fasting. Truly I tell you, they have received their reward. But when you fast, put oil on your head and wash your face, so that your fasting may be seen not by others but by your Father who is in secret; and your Father who sees in secret will reward you.'

- Religion can be used for selfish reasons, like being well thought of. God asks that we focus on his place in our lives through our faith. We need to recall the priority of God in our lives: that we come from him and go to him, and that he is the companion of our lives.

Thursday 23 February
Luke 9:22–25

Jesus said to his disciples, 'The Son of Man must undergo great suffering, and be rejected by the elders, chief priests and scribes, and be killed, and on the third day be raised.'

Then he said to them all, 'If any want to become my followers, let them deny themselves and take up their cross daily and follow me. For those who want to save their life will lose it, and those who lose their life for my sake will save it. What does it profit them if they gain the whole world, but lose or forfeit themselves?'

• We know from the Gospels that the disciples of Jesus would have been tempted – influenced by the expectation of their fellow Jews – by the prospect of their Master inaugurating a new political and national power. In another Gospel, Peter is roundly denounced by Jesus for attempting to draw him aside from the wholly unexpected path of suffering announced here (making reference to condemned persons often being forced to carry their own cross). We tend in our own minds to catalogue today's passage simply as a prophecy of suffering.

Friday 24 February
Matthew 9:14–15

Then the disciples of John came to him, saying, 'Why do we and the Pharisees fast often, but your disciples do not fast?' And Jesus said to them, 'The wedding-guests cannot mourn as long as the bridegroom is with them, can they? The days will come when the bridegroom is taken away from them, and then they will fast.'

• Jesus is often presented in the gospel as giving his life over to his Father. His convictions and preaching would lead to his death. His future resurrection was in the power of his Father. Much of what we want to hold on to in life can be swiftly taken away – our good health, our security of wealth, even our good name. What we share in love and in God cannot be taken away. Ask in prayer to value love, and to offer your life now and always in love and for love.

Saturday 25 February
Luke 5:27–32

After this he went out and saw a tax-collector named Levi, sitting at the tax booth; and he said to him, 'Follow me.' And he got up, left everything and followed him.

Then Levi gave a great banquet for him in his house; and there was a large crowd of tax-collectors and others sitting at the table with them. The Pharisees and their scribes were complaining to his disciples, saying, 'Why do you eat and drink with tax-collectors and sinners?' Jesus answered, 'Those who are well have no need of a physician, but those who are sick; I have come to call not the righteous but sinners to repentance.'

• Where are the Levis in my world? The drug-pushers, paedophiles, wife-batterers, rapists, those who cheat on tax or social welfare, those who are headlined for hatred in the tabloid press. Lord, these are the sick who need you as physician. Can I help you to reach out to them?

26 February–4 March 2023

Something to think and pray about each day this week:

The days of spring lengthen and Lent echoes nature, inviting us as well to a new springtime of faith. As in farming and gardening, there is work to be done if new growth is to flourish or even to happen at all. We have to look back and see what has done well and what has, in effect, died off. We need to make space by clearing the ground and looking at ourselves honestly. It would be good to identify what will feed and sustain us during this journey from the ashes of Ash Wednesday to the new birth of Easter.

Kieran J. O'Mahony OSA,
*Hearers of the Word: Praying and Exploring the
Readings for Lent and Holy Week*

The Presence of God
I pause for a moment and think of the love and the grace that God showers on me. I am created in the image and likeness of God; I am God's dwelling place.

Freedom
Lord, you granted me the great gift of freedom. In these times, O Lord, grant that I may be free from any form of racism or intolerance. Remind me that we are all equal in your loving eyes.

Consciousness
Knowing that God loves me unconditionally, I can afford to be honest about how I am. How has the day been, and how do I feel now? I share my feelings openly with the Lord.

The Word
I take my time to read the word of God slowly, a few times, allowing myself to dwell on anything that strikes me.
(Please turn to the Scripture on the following pages. Inspiration points are there, should you need them. When you are ready, return here to continue.)

Conversation
Sometimes I wonder what I might say if I were to meet you in person, Lord. I think I might say, 'Thank you' because you are always there for me.

Conclusion
I thank God for these moments we have spent together and for any insights I have been given concerning the text.

Sunday 26 February
First Sunday of Lent
Matthew 4:1–11

Then Jesus was led up by the Spirit into the wilderness to be tempted by the devil. He fasted for forty days and forty nights, and afterwards he was famished. The tempter came and said to him, 'If you are the Son of God, command these stones to become loaves of bread.' But he answered, 'It is written,

> "One does not live by bread alone,
>> but by every word that comes from the mouth of God."'

Then the devil took him to the holy city and placed him on the pinnacle of the temple, saying to him, 'If you are the Son of God, throw yourself down; for it is written,

> "He will command his angels concerning you",
>> and "On their hands they will bear you up,
> so that you will not dash your foot against a stone."'

Jesus said to him, 'Again it is written, "Do not put the Lord your God to the test."'

Again, the devil took him to a very high mountain and showed him all the kingdoms of the world and their splendour; and he said to him, 'All these I will give you, if you will fall down and worship me.' Jesus said to him, 'Away with you, Satan! for it is written,

> "Worship the Lord your God,
>> and serve only him."'

Then the devil left him, and suddenly angels came and waited on him.

- What is the spirit trying to tell me in this story? Am I aware of my own particular 'temptations' that make trouble for me in my life? Do I find wisdom and guidance in Scripture to help me cope with difficulties in my life? Let us consider where Jesus found inspiration and guidance throughout his life.

Monday 27 February
Matthew 25:31–46

Jesus said to them, 'When the Son of Man comes in his glory, and all the angels with him, then he will sit on the throne of his glory. All the nations will be gathered before him, and he will separate people one from another as a shepherd separates the sheep from the goats, and he will put the sheep at his right hand and the goats at the left. Then the king will say to those at his right hand, "Come, you that are blessed by my Father, inherit the kingdom prepared for you from the foundation of the world; for I was hungry and you gave me food, I was thirsty and you gave me something to drink, I was a stranger and you welcomed me, I was naked and you gave me clothing, I was sick and you took care of me, I was in prison and you visited me." Then the righteous will answer him, "Lord, when was it that we saw you hungry and gave you food, or thirsty and gave you something to drink? And when was it that we saw you a stranger and welcomed you, or naked and gave you clothing? And when was it that we saw you sick or in prison and visited you?" And the king will answer them, "Truly I tell you, just as you did it to one of the least of these who are members of my family, you did it to me." Then he will say to those at his left hand, "You that are accursed, depart from me into the eternal fire prepared for the devil and his angels; for I was hungry and you gave me no food, I was thirsty and you gave me nothing to drink, I was a stranger and you did not welcome me, naked and you did not give me clothing, sick and in prison and you did not visit me." Then they also will answer, "Lord, when was it that we saw you hungry or thirsty or a stranger or naked or sick or in prison, and did not take care of you?" Then he will answer them, "Truly I tell you, just as you did not do it to one of the least of these, you did not do it to me." And these will go away into eternal punishment, but the righteous into eternal life.'

• The things we are asked to do are so simple: give food and drink to 'Jesus' in those who are hungry and thirsty; to clothe 'Jesus' in those who are naked; to visit 'Jesus' in those who are sick and in jail. Whether we realise it or not, every time we spontaneously take care of a brother or sister in need it is Jesus himself we are serving.

Tuesday 28 February
Matthew 6:7–15

Jesus said to them, 'When you are praying, do not heap up empty phrases as the Gentiles do; for they think that they will be heard because of their many words. Do not be like them, for your Father knows what you need before you ask him.

'Pray then in this way:
Our Father in heaven,
hallowed be your name.
Your kingdom come.
Your will be done,
on earth as it is in heaven.
Give us this day our daily bread.
And forgive us our debts,
as we also have forgiven our debtors.
And do not bring us to the time of trial,
but rescue us from the evil one.

For if you forgive others their trespasses, your heavenly Father will also forgive you; but if you do not forgive others, neither will your Father forgive your trespasses.'

- The Our Father is so familiar it is hard to be really present to the words we say. Maybe try to just focus on one phrase like 'hallowed be your name'. What is this phrase saying to me right now?
- How might 'hallowing his name' look in my life today? Which phrases in the Our Father give me the greatest comfort and the greatest challenge?

Wednesday 1 March
Luke 11:29–32

When the crowds were increasing, he began to say, 'This generation is an evil generation; it asks for a sign, but no sign will be given to it except the sign of Jonah. For just as Jonah became a sign to the people of Nineveh, so the Son of Man will be to this generation. The queen of the South will rise at the judgement with the people of this generation and condemn them, because she came from the ends of the earth to listen to the wisdom of Solomon, and see, something greater than Solomon is here! The people of Nineveh will rise up at the judgement with this generation and condemn it, because they repented at the proclamation of Jonah, and see, something greater than Jonah is here!'

- Where do I see 'signs' of God's activity in my life? Maybe in nature; family; friends; random acts of kindness; poverty; the homeless?

- 'Something greater than Solomon is here'. Do I catch glimpses of this reality? Help me to have eyes to see and a heart open enough to allow me to become aware of your presence and action in my life.

Thursday 2 March
Matthew 7:7–11

Jesus said, 'Ask, and it will be given to you; search, and you will find; knock, and the door will be opened for you. For everyone who asks receives, and everyone who searches finds, and for everyone who knocks, the door will be opened. Is there anyone among you who, if your child asks for bread, will give a stone? Or if the child asks for a fish, will give a snake? If you then, who are evil, know how to give good gifts to your children, how much more will your Father in heaven give good things to those who ask him!'

- Prayer is never wasted. Good things come in prayer, but perhaps not what someone asks for. Prayer opens the heart for good things from God. Be grateful at the end of prayer for time spent with the God of all goodness. Prayer time is always productive time in making us people of more love.

Friday 3 March
Matthew 5:20–26

Jesus said to the crowds, 'For I tell you, unless your righteousness exceeds that of the scribes and Pharisees, you will never enter the kingdom of heaven.

'You have heard that it was said to those of ancient times, "You shall not murder"; and "whoever murders shall be liable to judgement." But I say to you that if you are angry with a brother or sister, you will be liable to judgement; and if you insult a brother or sister, you will be liable to the council; and if you say, "You fool", you will be liable to the hell of fire. So when you are offering your gift at the altar, if you remember that your brother or sister has something against you, leave your gift there before the altar and go; first be reconciled to your brother or sister, and then come and offer your gift. Come to terms quickly with your accuser while you are on the way to court with him, or your accuser may hand you over to the judge, and the judge to the guard, and you will be thrown into prison. Truly I tell you, you will never get out until you have paid the last penny.'

- Any illusion that Christianity is an 'easy' religion is dispelled here. Can I put any of these teachings of Jesus into action in my own life?

- Do I ever call myself a fool!? Let me not be too hard on myself today. I will ask Jesus to give me the grace to accept myself as I am.

Saturday 4 March
Matthew 5:43–48

Jesus taught them, saying, 'You have heard that it was said, "You shall love your neighbour and hate your enemy." But I say to you, Love your enemies and pray for those who persecute you, so that you may be children of your Father in heaven; for he makes his sun rise on the evil and on the good, and sends rain on the righteous and on the unrighteous. For if you love those who love you, what reward do you have? Do not even the tax-collectors do the same? And if you greet only your brothers and sisters, what more are you doing than others? Do not even the Gentiles do the same? Be perfect, therefore, as your heavenly Father is perfect.'

- As I sit with these lines what is my gut reaction? Is this a 'hard saying' for me? Can I even believe that it is possible for me? Is it good for me? I talk to Jesus about what is going on in my heart now.

- He, Jesus, loved till the end. I am called to be like him. Have I ever experienced the effect of actually praying for whoever has hurt me, to wish them well, wish them peace and healing?

Something to think and pray about each day this week:

Jesus says to his disciples: 'It is easier for a camel to pass through the eye of a needle than for someone rich to enter the kingdom of God' (Mark 10:25). With this Jesus puts his finger on a central aspect of Christian life: our willingness to become empty or to become poor before God. The disciples are shocked because they sense how difficult it is to be really empty and poor. This is the passage that, time and again, leads to misunderstandings: should we all be poor, not own anything, be ascetic? Does Jesus begrudge us everything? It is he who has promised us a life in fullness. The word 'emptiness' is not easily understood because it can be interpreted in so many different ways. For one thing it sounds negative. Yet it is exactly our willingness to become empty that is essential for our spiritual life. This is why it plays an integral role in contemplative retreats.

Joachim Hartmann and Annette Clara Unkelhäußer,
Joy in God: Rekindling an Inner Fire

The Presence of God
Dear Jesus, today I call on you, but not to ask for anything. I'd like only to dwell in your presence. May my heart respond to your love.

Freedom
God my creator, you gave me life and the gift of freedom. Through your love I exist in this world. May I never take the gift of life for granted. May I always respect others' right to life.

Consciousness
I ask how I am today. Am I particularly tired, stressed or anxious? If any of these characteristics apply, can I try to let go of the concerns that disturb me?

The Word
The word of God comes down to us through the Scriptures. May the Holy Spirit enlighten my mind and my heart to respond to the gospel teachings.
(Please turn to the Scripture on the following pages. Inspiration points are there, should you need them. When you are ready, return here to continue.)

Conversation
I begin to talk with Jesus about the Scripture I have just read. What part of it strikes a chord in me? Perhaps the words of a friend – or some story I have heard recently – will rise to the surface in my consciousness. If so, does the story throw light on what the Scripture passage may be saying to me?

Conclusion
Glory be to the Father, and to the Son, and to the Holy Spirit,
As it was in the beginning, is now and ever shall be,
World without end. Amen.

Sunday 5 March
Second Sunday of Lent
Matthew 17:1–9

Six days later, Jesus took with him Peter and James and his brother John and led them up a high mountain, by themselves. And he was transfigured before them, and his face shone like the sun, and his clothes became dazzling white. Suddenly there appeared to them Moses and Elijah, talking with him. Then Peter said to Jesus, 'Lord, it is good for us to be here; if you wish, I will make three dwellings here, one for you, one for Moses, and one for Elijah.' While he was still speaking, suddenly a bright cloud overshadowed them, and from the cloud a voice said, 'This is my Son, the Beloved; with him I am well pleased; listen to him!' When the disciples heard this, they fell to the ground and were overcome by fear. But Jesus came and touched them, saying, 'Get up and do not be afraid.' And when they looked up, they saw no one except Jesus himself alone.

As they were coming down the mountain, Jesus ordered them, 'Tell no one about the vision until after the Son of Man has been raised from the dead.'

• The disciples see Jesus revealed in all his divine glory. It is a special moment for them, as Peter confirms – 'it is good for us to be here'.

• Go with the disciples and our Lord, paying close attention to what they say and do. What would they have said to one another after the incident? Imagine one of them in later life giving an account and explanation of the incident.

Monday 6 March
Luke 6:36–38

Jesus said to his disciples, 'Be merciful, just as your Father is merciful.

'Do not judge, and you will not be judged; do not condemn, and you will not be condemned. Forgive, and you will be forgiven; give, and it will be given to you. A good measure, pressed down, shaken together, running over, will be put into your lap; for the measure you give will be the measure you get back.'

• Jesus invites us to be as God is – nothing less! He does not intend to overwhelm us or cause us feel frustrated by such an enormous invitation, but wants us to wonder at the immensity of God's capacity to love. In our humanity, we are not infinite, but we are called to great love and hope. The invitation reaches to us as we are in our lives, calling us into the life of God.

- Judgement, condemnation and lack of forgiveness inhibit good and bind up the spirit. Lord help me to be generous, not by forcing anything from myself, but by sharing fully what you give to me.

Tuesday 7 March
Matthew 23:1–12

Then Jesus said to the crowds and to his disciples, 'The scribes and the Pharisees sit on Moses' seat; therefore, do whatever they teach you and follow it; but do not do as they do, for they do not practise what they teach. They tie up heavy burdens, hard to bear, and lay them on the shoulders of others; but they themselves are unwilling to lift a finger to move them. They do all their deeds to be seen by others; for they make their phylacteries broad and their fringes long. They love to have the place of honour at banquets and the best seats in the synagogues, and to be greeted with respect in the market-places, and to have people call them rabbi. But you are not to be called rabbi, for you have one teacher, and you are all students. And call no one your father on earth, for you have one Father – the one in heaven. Nor are you to be called instructors, for you have one instructor, the Messiah. The greatest among you will be your servant. All who exalt themselves will be humbled, and all who humble themselves will be exalted.'

- Christianity should not be a wearying load to carry. Jesus, who said, 'My yoke is easy and my burden is light', was conscious of people's limitations. When I am tempted to pass judgement on another person's perceived failures, do I exercise the same compassion that Jesus did?

Wednesday 8 March
Matthew 20:17–28

While Jesus was going up to Jerusalem, he took the twelve disciples aside by themselves, and said to them on the way, 'See, we are going up to Jerusalem, and the Son of Man will be handed over to the chief priests and scribes, and they will condemn him to death; then they will hand him over to the Gentiles to be mocked and flogged and crucified; and on the third day he will be raised.'

Then the mother of the sons of Zebedee came to him with her sons, and kneeling before him, she asked a favour of him. And he said to her, 'What do you want?' She said to him, 'Declare that these two sons of mine will sit, one at your right hand and one at your left, in your kingdom.' But Jesus answered, 'You do not know what you are asking. Are you able to drink the cup that I am about to drink?' They said to him, 'We are able.' He said to them, 'You will indeed drink my cup, but to sit at my right hand and at my left, this is not mine to grant, but it is for those for whom it has been prepared by my Father.'

When the ten heard it, they were angry with the two brothers. But Jesus called them to him and said, 'You know that the rulers of the Gentiles lord it over them, and their great ones are tyrants over them. It will not be so among you; but whoever wishes to be great among you must be your servant, and whoever wishes to be first among you must be your slave; just as the Son of Man came not to be served but to serve, and to give his life a ransom for many.'

- To love is to serve. To love is to be called to go beyond myself and my needs for others. Jesus came among us to teach us how to live a fully human life.

- Have you ever experienced that 'going beyond' yourself for others? Talk to Jesus about this experience.

Thursday 9 March
Luke 16:19–31

Then Jesus said to his disciples, 'There was a rich man who was dressed in purple and fine linen and who feasted sumptuously every day. And at his gate lay a poor man named Lazarus, covered with sores, who longed to satisfy his hunger with what fell from the rich man's table; even the dogs would come and lick his sores. The poor man died and was carried away by the angels to be with Abraham. The rich man also died and was buried. In Hades, where he was being tormented, he looked up and saw Abraham far away with Lazarus by his side. He called out, "Father Abraham, have mercy on me, and send Lazarus to dip the tip of his finger in water and cool my tongue; for I am in agony in these flames." But

Abraham said, "Child, remember that during your lifetime you received your good things, and Lazarus in like manner evil things; but now he is comforted here, and you are in agony. Besides all this, between you and us a great chasm has been fixed, so that those who might want to pass from here to you cannot do so, and no one can cross from there to us." He said, "Then, father, I beg you to send him to my father's house – for I have five brothers – that he may warn them, so that they will not also come into this place of torment." Abraham replied, "They have Moses and the prophets; they should listen to them." He said, "No, father Abraham; but if someone goes to them from the dead, they will repent." He said to him, "If they do not listen to Moses and the prophets, neither will they be convinced even if someone rises from the dead."'

- This story reminds us of the huge inequality of people in Jesus' time and still today. The parable invites us to see ourselves as richer in the goods of the world than many millions. Even by having access to this text, you count among the privileged world. Praying on this story will simply challenge us into care for the needy, and, in whatever way we can, to improve the lives of very poor people.

Friday 10 March
Matthew 21:33–43, 45–46

Jesus said to them, 'Listen to another parable. There was a landowner who planted a vineyard, put a fence around it, dug a wine press in it, and built a watch-tower. Then he leased it to tenants and went to another country. When the harvest time had come, he sent his slaves to the tenants to collect his produce. But the tenants seized his slaves and beat one, killed another, and stoned another. Again he sent other slaves, more than the first; and they treated them in the same way. Finally he sent his son to them, saying, "They will respect my son." But when the tenants saw the son, they said to themselves, "This is the heir; come, let us kill him and get his inheritance." So they seized him, threw him out of the vineyard, and killed him. Now when the owner of the vineyard comes, what will he do to those tenants?' They said to him, 'He will put those wretches to a miserable death, and lease the vineyard to other tenants who will give him the produce at the harvest time.'

Jesus said to them, 'Have you never read in the scriptures:

"The stone that the builders rejected
has become the cornerstone;
this was the Lord's doing,
and it is amazing in our eyes"?

Therefore I tell you, the kingdom of God will be taken away from you and given to a people that produces the fruits of the kingdom.'

When the chief priests and the Pharisees heard his parables, they realised that he was speaking about them. They wanted to arrest him, but they feared the crowds, because they regarded him as a prophet.

• Jesus – the Son – comes to us so that we might receive our inheritance; we do not need to take anything by force, but can trust in Jesus' promise, message and presence.

Saturday 11 March
Luke 15:1–3, 11–32

Now all the tax-collectors and sinners were coming near to listen to him. And the Pharisees and the scribes were grumbling and saying, 'This fellow welcomes sinners and eats with them.'

So he told them this parable: 'There was a man who had two sons. The younger of them said to his father, "Father, give me the share of the property that will belong to me." So he divided his property between them. A few days later the younger son gathered all he had and travelled to a distant country, and there he squandered his property in dissolute living. When he had spent everything, a severe famine took place throughout that country, and he began to be in need. So he went and hired himself out to one of the citizens of that country, who sent him to his fields to feed the pigs. He would gladly have filled himself with the pods that the pigs were eating; and no one gave him anything. But when he came to himself he said, "How many of my father's hired hands have bread enough and to spare, but here I am dying of hunger! I will get up and go to my father, and I will say to him, 'Father, I have sinned against heaven and before you; I am no longer worthy to be called your son; treat me like one of your hired hands.'" So he set off and went to his father. But while he was still far off, his father saw him and was filled with compassion; he ran and put his arms around him and kissed him. Then the son said to him, "Father, I have sinned against heaven and before you; I am no longer worthy to be called your son." But the father said to his slaves, "Quickly, bring out a robe – the best one – and put it on him; put a ring on his finger and sandals on his feet. And get the fatted calf and kill it, and let us eat and celebrate; for this son of mine was dead and is alive again; he was lost and is found!" And they began to celebrate.

'Now his elder son was in the field; and when he came and approached the house, he heard music and dancing. He called one of the slaves and asked what was going on. He replied, "Your brother has come, and your father has killed the fatted calf, because he has got him back safe and sound." Then he became angry and refused to go in. His father came out and began to plead with him. But he answered his father, "Listen! For all these years I have been working like a slave for you, and I have never disobeyed your command; yet you have never given me even a young goat so that I might celebrate with my friends. But when this son of yours came back, who has devoured your property with prostitutes, you killed the fatted calf for him!" Then the father said to him, "Son, you are always with me, and all that is mine is yours. But we had to celebrate and rejoice, because this brother of yours was dead and has come to life; he was lost and has been found."'

• This classic parable has a universal appeal. The figures of the father and his two sons are portrayed vividly and memorably. The description of the relationships between them is psychologically acute. The central character is the father; it is he who is 'prodigal', not his younger son. The prodigality of the father's love is boundless and unconditional.

The Third Week of Lent
12–18 March 2023

Something to think and pray about each day this week:

We live in a very noisy, busy world, a culture marked by constant distraction. Even at the ordinary level of relationship, attending to the other – really hearing him or her – is a challenge. It happens when we choose to make space, to shut out the other noises and graciously attend to each other. Something similar may be said of the life of the spirit. Listening to the Son happens when we choose it and, by means of practical choices, create spaces in our lives for such encounters.

Kieran J. O'Mahony OSA,
Hearers of the Word: Praying and Exploring the
Readings for Lent and Holy Week

The Presence of God
God is with me, but even more astounding, God is within me.
Let me dwell for a moment on God's life-giving presence
in my body, in my mind, in my heart,
as I sit here, right now.

Freedom
Lord, may I never take the gift of freedom for granted. You gave me the
great blessing of freedom of spirit. Fill my spirit with your peace and joy.

Consciousness
I remind myself that I am in the presence of God, who is my strength in
times of weakness and my comforter in times of sorrow.

The Word
I take my time to read the word of God slowly, a few times, allowing
myself to dwell on anything that strikes me.
*(Please turn to the Scripture on the following pages. Inspiration points are there,
should you need them. When you are ready, return here to continue.)*

Conversation
Jesus, you always welcomed little children when you walked on this earth.
Teach me to have a childlike trust in you. Teach me to live in the knowl-
edge that you will never abandon me.

Conclusion
Glory be to the Father, and to the Son, and to the Holy Spirit,
As it was in the beginning, is now and ever shall be,
World without end. Amen.

Sunday 12 March
Third Sunday of Lent

John 4:5–42

So he came to a Samaritan city called Sychar, near the plot of ground that Jacob had given to his son Joseph. Jacob's well was there, and Jesus, tired out by his journey, was sitting by the well. It was about noon.

A Samaritan woman came to draw water, and Jesus said to her, 'Give me a drink'. (His disciples had gone to the city to buy food.) The Samaritan woman said to him, 'How is it that you, a Jew, ask a drink of me, a woman of Samaria?' (Jews do not share things in common with Samaritans.) Jesus answered her, 'If you knew the gift of God, and who it is that is saying to you, "Give me a drink", you would have asked him, and he would have given you living water.' The woman said to him, 'Sir, you have no bucket, and the well is deep. Where do you get that living water? Are you greater than our ancestor Jacob, who gave us the well, and with his sons and his flocks drank from it?' Jesus said to her, 'Everyone who drinks of this water will be thirsty again, but those who drink of the water that I will give them will never be thirsty. The water that I will give will become in them a spring of water gushing up to eternal life.' The woman said to him, 'Sir, give me this water, so that I may never be thirsty or have to keep coming here to draw water.'

Jesus said to her, 'Go, call your husband, and come back.' The woman answered him, 'I have no husband.' Jesus said to her, 'You are right in saying, "I have no husband"; for you have had five husbands, and the one you have now is not your husband. What you have said is true!' The woman said to him, 'Sir, I see that you are a prophet. Our ancestors worshipped on this mountain, but you say that the place where people must worship is in Jerusalem.' Jesus said to her, 'Woman, believe me, the hour is coming when you will worship the Father neither on this mountain nor in Jerusalem. You worship what you do not know; we worship what we know, for salvation is from the Jews. But the hour is coming, and is now here, when the true worshippers will worship the Father in spirit and truth, for the Father seeks such as these to worship him. God is spirit, and those who worship him must worship in spirit and truth.' The woman said to him, 'I know that Messiah is coming' (who is called Christ).

'When he comes, he will proclaim all things to us.' Jesus said to her, 'I am he, the one who is speaking to you.'

Just then his disciples came. They were astonished that he was speaking with a woman, but no one said, 'What do you want?' or, 'Why are you speaking with her?' Then the woman left her water-jar and went back to the city. She said to the people, 'Come and see a man who told me everything I have ever done! He cannot be the Messiah, can he?' They left the city and were on their way to him.

Meanwhile the disciples were urging him, 'Rabbi, eat something.' But he said to them, 'I have food to eat that you do not know about.' So the disciples said to one another, 'Surely no one has brought him something to eat?' Jesus said to them, 'My food is to do the will of him who sent me and to complete his work. Do you not say, "Four months more, then comes the harvest"? But I tell you, look around you, and see how the fields are ripe for harvesting. The reaper is already receiving wages and is gathering fruit for eternal life, so that sower and reaper may rejoice together. For here the saying holds true, "One sows and another reaps." I sent you to reap that for which you did not labour. Others have laboured, and you have entered into their labour.'

Many Samaritans from that city believed in him because of the woman's testimony, 'He told me everything I have ever done.' So when the Samaritans came to him, they asked him to stay with them; and he stayed there for two days. And many more believed because of his word. They said to the woman, 'It is no longer because of what you said that we believe, for we have heard for ourselves, and we know that this is truly the Saviour of the world.'

- Lord, I am going about my business like the Samaritan woman, and am taken aback when you accost me at the well. You interrupt my business, my getting and spending, and the routines of my day. Let me savour this encounter, imagine you probing my desires, showing you know the waywardness of my heart. At the end, like her, I am moved with such joy at meeting you that I cannot keep it to myself.

Monday 13 March
Luke 4:24–30

And he said, 'Truly I tell you, no prophet is accepted in the prophet's home town. But the truth is, there were many widows in Israel in the time of Elijah, when the heaven was shut up for three years and six months, and there was a severe famine over all the land; yet Elijah was sent to none of them except to a widow at Zarephath in Sidon. There were also many lepers in Israel in the time of the prophet Elisha, and none of them was cleansed except Naaman the Syrian.' When they heard this, all in the synagogue were filled with rage. They got up, drove him out of the town, and led him to the brow of the hill on which their town was built, so that they might hurl him off the cliff. But he passed through the midst of them and went on his way.

• This is about the expectation of miracles and cures. The self-important Naaman feels he has been slighted: he meets only a messenger, not the prophet himself; and the cure depends on Naaman washing himself in the river, instead of receiving hands-on treatment by Elisha.

• I am the same, Lord. Even in my neediness my ego pushes through. I want to be not just a victim but a celebrity victim. I want not just a cure, but to be the centre of attention. Help me to centre on you, not on me.

Tuesday 14 March
Matthew 18:21–35

Then Peter came and said to him, 'Lord, if another member of the church sins against me, how often should I forgive? As many as seven times?' Jesus said to him, 'Not seven times, but, I tell you, seventy-seven times.

'For this reason the kingdom of heaven may be compared to a king who wished to settle accounts with his slaves. When he began the reckoning, one who owed him ten thousand talents was brought to him; and, as he could not pay, his lord ordered him to be sold, together with his wife and children and all his possessions, and payment to be made. So the slave fell on his knees before him, saying, "Have patience with me, and I will pay you everything." And out of pity for him, the lord of that slave released him and forgave him the debt. But that same slave, as he went out, came upon one of his fellow-slaves who owed him a hundred denarii; and seizing him by the throat, he said, "Pay what you owe." Then his fellow-slave fell down and pleaded with him, "Have patience with me, and I will pay you." But he refused; then he went and threw him into prison until he should pay the debt. When his fellow-slaves saw what had happened, they were greatly distressed, and they went and reported to their lord all that had taken place. Then his lord summoned him and said to him, "You wicked slave! I forgave you all that debt because you pleaded with me. Should you not have had mercy on your fellow-slave, as I had mercy on you?" And in anger his lord handed him over to be tortured until he should pay his entire debt. So my heavenly Father will also do to every one of you, if you do not forgive your brother or sister from your heart.'

- As Jesus continues to emphasise forgiveness, I humbly bring myself before God who forgives me everything, who loves me beyond any sin. The forgiveness that God gives is often difficult for me to receive. I think of how it is given generously to me so that I may give it freely to others.

- I pray for those who have caused me hurt and, even if I can't wish them well now, I pray that one day I might.

Wednesday 15 March
Matthew 5:17–19

Jesus said to his disciples, 'Do not think that I have come to abolish the law or the prophets; I have come not to abolish but to fulfil. For truly I tell you, until heaven and earth pass away, not one letter, not one stroke of a letter, will pass from the law until all is accomplished. Therefore, whoever breaks one of the least of these commandments, and teaches others to do the same, will be called least in the kingdom of heaven; but whoever does them and teaches them will be called great in the kingdom of heaven.'

- I consider how it is that my way of living has an influence on others. I pray in thanksgiving for those places in my life in which I can imagine that I have a good influence. I ask God's help in the areas in which my example and inspiration might be better.

Thursday 16 March
Luke 11:14–23

Now he was casting out a demon that was mute; when the demon had gone out, the one who had been mute spoke, and the crowds were amazed. But some of them said, 'He casts out demons by Beelzebul, the ruler of the demons.' Others, to test him, kept demanding from him a sign from heaven. But he knew what they were thinking and said to them, 'Every kingdom divided against itself becomes a desert, and house falls on house. If Satan also is divided against himself, how will his kingdom stand? – for you say that I cast out the demons by Beelzebul. Now if I cast out the demons by Beelzebul, by whom do your exorcists cast them out? Therefore they will be your judges. But if it is by the finger of God that I cast out the demons, then the kingdom of God has come to you. When a strong man, fully armed, guards his castle, his property is safe. But when one stronger than he attacks him and overpowers him, he takes away his armour in which he trusted and divides his plunder. Whoever is not with me is against me, and whoever does not gather with me scatters.'

- You know how painful it is if your motives are misunderstood, if a twisted interpretation is put on your good intentions. Such experiences help you identify with Jesus and feel with him. Be there with him; share your experiences with him.

Friday 17 March
St Patrick, Bishop and Patron of Ireland
Mark 12:28–34

One of the scribes came near and heard them disputing with one another, and seeing that he answered them well, he asked him, 'Which commandment is the first of all?' Jesus answered, 'The first is, "Hear, O Israel: the Lord our God, the Lord is one; you shall love the Lord your God with all your heart, and with all your soul, and with all your mind, and with all your strength." The second is this, "You shall love your neighbour as yourself." There is no other commandment greater than these.' Then the scribe said to him, 'You are right, Teacher; you have truly said that "he is one, and besides him there is no other"; and "to love him with all the heart, and with all the understanding, and with all the strength", and "to love one's neighbour as oneself", – this is much more important than all whole burnt-offerings and sacrifices.' When Jesus saw that he answered wisely, he said to him, 'You are not far from the kingdom of God.' After that no one dared to ask him any question.

- 'Love your neighbour as yourself' – just how do I love myself? I am not just aware of present pleasure or pain. I think ahead, protect my routines and give energy to ensuring my comfort. Lord, if you are asking me to do all that for my neighbour, I will need to try much harder than I am doing.

Saturday 18 March
Luke 18:9–14

He also told this parable to some who trusted in themselves that they were righteous and regarded others with contempt: 'Two men went up to the temple to pray, one a Pharisee and the other a tax-collector. The Pharisee, standing by himself, was praying thus, "God, I thank you that I am not like other people: thieves, rogues, adulterers, or even like this tax-collector. I fast twice a week; I give a tenth of all my income." But the tax-collector, standing far off, would not even look up to heaven, but was beating his breast and saying, "God, be merciful to me, a sinner!" I tell you, this man went down to his home justified rather than the other; for all who exalt themselves will be humbled, but all who humble themselves will be exalted.'

- Am I shocked and scandalised by this parable, or do I discover a Pharisee and a publican in my heart too? Sometimes I cannot avoid feeling morally superior and holier than others, or even to a particular person, however much I try not to. I feel I tick all the boxes, unlike others. I humbly ask for light to see and feel the deep roots pride has in my heart, and for the grace of real humility.

The Fourth Week of Lent
19–25 March

Something to think and pray about each day this week:

Some saw a blind man being cured and walked on amazed. Others saw the same cures and found faith. We can see things – everyday things – with different eyes. A sick woman may be seen with the eye of compassion for illness, hope for a cure, profit for a profession. The Christian tries to see the world with the eye of faith.

We learn to see and love with the eye of faith by looking at the look of Jesus towards us. It is often a big jump to believe in what we cannot see. Jesus looks at each of us with faith in our goodness and with love.

Maybe we can walk around in this atmosphere of faith, 'seeing' God in a flower, in a parent holding a child's hand, in a person pushing a wheelchair with courage, and notice that in many ways God is near and the presence of Jesus is at hand.

Donal Neary SJ,
Gospel Reflections for Sundays of Year A

The Presence of God
Dear Lord, as I come to you today, fill my heart, my whole being, with the wonder of your presence. Help me remain receptive to you as I put aside the cares of this world. Fill my mind with your peace.

Freedom
Lord, grant me the grace to be free from the excesses of this life. Let me not get caught up with the desire for wealth. Keep my heart and mind free to love and serve you.

Consciousness
I exist in a web of relationships: links to nature, people, God.
I trace out these links, giving thanks for the life that flows through them.
Some links are twisted or broken; I may feel regret, anger, disappointment.
I pray for the gift of acceptance and forgiveness.

The Word
God speaks to each of us individually. I listen attentively to hear what he is saying to me. Read the text a few times, then listen.
(Please turn to the Scripture on the following pages. Inspiration points are there, should you need them. When you are ready, return here to continue.)

Conversation
Jesus, you speak to me through the words of the Gospels. May I respond to your call today. Teach me to recognise your hand at work in my daily living.

Conclusion
I thank God for these moments we have spent together and for any insights I have been given concerning the text.

Sunday 19 March
Fourth Sunday of Lent
John 9:1–41

As he walked along, he saw a man blind from birth. His disciples asked him, 'Rabbi, who sinned, this man or his parents, that he was born blind?' Jesus answered, 'Neither this man nor his parents sinned; he was born blind so that God's works might be revealed in him. We must work the works of him who sent me while it is day; night is coming when no one can work. As long as I am in the world, I am the light of the world.' When he had said this, he spat on the ground and made mud with the saliva and spread the mud on the man's eyes, saying to him, 'Go, wash in the pool of Siloam' (which means Sent). Then he went and washed and came back able to see. The neighbours and those who had seen him before as a beggar began to ask, 'Is this not the man who used to sit and beg?' Some were saying, 'It is he.' Others were saying, 'No, but it is someone like him.' He kept saying, 'I am the man.' But they kept asking him, 'Then how were your eyes opened?' He answered, 'The man called Jesus made mud, spread it on my eyes, and said to me, "Go to Siloam and wash." Then I went and washed and received my sight.' They said to him, 'Where is he?' He said, 'I do not know.'

They brought to the Pharisees the man who had formerly been blind. Now it was a sabbath day when Jesus made the mud and opened his eyes. Then the Pharisees also began to ask him how he had received his sight. He said to them, 'He put mud on my eyes. Then I washed, and now I see.' Some of the Pharisees said, 'This man is not from God, for he does not observe the sabbath.' But others said, 'How can a man who is a sinner perform such signs?' And they were divided. So they said again to the blind man, 'What do you say about him? It was your eyes he opened.' He said, 'He is a prophet.'

The Jews did not believe that he had been blind and had received his sight until they called the parents of the man who had received his sight and asked them, 'Is this your son, who you say was born blind? How then does he now see?' His parents answered, 'We know that this is our son, and that he was born blind; but we do not know how it is that now he sees, nor do we know who opened his eyes. Ask him; he is of age. He will speak for himself.' His parents said this because they were afraid of the Jews; for the Jews had already agreed that anyone who confessed Jesus to be the Messiah would be put out of the synagogue. Therefore his parents said, 'He is of age; ask him.'

So for the second time they called the man who had been blind, and they said to him, 'Give glory to God! We know that this man is a sinner.' He answered, 'I do not know whether he is a sinner. One thing I do know, that though I was blind, now I see.' They said to him, 'What did he do to you? How did he open your eyes?' He answered them, 'I have told you already, and you would not listen. Why do you want to hear it again? Do you also want to become his disciples?' Then they reviled him, saying, 'You are his disciple, but we are disciples of Moses. We know that God has spoken to Moses, but as for this man, we do not know where he comes from.' The man answered, 'Here is an astonishing thing! You do not know where he comes from, and yet he opened my eyes. We know that God does not listen to sinners, but he does listen to one who worships him and obeys his will. Never since the world began has it been heard that anyone opened the eyes of a person born blind. If this man were not from God, he could do nothing.' They answered him, 'You were born entirely in sins, and are you trying to teach us?' And they drove him out.

Jesus heard that they had driven him out, and when he found him, he said, 'Do you believe in the Son of Man?' He answered, 'And who is he, sir? Tell me, so that I may believe in him.' Jesus said to him, 'You have seen him, and the one speaking with you is he.' He said, 'Lord, I believe.' And he worshipped him. Jesus said, 'I came into this world for judgement so that those who do not see may see, and those who do see may become blind.' Some of the Pharisees near him heard this and said to him, 'Surely we are not blind, are we?' Jesus said to them, 'If you were blind, you would not have sin. But now that you say, "We see", your sin remains.'

- What did he see? His eyes were opened to the light of faith, that Jesus was the Son of man. Can we pray that our eyes are opened to see the face of God in everyone we meet? And in everyone, friend or foe, for whom we pray?

Monday 20 March
St Joseph, Spouse of the Blessed Virgin Mary
Luke 2:41–51

Now every year his parents went to Jerusalem for the festival of the Passover. And when he was twelve years old, they went up as usual for the festival. When the festival was ended and they started to return, the boy Jesus stayed behind in Jerusalem, but his parents did not know it. Assuming that he was in the group of travellers, they went a day's journey. Then they started to look for him among their relatives and friends. When they did not find him, they returned to Jerusalem to search for him. After three days they found him in the temple, sitting among the teachers, listening to them and asking them questions. And all who heard him were amazed at his understanding and his answers. When his parents saw him they were astonished; and his mother said to him, 'Child, why have you treated us like this? Look, your father and I have been searching for you in great anxiety.' He said to them, 'Why were you searching for me? Did you not know that I must be in my Father's house?' But they did not understand what he said to them. Then he went down with them and came to Nazareth, and was obedient to them. His mother treasured all these things in her heart.

• Most people, in one way or another, leave their family environment. While our family always has a central place in our concerns, we are also called to serve the wider family. All of us, and especially Christians, are called to follow the example of Jesus and align ourselves with the family of the world. We are all brothers and sisters to each other and are called to care for and love each other.

Tuesday 21 March
John 5:1–16

After this there was a festival of the Jews, and Jesus went up to Jerusalem.

Now in Jerusalem by the Sheep Gate there is a pool, called in Hebrew Beth-zatha, which has five porticoes. In these lay many invalids – blind, lame, and paralysed. One man was there who had been ill for thirty-eight years. When Jesus saw him lying there and knew that he had been there a long time, he said to him, 'Do you want to be made well?' The sick man answered him, 'Sir, I have no one to put me into the pool when the water is stirred up; and while I am making my way, someone else steps down ahead of me.' Jesus said to him, 'Stand up, take your mat and walk.' At once the man was made well, and he took up his mat and began to walk.

Now that day was a sabbath. So the Jews said to the man who had been cured, 'It is the sabbath; it is not lawful for you to carry your mat.' But he answered them, 'The man who made me well said to me, "Take up your mat and walk."' They asked him, 'Who is the man who said to you, "Take it up and walk"?' Now the man who had been healed did not know who it was, for Jesus had disappeared in the crowd that was there. Later Jesus found him in the temple and said to him, 'See, you have been made well! Do not sin any more, so that nothing worse happens to you.' The man went away and told the Jews that it was Jesus who had made him well. Therefore the Jews started persecuting Jesus, because he was doing such things on the sabbath.

- Are there sick people in your family, among your friends? Bring them, one by one, before the Lord asking him to do what is best for them. Maybe you are worried about your own health? Tell the Lord of your anxieties and leave them with him. 'Cast all your anxiety on him, because he cares for you' (1 Peter 5:7).

- What might the Lord say in response to your prayer?

Wednesday 22 March
John 5:17–30

But Jesus answered them, 'My Father is still working, and I also am working.' For this reason the Jews were seeking all the more to kill him, because he was not only breaking the sabbath, but was also calling God his own Father, thereby making himself equal to God.

Jesus said to them, 'Very truly, I tell you, the Son can do nothing on his own, but only what he sees the Father doing; for whatever the Father does, the Son does likewise. The Father loves the Son and shows him all that he himself is doing; and he will show him greater works than these, so that you will be astonished. Indeed, just as the Father raises the dead and gives them life, so also the Son gives life to whomsoever he wishes. The Father judges no one but has given all judgement to the Son, so that all may honour the Son just as they honour the Father. Anyone who does not honour the Son does not honour the Father who sent him. Very truly, I tell you, anyone who hears my word and believes him who sent me has eternal life, and does not come under judgement, but has passed from death to life.

'Very truly, I tell you, the hour is coming, and is now here, when the dead will hear the voice of the Son of God, and those who hear will live. For just as the Father has life in himself, so he has granted the Son also to have life in himself; and he has given him authority to execute judgement, because he is the Son of Man. Do not be astonished at this; for the hour is coming when all who are in their graves will hear his voice and will come out – those who have done good, to the resurrection of life, and those who have done evil, to the resurrection of condemnation.

'I can do nothing on my own. As I hear, I judge; and my judgement is just, because I seek to do not my own will but the will of him who sent me.'

- The Creator has handed over all judgement to his Son. This means that the words that Jesus speaks judge us. We need to listen to them, accept them deeply and live by them. They show us up – how good or how insensitive and erring we are.

Thursday 23 March
John 5:31–47

Jesus answered them, 'If I testify about myself, my testimony is not true. There is another who testifies on my behalf, and I know that his testimony to me is true. You sent messengers to John, and he testified to the truth. Not that I accept such human testimony, but I say these things so that you may be saved. He was a burning and shining lamp, and you were willing to rejoice for a while in his light. But I have a testimony greater than John's. The works that the Father has given me to complete, the very works that I am doing, testify on my behalf that the Father has sent me. And the Father who sent me has himself testified on my behalf. You have never heard his voice or seen his form, and you do not have his word abiding in you, because you do not believe him whom he has sent.

'You search the scriptures because you think that in them you have eternal life; and it is they that testify on my behalf. Yet you refuse to come to me to have life. I do not accept glory from human beings. But I know that you do not have the love of God in you. I have come in my Father's name, and you do not accept me; if another comes in his own name, you will accept him. How can you believe when you accept glory from one another and do not seek the glory that comes from the one who alone is God? Do not think that I will accuse you before the Father; your accuser is Moses, on whom you have set your hope. If you believed Moses, you would believe me, for he wrote about me. But if you do not believe what he wrote, how will you believe what I say?'

- Thank the Lord for the encouragement that came from home, school and friends. Seek to forgive those who were a source of discouragement.

- Ask for the grace to keep growing in the freedom to be your own person, to speak your truth and witness to the risen Jesus.

Friday 24 March

John 7:1-2, 10, 25–30

After this Jesus went about in Galilee. He did not wish to go about in Judea because the Jews were looking for an opportunity to kill him. Now the Jewish festival of Booths was near.

But after his brothers had gone to the festival, then he also went, not publicly but as it were in secret.

Now some of the people of Jerusalem were saying, 'Is not this the man whom they are trying to kill? And here he is, speaking openly, but they say nothing to him! Can it be that the authorities really know that this is the Messiah? Yet we know where this man is from; but when the Messiah comes, no one will know where he is from.' Then Jesus cried out as he was teaching in the temple, 'You know me, and you know where I am from. I have not come on my own. But the one who sent me is true, and you do not know him. I know him, because I am from him, and he sent me.' Then they tried to arrest him, but no one laid hands on him, because his hour had not yet come.

- The one who sent Jesus contains all truth. But Jesus himself is that truth. Those who listened to him did not really know what truth is. To accept Jesus is to have the truth at its deepest level.

Saturday 25 March
The Annunciation of the Lord
Luke 1:26–38

In the sixth month the angel Gabriel was sent by God to a town in Galilee called Nazareth, to a virgin engaged to a man whose name was Joseph, of the house of David. The virgin's name was Mary. And he came to her and said, 'Greetings, favoured one! The Lord is with you.' But she was much perplexed by his words and pondered what sort of greeting this might be. The angel said to her, 'Do not be afraid, Mary, for you have found favour with God. And now, you will conceive in your womb and bear a son, and you will name him Jesus. He will be great, and will be called the Son of the Most High, and the Lord God will give to him the throne of his ancestor David. He will reign over the house of Jacob for ever, and of his kingdom there will be no end.' Mary said to the angel, 'How can this be, since I am a virgin?' The angel said to her, 'The Holy Spirit will come upon you, and the power of the Most High will overshadow you; therefore the child to be born will be holy; he will be called Son of God. And now, your relative Elizabeth in her old age has also conceived a son; and this is the sixth month for her who was said to be barren. For nothing will be impossible with God.' Then Mary said, 'Here am I, the servant of the Lord; let it be with me according to your word.' Then the angel departed from her.

- Lord, when the silence seems heavy and impenetrable, I recall how it can be broken at the most unexpected time and in the most unexpected circumstances. Like Mary, I must be still enough to hear the voice; courageous enough to act on it.

The Fifth Week of Lent
26 March–2 April 2023

Something to think and pray about each day this week:

A friend of mine from the Lutheran tradition has a very interesting question about Catholic Lent. 'Why do you need to do these things once a year – why don't you do all these good things all year?' I must say I had no answer.

When you cut to the quick, there is no doubt that for a Christian the entire year should be Lenten in spirit, but we are frail people and we need a good kick in the backside every so often, and an opportunity to benefit from that self-same kick. In fact, many of the great spiritual writers would hold the view that we should have a Lenten mindset all year round.

Some of these same writers would point out that Lent falls at a time of year when the pantry is running low. When the pantry was all you had, there was a sense of 'making do' until spring produced fresh produce. Lent helped this process. Rather than Lent being an occasion to make a personal decision to give something up it was a chance to live with the reality that the resources of the earth are scarce, and that we live in a fragile world.

Alan Hilliard,
Dipping into Lent

The Presence of God

Dear Jesus, I come to you today longing for your presence. I desire to love you as you love me. May nothing ever separate me from you.

Freedom

Lord, grant me the grace to have freedom of the spirit. Cleanse my heart and soul so that I may live joyously in your love.

Consciousness

Where am I with God? With others?
Do I have something to be grateful for? Then I give thanks.
Is there something I am sorry for? Then I ask forgiveness.

The Word

The word of God comes down to us through the Scriptures. May the Holy Spirit enlighten my mind and my heart to respond to the gospel teachings.

(Please turn to the Scripture on the following pages. Inspiration points are there, should you need them. When you are ready, return here to continue.)

Conversation

How has God's word moved me? Has it left me cold?
Has it consoled me or moved me to act in a new way?
I imagine Jesus standing or sitting beside me;
I turn and share my feelings with him

Conclusion

I thank God for these moments we have spent together and for any insights I have been given concerning the text.

Sunday 26 March
Fifth Sunday of Lent
John 11:1–45

Now a certain man was ill, Lazarus of Bethany, the village of Mary and her sister Martha. Mary was the one who anointed the Lord with perfume and wiped his feet with her hair; her brother Lazarus was ill. So the sisters sent a message to Jesus, 'Lord, he whom you love is ill.' But when Jesus heard it, he said, 'This illness does not lead to death; rather it is for God's glory, so that the Son of God may be glorified through it.' Accordingly, though Jesus loved Martha and her sister and Lazarus, after having heard that Lazarus was ill, he stayed two days longer in the place where he was.

Then after this he said to the disciples, 'Let us go to Judea again.' The disciples said to him, 'Rabbi, the Jews were just now trying to stone you, and are you going there again?' Jesus answered, 'Are there not twelve hours of daylight? Those who walk during the day do not stumble, because they see the light of this world. But those who walk at night stumble, because the light is not in them.' After saying this, he told them, 'Our friend Lazarus has fallen asleep, but I am going there to awaken him.' The disciples said to him, 'Lord, if he has fallen asleep, he will be all right.' Jesus, however, had been speaking about his death, but they thought that he was referring merely to sleep. Then Jesus told them plainly, 'Lazarus is dead. For your sake I am glad I was not there, so that you may believe. But let us go to him.' Thomas, who was called the Twin, said to his fellow-disciples, 'Let us also go, that we may die with him.'

When Jesus arrived, he found that Lazarus had already been in the tomb for four days. Now Bethany was near Jerusalem, some two miles away, and many of the Jews had come to Martha and Mary to console them about their brother. When Martha heard that Jesus was coming, she went and met him, while Mary stayed at home. Martha said to Jesus, 'Lord, if you had been here, my brother would not have died. But even now I know that God will give you whatever you ask of him.' Jesus said to her, 'Your brother will rise again.' Martha said to him, 'I know that he will rise again in the resurrection on the last day.' Jesus said to her, 'I am the resurrection and the life. Those who believe in me, even though they die, will live, and everyone who lives and believes in me will never die.

Do you believe this?' She said to him, 'Yes, Lord, I believe that you are the Messiah, the Son of God, the one coming into the world.'

When she had said this, she went back and called her sister Mary, and told her privately, 'The Teacher is here and is calling for you.' And when she heard it, she got up quickly and went to him. Now Jesus had not yet come to the village, but was still at the place where Martha had met him. The Jews who were with her in the house, consoling her, saw Mary get up quickly and go out. They followed her because they thought that she was going to the tomb to weep there. When Mary came where Jesus was and saw him, she knelt at his feet and said to him, 'Lord, if you had been here, my brother would not have died.' When Jesus saw her weeping, and the Jews who came with her also weeping, he was greatly disturbed in spirit and deeply moved. He said, 'Where have you laid him?' They said to him, 'Lord, come and see.' Jesus began to weep. So the Jews said, 'See how he loved him!' But some of them said, 'Could not he who opened the eyes of the blind man have kept this man from dying?'

Then Jesus, again greatly disturbed, came to the tomb. It was a cave, and a stone was lying against it. Jesus said, 'Take away the stone.' Martha, the sister of the dead man, said to him, 'Lord, already there is a stench because he has been dead for four days.' Jesus said to her, 'Did I not tell you that if you believed, you would see the glory of God?' So they took away the stone. And Jesus looked upwards and said, 'Father, I thank you for having heard me. I knew that you always hear me, but I have said this for the sake of the crowd standing here, so that they may believe that you sent me.' When he had said this, he cried with a loud voice, 'Lazarus, come out!' The dead man came out, his hands and feet bound with strips of cloth, and his face wrapped in a cloth. Jesus said to them, 'Unbind him, and let him go.'

Many of the Jews therefore, who had come with Mary and had seen what Jesus did, believed in him.

• Do I have some sense of being 'dead' in some areas of my life? What is keeping me in the grip of death? Do I have any awareness of what would need to change in my life for me to begin to become more alive again?

Monday 27 March

John 8:1–11

Early in the morning Jesus came again to the temple. All the people came to him and he sat down and began to teach them. The scribes and the Pharisees brought a woman who had been caught in adultery; and making her stand before all of them, they said to him, 'Teacher, this woman was caught in the very act of committing adultery. Now in the law Moses commanded us to stone such women. Now what do you say?' They said this to test him, so that they might have some charge to bring against him. Jesus bent down and wrote with his finger on the ground. When they kept on questioning him, he straightened up and said to them, 'Let anyone among you who is without sin be the first to throw a stone at her.' And once again he bent down and wrote on the ground. When they heard it, they went away, one by one, beginning with the elders; and Jesus was left alone with the woman standing before him. Jesus straightened up and said to her, 'Woman, where are they? Has no one condemned you?' She said, 'No one, sir.' And Jesus said, 'Neither do I condemn you. Go your way, and from now on do not sin again.'

• Have you experienced being challenged for doing something wrong by someone who loves you or by someone who is hostile to you? What has been the difference? To forgive and be forgiven is a wonderful healing.

Tuesday 28 March

John 8:21–30

Again he said to them, 'I am going away, and you will search for me, but you will die in your sin. Where I am going, you cannot come.' Then the Jews said, 'Is he going to kill himself? Is that what he means by saying, "Where I am going, you cannot come"?' He said to them, 'You are from below, I am from above; you are of this world, I am not of this world. I told you that you would die in your sins, for you will die in your sins unless you believe that I am he.' They said to him, 'Who are you?' Jesus said to them, 'Why do I speak to you at all? I have much to say about you and much to condemn; but the one who sent me is true, and I declare to the world what I have heard from him.' They did not understand that he was speaking to them about the Father. So Jesus said, 'When you have lifted up the Son of Man, then you will realise that I am he, and that I do nothing on my own, but I speak these things as the Father instructed me. And the one who sent me is with me; he has not left me alone, for I always do what is pleasing to him.' As he was saying these things, many believed in him.

- Jesus' hearers were either unable or unwilling to understand his teaching up to this point. He is still revealing his identity but he is also explaining the indentity of those he is addressing.

Wednesday 29 March
John 8:31–42

Then Jesus said to the Jews who had believed in him, 'If you continue in my word, you are truly my disciples; and you will know the truth, and the truth will make you free.' They answered him, 'We are descendants of Abraham and have never been slaves to anyone. What do you mean by saying, "You will be made free"?'

Jesus answered them, 'Very truly, I tell you, everyone who commits sin is a slave to sin. The slave does not have a permanent place in the household; the son has a place there for ever. So if the Son makes you free, you will be free indeed. I know that you are descendants of Abraham; yet you look for an opportunity to kill me, because there is no place in you for my word. I declare what I have seen in the Father's presence; as for you, you should do what you have heard from the Father.'

They answered him, 'Abraham is our father.' Jesus said to them, 'If you were Abraham's children, you would be doing what Abraham did, but now you are trying to kill me, a man who has told you the truth that I heard from God. This is not what Abraham did. You are indeed doing what your father does.' They said to him, 'We are not illegitimate children; we have one father, God himself.' Jesus said to them, 'If God were your Father, you would love me, for I came from God and now I am here. I did not come on my own, but he sent me.'

- Jesus stresses the importance of keeping his word. Doing this shows that one is a genuine follower of his. It means having the truth – or seeing things like God. This also means being free – from all dark deceptions. There is much to ponder in this.

Thursday 30 March
John 8:51–59

Jesus said to them. 'Very truly, I tell you, whoever keeps my word will never see death.' The Jews said to him, 'Now we know that you have a demon. Abraham died, and so did the prophets; yet you say, "Whoever keeps my word will never taste death." Are you greater than our father Abraham, who died? The prophets also died. Who do you claim to be?' Jesus answered, 'If I glorify myself, my glory is nothing. It is my Father who glorifies me, he of whom you say, "He is our God", though you do not know him. But I know him; if I were to say that I do not know him, I would be a liar like you. But I do know him and I keep his word. Your ancestor Abraham rejoiced that he would see my day; he saw it and was glad.' Then the Jews said to him, 'You are not yet fifty years old, and have you seen Abraham?' Jesus said to them, 'Very truly, I tell you, before Abraham was, I am.' So they picked up stones to throw at him, but Jesus hid himself and went out of the temple.

- The gospel today highlights the difference between the way of Jesus and the way of the authorities. The divine way of looking at things is the deep meaning that Jesus brings to life. His statement 'before Abraham ever was, I Am' pinpoints this difference. Ask Jesus to help you believe in his incarnation as he gives the gift of himself to us.

Friday 31 March
John 10:31–42

The Jews took up stones again to stone him. Jesus replied, 'I have shown you many good works from the Father. For which of these are you going to stone me?' The Jews answered, 'It is not for a good work that we are going to stone you, but for blasphemy, because you, though only a human being, are making yourself God.' Jesus answered, 'Is it not written in your law, "I said, you are gods"? If those to whom the word of God came were called "gods" – and the scripture cannot be annulled – can you say that the one whom the Father has sanctified and sent into the world is blaspheming because I said, "I am God's Son"? If I am not doing the works of my Father, then do not believe me. But if I do them, even though you do not believe me, believe the works, so that you may know and understand that the Father is in me and I am in the Father.' Then they tried to arrest him again, but he escaped from their hands.

He went away again across the Jordan to the place where John had been baptising earlier, and he remained there. Many came to him, and they were saying, 'John performed no sign, but everything that John said about this man was true.' And many believed in him there.

- The miracles that Jesus was working showed that there was something special about him. They were what the Father had given him to do. They were an indication of a mysterious relationship – that the Father is in him and he is in the Father. This knowledge called for wonder and astonishment. Aren't we all quick to reject and slow to learn?

Saturday 1 April
John 11:45–56

Many of the Jews therefore, who had come with Mary and had seen what Jesus did, believed in him. But some of them went to the Pharisees and told them what he had done. So the chief priests and the Pharisees called a meeting of the council, and said, 'What are we to do? This man is performing many signs. If we let him go on like this, everyone will believe in him, and the Romans will come and destroy both our holy place and our nation.' But one of them, Caiaphas, who was high priest that year, said to them, 'You know nothing at all! You do not understand that it is better for you to have one man die for the people than to have the whole nation destroyed.' He did not say this on his own, but being high priest that year he prophesied that Jesus was about to die for the nation, and not for the nation only, but to gather into one the dispersed children of God. So from that day on they planned to put him to death.

Jesus therefore no longer walked about openly among the Jews, but went from there to a town called Ephraim in the region near the wilderness; and he remained there with the disciples.

Now the Passover of the Jews was near, and many went up from the country to Jerusalem before the Passover to purify themselves. They were looking for Jesus and were asking one another as they stood in the temple, 'What do you think? Surely he will not come to the festival, will he?'

- I imagine the tension that reigned among Jesus and his group: a few days after their triumphant entry into Jerusalem, they could no longer walk openly in the city without exposing themselves to serious risk. And all this for my sake.

Something to think and pray about each day this week:

Jesus, it seems to me, lived his life in borrowed places.

Born in a borrowed stable, early life lived in a borrowed country, hospitality borrowed from people like Martha, Mary and Lazarus, Passover meal in a borrowed room and death saw him rest in a borrowed tomb. As we reflect on Holy Week, could it be the case he wants to borrow something from you? Something precious and totally your gift to share with him? I think so. He is borrowing not anything you have but all that you are. He is borrowing you! Borrowing you, that like the stable, the foreign country, the friends' home, the Upper Room and the tomb, he may bring something of himself to you in these most sacred days.

Vincent Sherlock,
Celebrating Holy Week

The Presence of God

As I sit here, the beating of my heart,
the ebb and flow of my breathing, the movements of my mind
are all signs of God's ongoing creation of me.
I pause for a moment and become aware
of this presence of God within me.

Freedom

I will ask God's help
to be free from my own preoccupations,
to be open to God in this time of prayer,
to come to know, love and serve God more.

Consciousness

At this moment, Lord, I turn my thoughts to you.
I will leave aside my chores and preoccupations.
I will take rest and refreshment in your presence.

The Word

Now I turn to the Scripture set out for me this day. I read slowly over the
words and see if any sentence or sentiment appeals to me.
*(Please turn to the Scripture on the following pages. Inspiration points are there,
should you need them. When you are ready, return here to continue.)*

Conversation

Begin to talk to Jesus about the Scripture you have just read. What part
of it strikes a chord in you? Perhaps the words of a friend – or some story
you have heard recently – will slowly rise to the surface of your consciousness. If so, does the story throw light on what the Scripture passage may
be saying to you?

Conclusion

Glory be to the Father, and to the Son, and to the Holy Spirit,
As it was in the beginning, is now and ever shall be,
World without end. Amen.

Sunday 2 April
Palm Sunday of the Passion of the Lord
Matthew 26:14–27:66

Then one of the twelve, who was called Judas Iscariot, went to the chief priests and said, 'What will you give me if I betray him to you?' They paid him thirty pieces of silver. And from that moment he began to look for an opportunity to betray him.

On the first day of Unleavened Bread the disciples came to Jesus, saying, 'Where do you want us to make the preparations for you to eat the Passover?' He said, 'Go into the city to a certain man, and say to him, "The Teacher says, My time is near; I will keep the Passover at your house with my disciples."' So the disciples did as Jesus had directed them, and they prepared the Passover meal.

When it was evening, he took his place with the twelve; and while they were eating, he said, 'Truly I tell you, one of you will betray me.' And they became greatly distressed and began to say to him one after another, 'Surely not I, Lord?' He answered, 'The one who has dipped his hand into the bowl with me will betray me. The Son of Man goes as it is written of him, but woe to that one by whom the Son of Man is betrayed! It would have been better for that one not to have been born.' Judas, who betrayed him, said, 'Surely not I, Rabbi?' He replied, 'You have said so.'

While they were eating, Jesus took a loaf of bread, and after blessing it he broke it, gave it to the disciples, and said, 'Take, eat; this is my body.' Then he took a cup, and after giving thanks he gave it to them, saying, 'Drink from it, all of you; for this is my blood of the covenant, which is poured out for many for the forgiveness of sins. I tell you, I will never again drink of this fruit of the vine until that day when I drink it new with you in my Father's kingdom.'

When they had sung the hymn, they went out to the Mount of Olives.

Then Jesus said to them, 'You will all become deserters because of me this night; for it is written,

"I will strike the shepherd,
    and the sheep of the flock will be scattered."

But after I am raised up, I will go ahead of you to Galilee.' Peter said to him, 'Though all become deserters because of you, I will never desert you.' Jesus said to him, 'Truly I tell you, this very night, before the cock crows, you will deny me three times.' Peter said to him, 'Even though I must die with you, I will not deny you.' And so said all the disciples.

Then Jesus went with them to a place called Gethsemane; and he said to his disciples, 'Sit here while I go over there and pray.' He took with him Peter and the two sons of Zebedee, and began to be grieved and agitated. Then he said to them, 'I am deeply grieved, even to death; remain here, and stay awake with me.' And going a little farther, he threw himself on the ground and prayed, 'My Father, if it is possible, let this cup pass from me; yet not what I want but what you want.' Then he came to the disciples and found them sleeping; and he said to Peter, 'So, could you not stay awake with me one hour? Stay awake and pray that you may not come into the time of trial; the spirit indeed is willing, but the flesh is weak.' Again he went away for the second time and prayed, 'My Father, if this cannot pass unless I drink it, your will be done.' Again he came and found them sleeping, for their eyes were heavy. So leaving them again, he went away and prayed for the third time, saying the same words. Then he came to the disciples and said to them, 'Are you still sleeping and taking your rest? See, the hour is at hand, and the Son of Man is betrayed into the hands of sinners. Get up, let us be going. See, my betrayer is at hand.'

While he was still speaking, Judas, one of the twelve, arrived; with him was a large crowd with swords and clubs, from the chief priests and the elders of the people. Now the betrayer had given them a sign, saying, 'The one I will kiss is the man; arrest him.' At once he came up to Jesus and said, 'Greetings, Rabbi!' and kissed him. Jesus said to him, 'Friend, do what you are here to do.' Then they came and laid hands on Jesus and arrested him. Suddenly, one of those with Jesus put his hand on his sword, drew it, and struck the slave of the high priest, cutting off his ear. Then Jesus said to him, 'Put your sword back into its place; for all who take the sword will perish by the sword. Do you think that I cannot appeal to my Father, and he will at once send me more than twelve legions of angels? But how then would the scriptures be fulfilled, which say it must happen in this way?' At that hour Jesus said to the crowds, 'Have you come out with swords and clubs to arrest me as though I were a bandit? Day after day I sat in the temple teaching, and you did not arrest me. But all this has taken place, so that the scriptures of the prophets may be fulfilled.' Then all the disciples deserted him and fled.

Those who had arrested Jesus took him to Caiaphas the high priest, in whose house the scribes and the elders had gathered. But Peter was following him at a distance, as far as the courtyard of the high priest; and going inside, he sat with the guards in order to see how this would end. Now the chief priests and the whole council were looking for false testimony against Jesus so that they might put him to death, but they found none, though many false witnesses came forward. At last two came forward and said, 'This fellow said, "I am able to destroy the temple of God and to build it in three days."' The high priest stood up and said, 'Have you no answer? What is it that they testify against you?' But Jesus was silent. Then the high priest said to him, 'I put you under oath before the living God, tell us if you are the Messiah, the Son of God.' Jesus said to him, 'You have said so. But I tell you,

From now on you will see the Son of Man
seated at the right hand of Power
and coming on the clouds of heaven.'

Then the high priest tore his clothes and said, 'He has blasphemed! Why do we still need witnesses? You have now heard his blasphemy. What is your verdict?' They answered, 'He deserves death.' Then they spat in his face and struck him; and some slapped him, saying, 'Prophesy to us, you Messiah! Who is it that struck you?'

Now Peter was sitting outside in the courtyard. A servant-girl came to him and said, 'You also were with Jesus the Galilean.' But he denied it before all of them, saying, 'I do not know what you are talking about.' When he went out to the porch, another servant-girl saw him, and she said to the bystanders, 'This man was with Jesus of Nazareth.' Again he denied it with an oath, 'I do not know the man.' After a little while the bystanders came up and said to Peter, 'Certainly you are also one of them, for your accent betrays you.' Then he began to curse, and he swore an oath, 'I do not know the man!' At that moment the cock crowed. Then Peter remembered what Jesus had said: 'Before the cock crows, you will deny me three times.' And he went out and wept bitterly.

When morning came, all the chief priests and the elders of the people conferred together against Jesus in order to bring about his death. They bound him, led him away, and handed him over to Pilate the governor.

When Judas, his betrayer, saw that Jesus was condemned, he repented and brought back the thirty pieces of silver to the chief priests and the elders. He said, 'I have sinned by betraying innocent blood.' But they said, 'What is that to us? See to it yourself.' Throwing down the pieces of silver in the temple, he departed; and he went and hanged himself. But the chief priests, taking the pieces of silver, said, 'It is not lawful to put them into the treasury, since they are blood money.' After conferring together, they used them to buy the potter's field as a place to bury foreigners. For this reason that field has been called the Field of Blood to this day. Then was fulfilled what had been spoken through the prophet Jeremiah, 'And they took the thirty pieces of silver, the price of the one on whom a price had been set, on whom some of the people of Israel had set a price, and they gave them for the potter's field, as the Lord commanded me.'

Now Jesus stood before the governor; and the governor asked him, 'Are you the King of the Jews?' Jesus said, 'You say so.' But when he was accused by the chief priests and elders, he did not answer. Then Pilate said to him, 'Do you not hear how many accusations they make against you?' But he gave him no answer, not even to a single charge, so that the governor was greatly amazed.

Now at the festival the governor was accustomed to release a prisoner for the crowd, anyone whom they wanted. At that time they had a notorious prisoner, called Jesus Barabbas. So after they had gathered, Pilate said to them, 'Whom do you want me to release for you, Jesus Barabbas or Jesus who is called the Messiah?' For he realised that it was out of jealousy that they had handed him over. While he was sitting on the judgement seat, his wife sent word to him, 'Have nothing to do with that innocent man, for today I have suffered a great deal because of a dream about him.' Now the chief priests and the elders persuaded the crowds to ask for Barabbas and to have Jesus killed. The governor again said to them, 'Which of the two do you want me to release for you?' And they said, 'Barabbas.' Pilate said to them, 'Then what should I do with Jesus who is called the Messiah?' All of them said, 'Let him be crucified!' Then he asked, 'Why, what evil has he done?' But they shouted all the more, 'Let him be crucified!'

So when Pilate saw that he could do nothing, but rather that a riot was beginning, he took some water and washed his hands before the crowd, saying, 'I am innocent of this man's blood; see to it yourselves.' Then the people as a whole answered, 'His blood be on us and on our children!' So he released Barabbas for them; and after flogging Jesus, he handed him over to be crucified.

Then the soldiers of the governor took Jesus into the governor's headquarters, and they gathered the whole cohort around him. They stripped him and put a scarlet robe on him, and after twisting some thorns into a crown, they put it on his head. They put a reed in his right hand and knelt before him and mocked him, saying, 'Hail, King of the Jews!' They spat on him, and took the reed and struck him on the head. After mocking him, they stripped him of the robe and put his own clothes on him. Then they led him away to crucify him.

As they went out, they came upon a man from Cyrene named Simon; they compelled this man to carry his cross. And when they came to a place called Golgotha (which means Place of a Skull), they offered him wine to drink, mixed with gall; but when he tasted it, he would not drink it. And when they had crucified him, they divided his clothes among themselves by casting lots; then they sat down there and kept watch over him. Over his head they put the charge against him, which read, 'This is Jesus, the King of the Jews.'

Then two bandits were crucified with him, one on his right and one on his left. Those who passed by derided him, shaking their heads and saying, 'You who would destroy the temple and build it in three days, save yourself! If you are the Son of God, come down from the cross.' In the same way the chief priests also, along with the scribes and elders, were mocking him, saying, 'He saved others; he cannot save himself. He is the King of Israel; let him come down from the cross now, and we will believe in him. He trusts in God; let God deliver him now, if he wants to; for he said, "I am God's Son."' The bandits who were crucified with him also taunted him in the same way.

From noon on, darkness came over the whole land until three in the afternoon. And about three o'clock Jesus cried with a loud voice, 'Eli, Eli, lama sabachthani?' that is, 'My God, my God, why have you forsaken me?' When some of the bystanders heard it, they said, 'This man is calling for Elijah.' At once one of them ran and got a sponge, filled it with sour wine, put it on a stick, and gave it to him to drink. But the others said, 'Wait, let us see whether Elijah will come to save him.' Then Jesus cried again with a loud voice and breathed his last. At that moment the curtain of the temple was torn in two, from top to bottom. The earth shook, and the rocks were split. The tombs also were opened, and many bodies of the saints who had fallen asleep were raised. After his resurrection they came out of the tombs and entered the holy city and appeared to many. Now when the centurion and those with him, who were keeping watch over Jesus, saw the earthquake and what took place, they were terrified and said, 'Truly this man was God's Son!'

Many women were also there, looking on from a distance; they had followed Jesus from Galilee and had provided for him. Among them were Mary Magdalene, and Mary the mother of James and Joseph, and the mother of the sons of Zebedee.

When it was evening, there came a rich man from Arimathea, named Joseph, who was also a disciple of Jesus. He went to Pilate and asked for the body of Jesus; then Pilate ordered it to be given to him. So Joseph took the body and wrapped it in a clean linen cloth and laid it in his own new tomb, which he had hewn in the rock. He then rolled a great stone to the door of the tomb and went away. Mary Magdalene and the other Mary were there, sitting opposite the tomb.

The next day, that is, after the day of Preparation, the chief priests and the Pharisees gathered before Pilate and said, 'Sir, we remember what that impostor said while he was still alive, "After three days I will rise again." Therefore command that the tomb be made secure until the third day; otherwise his disciples may go and steal him away, and tell the people, "He has been raised from the dead", and the last deception would be worse than the first.' Pilate said to them, 'You have a guard of soldiers; go, make it as secure as you can.' So they went with the guard and made the tomb secure by sealing the stone.

- The concept of betrayal, referenced here five times, is central in the Passion. Recall an experience you have had of being betrayed – perhaps you were let down by a friend, or a partner, or perhaps like many Catholics today you feel let down by the Church. How did you react? Did you retaliate, walk away or do your best to forgive?

Monday 3 April

John 12:1–11

Six days before the Passover Jesus came to Bethany, the home of Lazarus, whom he had raised from the dead. There they gave a dinner for him. Martha served, and Lazarus was one of those at the table with him. Mary took a pound of costly perfume made of pure nard, anointed Jesus' feet, and wiped them with her hair. The house was filled with the fragrance of the perfume. But Judas Iscariot, one of his disciples (the one who was about to betray him), said, 'Why was this perfume not sold for three hundred denarii and the money given to the poor?' (He said this not because he cared about the poor, but because he was a thief; he kept the common purse and used to steal what was put into it.) Jesus said, 'Leave her alone. She bought it so that she might keep it for the day of my burial. You always have the poor with you, but you do not always have me.'

When the great crowd of the Jews learned that he was there, they came not only because of Jesus but also to see Lazarus, whom he had raised from the dead. So the chief priests planned to put Lazarus to death as well, since it was on account of him that many of the Jews were deserting and were believing in Jesus.

• Mary is praying with her body and with her heart. It is a way we seldom pray. Her prayer is part of a tradition as old as the passionate, lyrical and sensuous Song of Solomon. Yet there is nothing to stop us praying this way – a gentle touch of understanding, a hug of reassurance, a smile of love – these, too, are prayers.

Tuesday 4 April

John 13:21–33, 36–38

After saying this Jesus was troubled in spirit, and declared, 'Very truly, I tell you, one of you will betray me.' The disciples looked at one another, uncertain of whom he was speaking. One of his disciples – the one whom Jesus loved – was reclining next to him; Simon Peter therefore motioned to him to ask Jesus of whom he was speaking. So while reclining next to Jesus, he asked him, 'Lord, who is it?' Jesus answered, 'It is the one to whom I give this piece of bread when I have dipped it in the dish.' So when he had dipped the piece of bread, he gave it to Judas son of Simon Iscariot. After he received the piece of bread, Satan entered into him.

Jesus said to him, 'Do quickly what you are going to do.' Now no one at the table knew why he said this to him. Some thought that, because Judas had the common purse, Jesus was telling him, 'Buy what we need for the festival'; or, that he should give something to the poor. So, after receiving the piece of bread, he immediately went out. And it was night.

When he had gone out, Jesus said, 'Now the Son of Man has been glorified, and God has been glorified in him. If God has been glorified in him, God will also glorify him in himself and will glorify him at once. Little children, I am with you only a little longer. You will look for me; and as I said to the Jews so now I say to you, "Where I am going, you cannot come."'

Simon Peter said to him, 'Lord, where are you going?' Jesus answered, 'Where I am going, you cannot follow me now; but you will follow afterwards.' Peter said to him, 'Lord, why can I not follow you now? I will lay down my life for you.' Jesus answered, 'Will you lay down your life for me? Very truly, I tell you, before the cock crows, you will have denied me three times.'

- Christ tells his disciples that he is going away, and that for the moment they cannot come with him. Peter asserts that he will be with Jesus come what may, but he is unaware of his own frailty. Our good intentions are often not carried out.

Wednesday 5 April
Matthew 26:14–25

Then one of the twelve, who was called Judas Iscariot, went to the chief priests and said, 'What will you give me if I betray him to you?' They paid him thirty pieces of silver. And from that moment he began to look for an opportunity to betray him.

On the first day of Unleavened Bread the disciples came to Jesus, saying, 'Where do you want us to make the preparations for you to eat the Passover?' He said, 'Go into the city to a certain man, and say to him, "The Teacher says, My time is near; I will keep the Passover at your house with my disciples."' So the disciples did as Jesus had directed them, and they prepared the Passover meal.

When it was evening, he took his place with the twelve; and while they were eating, he said, 'Truly I tell you, one of you will betray me.' And they became greatly distressed and began to say to him one after another, 'Surely not I, Lord?' He answered, 'The one who has dipped his hand into the bowl with me will betray me. The Son of Man goes as it is written of him, but woe to that one by whom the Son of Man is betrayed! It would have been better for that one not to have been born.' Judas, who betrayed him, said, 'Surely not I, Rabbi?' He replied, 'You have said so.'

• Holy Week is an invitation to walk closely with Jesus: we fix our gaze on him and accompany him in his suffering; we let him look closely at us and see us as we really are. We do not have to present a brave face to him, but can tell him about where we have been disappointed, let down – perhaps even betrayed. We avoid getting stuck in our own misfortune by seeing as he sees, by learning from his heart.

Thursday 6 April
Holy Thursday
John 13:1–15

Now before the festival of the Passover, Jesus knew that his hour had come to depart from this world and go to the Father. Having loved his own who were in the world, he loved them to the end. The devil had already put it into the heart of Judas son of Simon Iscariot to betray him. And during supper Jesus, knowing that the Father had given all things into his hands, and that he had come from God and was going to God, got up from the table, took off his outer robe, and tied a towel around himself. Then he poured water into a basin and began to wash the disciples' feet and to wipe them with the towel that was tied around him. He came to Simon Peter, who said to him, 'Lord, are you going to wash my feet?' Jesus answered, 'You do not know now what I am doing, but later you will understand.' Peter said to him, 'You will never wash my feet.' Jesus answered, 'Unless I wash you, you have no share with me.' Simon Peter said to him, 'Lord, not my feet only but also my hands and my head!' Jesus said to him, 'One who has bathed does not need to wash, except for the feet, but is entirely clean. And you are clean, though not all of you.' For he knew who was to betray him; for this reason he said, 'Not all of you are clean.'

After he had washed their feet, had put on his robe, and had returned to the table, he said to them, 'Do you know what I have done to you? You call me Teacher and Lord – and you are right, for that is what I am. So if I, your Lord and Teacher, have washed your feet, you also ought to wash one another's feet. For I have set you an example, that you also should do as I have done to you.'

• Do I feel like Peter, when Jesus kneels at my feet? Let me hear him whisper to me: 'Unless I wash you, you have no share with me.' Have I the courage and the generosity to accept his humble service and unconditional love?

Friday 7 April
Good Friday
John 18:1–19:42

After Jesus had spoken these words, he went out with his disciples across the Kidron valley to a place where there was a garden, which he and his disciples entered. Now Judas, who betrayed him, also knew the place, because Jesus often met there with his disciples. So Judas brought a detachment of soldiers together with police from the chief priests and the Pharisees, and they came there with lanterns and torches and weapons. Then Jesus, knowing all that was to happen to him, came forward and asked them, 'For whom are you looking?' They answered, 'Jesus of Nazareth.' Jesus replied, 'I am he.' Judas, who betrayed him, was standing with them. When Jesus said to them, 'I am he', they stepped back and fell to the ground. Again he asked them, 'For whom are you looking?' And they said, 'Jesus of Nazareth.' Jesus answered, 'I told you that I am he. So if you are looking for me, let these men go.' This was to fulfil the word that he had spoken, 'I did not lose a single one of those whom you gave me.' Then Simon Peter, who had a sword, drew it, struck the high priest's slave, and cut off his right ear. The slave's name was Malchus. Jesus said to Peter, 'Put your sword back into its sheath. Am I not to drink the cup that the Father has given me?'

So the soldiers, their officer, and the Jewish police arrested Jesus and bound him. First they took him to Annas, who was the father-in-law of Caiaphas, the high priest that year. Caiaphas was the one who had advised the Jews that it was better to have one person die for the people.

Simon Peter and another disciple followed Jesus. Since that disciple was known to the high priest, he went with Jesus into the courtyard of the high priest, but Peter was standing outside at the gate. So the other disciple, who was known to the high priest, went out, spoke to the woman who guarded the gate, and brought Peter in. The woman said to Peter, 'You are not also one of this man's disciples, are you?' He said, 'I am not.' Now the slaves and the police had made a charcoal fire because it was cold, and they were standing round it and warming themselves. Peter also was standing with them and warming himself.

Then the high priest questioned Jesus about his disciples and about his teaching. Jesus answered, 'I have spoken openly to the world; I have always taught in synagogues and in the temple, where all the Jews come together. I have said nothing in secret. Why do you ask me? Ask those who heard what I said to them; they know what I said.' When he had said this, one of the police standing nearby struck Jesus on the face, saying, 'Is that how you answer the high priest?' Jesus answered, 'If I have spoken wrongly, testify to the wrong. But if I have spoken rightly, why do you strike me?' Then Annas sent him bound to Caiaphas the high priest.

Now Simon Peter was standing and warming himself. They asked him, 'You are not also one of his disciples, are you?' He denied it and said, 'I am not.' One of the slaves of the high priest, a relative of the man whose ear Peter had cut off, asked, 'Did I not see you in the garden with him?' Again Peter denied it, and at that moment the cock crowed.

Then they took Jesus from Caiaphas to Pilate's headquarters. It was early in the morning. They themselves did not enter the headquarters, so as to avoid ritual defilement and to be able to eat the Passover. So Pilate went out to them and said, 'What accusation do you bring against this man?' They answered, 'If this man were not a criminal, we would not have handed him over to you.' Pilate said to them, 'Take him yourselves and judge him according to your law.' The Jews replied, 'We are not permitted to put anyone to death.' (This was to fulfil what Jesus had said when he indicated the kind of death he was to die.)

Then Pilate entered the headquarters again, summoned Jesus, and asked him, 'Are you the King of the Jews?' Jesus answered, 'Do you ask this on your own, or did others tell you about me?' Pilate replied, 'I am not a Jew, am I? Your own nation and the chief priests have handed you over to me. What have you done?' Jesus answered, 'My kingdom is not from this world. If my kingdom were from this world, my followers would be fighting to keep me from being handed over to the Jews. But as it is, my kingdom is not from here.' Pilate asked him, 'So you are a king?' Jesus answered, 'You say that I am a king. For this I was born, and for this I came into the world, to testify to the truth. Everyone who belongs to the truth listens to my voice.' Pilate asked him, 'What is truth?'

After he had said this, he went out to the Jews again and told them, 'I find no case against him. But you have a custom that I release someone for you at the Passover. Do you want me to release for you the King of the Jews?' They shouted in reply, 'Not this man, but Barabbas!' Now Barabbas was a bandit.

Then Pilate took Jesus and had him flogged. And the soldiers wove a crown of thorns and put it on his head, and they dressed him in a purple robe. They kept coming up to him, saying, 'Hail, King of the Jews!' and striking him on the face. Pilate went out again and said to them, 'Look, I am bringing him out to you to let you know that I find no case against him.' So Jesus came out, wearing the crown of thorns and the purple robe. Pilate said to them, 'Here is the man!' When the chief priests and the police saw him, they shouted, 'Crucify him! Crucify him!' Pilate said to them, 'Take him yourselves and crucify him; I find no case against him.' The Jews answered him, 'We have a law, and according to that law he ought to die because he has claimed to be the Son of God.'

Now when Pilate heard this, he was more afraid than ever. He entered his headquarters again and asked Jesus, 'Where are you from?' But Jesus gave him no answer. Pilate therefore said to him, 'Do you refuse to speak to me? Do you not know that I have power to release you, and power to crucify you?' Jesus answered him, 'You would have no power over me unless it had been given you from above; therefore the one who handed me over to you is guilty of a greater sin.' From then on Pilate tried to release him, but the Jews cried out, 'If you release this man, you are no friend of the emperor. Everyone who claims to be a king sets himself against the emperor.'

When Pilate heard these words, he brought Jesus outside and sat on the judge's bench at a place called The Stone Pavement, or in Hebrew Gabbatha. Now it was the day of Preparation for the Passover; and it was about noon. He said to the Jews, 'Here is your King!' They cried out, 'Away with him! Away with him! Crucify him!' Pilate asked them, 'Shall I crucify your King?' The chief priests answered, 'We have no king but the emperor.' Then he handed him over to them to be crucified.

So they took Jesus; and carrying the cross by himself, he went out to what is called The Place of the Skull, which in Hebrew is called Golgotha. There they crucified him, and with him two others, one on either side, with Jesus between them. Pilate also had an inscription written and put on the cross. It read, 'Jesus of Nazareth, the King of the Jews.' Many of the Jews read this inscription, because the place where Jesus was crucified was near the city; and it was written in Hebrew, in Latin and in Greek. Then the chief priests of the Jews said to Pilate, 'Do not write, "The King of the Jews", but, "This man said, I am King of the Jews."' Pilate answered, 'What I have written I have written.' When the soldiers had crucified Jesus, they took his clothes and divided them into four parts, one for each soldier. They also took his tunic; now the tunic was seamless, woven in one piece from the top. So they said to one another, 'Let us not tear it, but cast lots for it to see who will get it.' This was to fulfil what the scripture says,

> 'They divided my clothes among themselves,
>   and for my clothing they cast lots.'

And that is what the soldiers did.

Meanwhile, standing near the cross of Jesus were his mother, and his mother's sister, Mary the wife of Clopas, and Mary Magdalene. When Jesus saw his mother and the disciple whom he loved standing beside her, he said to his mother, 'Woman, here is your son.' Then he said to the disciple, 'Here is your mother.' And from that hour the disciple took her into his own home.

After this, when Jesus knew that all was now finished, he said (in order to fulfil the scripture), 'I am thirsty.' A jar full of sour wine was standing there. So they put a sponge full of the wine on a branch of hyssop and held it to his mouth. When Jesus had received the wine, he said, 'It is finished.' Then he bowed his head and gave up his spirit.

Since it was the day of Preparation, the Jews did not want the bodies left on the cross during the sabbath, especially because that sabbath was a day of great solemnity. So they asked Pilate to have the legs of the crucified men broken and the bodies removed. Then the soldiers came and broke the legs of the first and of the other who had been crucified with him. But when they came to Jesus and saw that he was already dead, they did not break his legs. Instead, one of the soldiers pierced his side with a spear, and at once blood and water came out. (He who saw this has testified so that you also may believe. His testimony is true, and he knows that he tells the truth.) These things occurred so that the scripture might be fulfilled, 'None of his bones shall be broken.' And again another passage of scripture says, 'They will look on the one whom they have pierced.'

After these things, Joseph of Arimathea, who was a disciple of Jesus, though a secret one because of his fear of the Jews, asked Pilate to let him take away the body of Jesus. Pilate gave him permission; so he came and removed his body. Nicodemus, who had at first come to Jesus by night, also came, bringing a mixture of myrrh and aloes, weighing about a hundred pounds. They took the body of Jesus and wrapped it with the spices in linen cloths, according to the burial custom of the Jews. Now there was a garden in the place where he was crucified, and in the garden there was a new tomb in which no one had ever been laid. And so, because it was the Jewish day of Preparation, and the tomb was nearby, they laid Jesus there.

• They took Jesus to Calvary and crucified him there. It looked a brutal act, but what splendour was shining through it! The cross ever stands as a symbol of power in weakness. The thirst of Christ on the cross is only a mirror of the depths of his prayer and longing.

Saturday 8 April
Holy Saturday
Matthew 28:1–10

After the sabbath, as the first day of the week was dawning, Mary Magdalene and the other Mary went to see the tomb. And suddenly there was a great earthquake; for an angel of the Lord, descending from heaven, came and rolled back the stone and sat on it. His appearance was like lightning, and his clothing white as snow. For fear of him the guards shook and became like dead men. But the angel said to the women, 'Do not be afraid; I know that you are looking for Jesus who was crucified. He is not here; for he has been raised, as he said. Come, see the place where he lay. Then go quickly and tell his disciples, "He has been raised from the dead, and indeed he is going ahead of you to Galilee; there you will see him." This is my message for you.' So they left the tomb quickly with fear and great joy, and ran to tell his disciples. Suddenly Jesus met them and said, 'Greetings!' And they came to him, took hold of his feet, and worshipped him. Then Jesus said to them, 'Do not be afraid; go and tell my brothers to go to Galilee; there they will see me.'

• It cannot but impress us that the Gospels, which provide such a detailed account of the Passion, do not contain one single word describing the Resurrection. We only read of the women going to the tomb and finding it empty. They are told that Jesus is not there, for he is risen. You will meet him in Galilee, in the land of your ordinary life. I pray to be able to find him in my life, for he is already there.

9–15 April 2023

Something to think and pray about each day this week:

The reason for the joy of Easter is that Christ is risen – the women who came to the tomb found their joy in this. They may have found joy also in a beautiful dawn in the garden, or in their friendships, but the joy of Easter is a joy of faith, which nothing need take away.

The joy of the resurrection is a joy in giving the life we have received from God: 'Life grows by being given away, and it weakens in isolation and comfort. Indeed, those who enjoy life most are those who leave security on the shore and become excited by the mission of communicating life to others' (Pope Francis). The Alleluia is for singing, not for humming; it is to be heard from the voice of the heart, and should lift the hearts of those who hear: 'Jesus Christ is risen. He is risen indeed. Alleluia!'

Donal Neary SJ,
Gospel Reflections for Sundays of Year A

The Presence of God

'Be still, and know that I am God!' (Psalm 46:10) Lord, your words lead us to the calmness and greatness of your presence.

Freedom

God is not foreign to my freedom. The Spirit breathes life into my most intimate desires, gently nudging me towards all that is good. I ask for the grace to let myself be enfolded by the Spirit.

Consciousness

Where do I sense hope, encouragement and growth in my life? By looking back over the past few months, I may be able to see which activities and occasions have produced rich fruit. If I do notice such areas, I will determine to give those areas both time and space in the future.

The Word

The word of God comes down to us through the Scriptures. May the Holy Spirit enlighten my mind and my heart to respond to the gospel teachings.

(Please turn to the Scripture on the following pages. Inspiration points are there, should you need them. When you are ready, return here to continue.)

Conversation

What is stirring in me as I pray? Am I consoled, troubled, left cold? I imagine Jesus standing or sitting at my side, and I share my feelings with him.

Conclusion

Glory be to the Father, and to the Son, and to the Holy Spirit,
As it was in the beginning, is now and ever shall be,
World without end. Amen.

Sunday 9 April
Easter Sunday of the Resurrection of the Lord
John 20:1–9

After the sabbath, as the first day of the week was dawning, Mary Magdalene and the other Mary went to see the tomb. And suddenly there was a great earthquake; for an angel of the Lord, descending from heaven, came and rolled back the stone and sat on it. His appearance was like lightning, and his clothing white as snow. For fear of him the guards shook and became like dead men. But the angel said to the women, 'Do not be afraid; I know that you are looking for Jesus who was crucified. He is not here; for he has been raised, as he said. Come, see the place where he lay. Then go quickly and tell his disciples, "He has been raised from the dead, and indeed he is going ahead of you to Galilee; there you will see him." This is my message for you.' So they left the tomb quickly with fear and great joy, and ran to tell his disciples. Suddenly Jesus met them and said, 'Greetings!' And they came to him, took hold of his feet, and worshipped him. Then Jesus said to them, 'Do not be afraid; go and tell my brothers to go to Galilee; there they will see me.'

• This is the day that the Lord has made, let us rejoice and be glad. Jesus is risen, never to die again. After the anguish of the last few days, it is the time of unbounded joy. I ask for the grace to enter into the joy of Jesus himself, the seed that fell to the ground and died, and is now bearing abundant fruit, full of new life.

Monday 10 April
Matthew 28:8–15

So they left the tomb quickly with fear and great joy, and ran to tell his disciples. Suddenly Jesus met them and said, 'Greetings!' And they came to him, took hold of his feet, and worshipped him. Then Jesus said to them, 'Do not be afraid; go and tell my brothers to go to Galilee; there they will see me.'

While they were going, some of the guard went into the city and told the chief priests everything that had happened. After the priests had assembled with the elders, they devised a plan to give a large sum of money to the soldiers, telling them, 'You must say, "His disciples came by night and stole him away while we were asleep." If this comes to the governor's ears, we will satisfy him and keep you out of trouble.' So they took the money and did as they were directed. And this story is still told among the Jews to this day.

- It seems strange that the authorities were ready to pay money to hide the fact of the Resurrection. Yet it is such a momentous event that turns upside down many of our usual ways of seeing things, that it is better to offer an implausible explanation than deal with its reality. I ask for the gift of faith, an open heart ready to meet the Risen Jesus.

Tuesday 11 April
John 20:11–18

But Mary stood weeping outside the tomb. As she wept, she bent over to look into the tomb; and she saw two angels in white, sitting where the body of Jesus had been lying, one at the head and the other at the feet. They said to her, 'Woman, why are you weeping?' She said to them, 'They have taken away my Lord, and I do not know where they have laid him.' When she had said this, she turned round and saw Jesus standing there, but she did not know that it was Jesus. Jesus said to her, 'Woman, why are you weeping? For whom are you looking?' Supposing him to be the gardener, she said to him, 'Sir, if you have carried him away, tell me where you have laid him, and I will take him away.' Jesus said to her, 'Mary!' She turned and said to him in Hebrew, 'Rabbouni!' (which means Teacher). Jesus said to her, 'Do not hold on to me, because I have not yet ascended to the Father. But go to my brothers and say to them, "I am ascending to my Father and your Father, to my God and your God."' Mary Magdalene went and announced to the disciples, 'I have seen the Lord'; and she told them that he had said these things to her.

- Lord, you offer me a parable of your dealings with me. Like Mary I am looking for you, following the call of love, but not recognising you because I am too caught up in my own emotions. But all the time you are looking at me, and it is when you call me by my name, and reach me with some intimately personal experience, that I recognise you with joy as my Rabbouni.

Wednesday 12 April
Luke 24:13–35

Now on that same day two of them were going to a village called Emmaus, about seven miles from Jerusalem, and talking with each other about all these things that had happened. While they were talking and discussing, Jesus himself came near and went with them, but their eyes were kept from recognising him. And he said to them, 'What are you discussing with each other while you walk along?' They stood still, looking sad. Then one of them, whose name was Cleopas, answered him, 'Are you the only stranger in Jerusalem who does not know the things that have taken place there in these days?' He asked them, 'What things?' They replied, 'The things about Jesus of Nazareth, who was a prophet mighty in deed and word before God and all the people, and how our chief priests and leaders handed him over to be condemned to death and crucified him. But we had hoped that he was the one to redeem Israel. Yes, and besides all this, it is now the third day since these things took place. Moreover, some women of our group astounded us. They were at the tomb early this morning, and when they did not find his body there, they came back and told us that they had indeed seen a vision of angels who said that he was alive. Some of those who were with us went to the tomb and found it just as the women had said; but they did not see him.' Then he said to them, 'Oh, how foolish you are, and how slow of heart to believe all that the prophets have declared! Was it not necessary that the Messiah should suffer these things and then enter into his glory?' Then beginning with Moses and all the prophets, he interpreted to them the things about himself in all the scriptures.

As they came near the village to which they were going, he walked ahead as if he were going on. But they urged him strongly, saying, 'Stay with us, because it is almost evening and the day is now nearly over.' So he went in to stay with them. When he was at the table with them, he took bread, blessed and broke it, and gave it to them. Then their eyes were opened, and they recognised him; and he vanished from their sight. They said to each other, 'Were not our hearts burning within us while he was talking to us on the road, while he was opening the scriptures to us?' That same hour they got up and returned to Jerusalem; and they found the eleven and their companions gathered together. They were saying,

'The Lord has risen indeed, and he has appeared to Simon!' Then they told what had happened on the road, and how he had been made known to them in the breaking of the bread.

- I reflect on this episode and on the mood of the two disciples, and realise how often I am in the same situation. How often I feel deeply disappointed and disoriented by the events around me, how often I am angry and frustrated like these two. The Resurrection seems something vague, that does not really fill me with hope. Yet I too feel this deep yearning to meet Jesus, whom I had hoped would be light of my life, giving it direction and meaning.

Thursday 13 April
Luke 24:35–48

Then they told what had happened on the road, and how he had been made known to them in the breaking of the bread.

While they were talking about this, Jesus himself stood among them and said to them, 'Peace be with you.' They were startled and terrified, and thought that they were seeing a ghost. He said to them, 'Why are you frightened, and why do doubts arise in your hearts? Look at my hands and my feet; see that it is I myself. Touch me and see; for a ghost does not have flesh and bones as you see that I have.' And when he had said this, he showed them his hands and his feet. While in their joy they were disbelieving and still wondering, he said to them, 'Have you anything here to eat?' They gave him a piece of broiled fish, and he took it and ate in their presence.

Then he said to them, 'These are my words that I spoke to you while I was still with you – that everything written about me in the law of Moses, the prophets and the psalms must be fulfilled.' Then he opened their minds to understand the scriptures, and he said to them, 'Thus it is written, that the Messiah is to suffer and to rise from the dead on the third day, and that repentance and forgiveness of sins is to be proclaimed in his name to all nations, beginning from Jerusalem. You are witnesses of these things.'

- Peace is not just the absence of conflict, but a deep sense of knowing all will be well! When he appears he so often says, 'Do not be afraid'! Am I fearful? Do I need to pray for trust in God, trust in my life, maybe an important relationship which is strained?

Friday 14 April

John 21:1–14

After these things Jesus showed himself again to the disciples by the Sea of Tiberias; and he showed himself in this way. Gathered there together were Simon Peter, Thomas called the Twin, Nathanael of Cana in Galilee, the sons of Zebedee, and two others of his disciples. Simon Peter said to them, 'I am going fishing.' They said to him, 'We will go with you.' They went out and got into the boat, but that night they caught nothing.

Just after daybreak, Jesus stood on the beach; but the disciples did not know that it was Jesus. Jesus said to them, 'Children, you have no fish, have you?' They answered him, 'No.' He said to them, 'Cast the net to the right side of the boat, and you will find some.' So they cast it, and now they were not able to haul it in because there were so many fish. That disciple whom Jesus loved said to Peter, 'It is the Lord!' When Simon Peter heard that it was the Lord, he put on some clothes, for he was naked, and jumped into the lake. But the other disciples came in the boat, dragging the net full of fish, for they were not far from the land, only about a hundred yards off.

When they had gone ashore, they saw a charcoal fire there, with fish on it, and bread. Jesus said to them, 'Bring some of the fish that you have just caught.' So Simon Peter went aboard and hauled the net ashore, full of large fish, a hundred and fifty-three of them; and though there were so many, the net was not torn. Jesus said to them, 'Come and have breakfast.' Now none of the disciples dared to ask him, 'Who are you?' because they knew it was the Lord. Jesus came and took the bread and gave it to them, and did the same with the fish. This was now the third time that Jesus appeared to the disciples after he was raised from the dead.

- 'Come and have breakfast.' How simply and sensitively Jesus deals with us! He knows our needs and our hunger. He knows too that we can only manage the revelations of the divine in small portions. I could do well before my daily breakfast to listen to the Lord speaking my name and saying 'Come and have breakfast.' Imagine him serving me, if not with bread and fish, perhaps with a muffin and coffee! I begin to notice that throughout the day he continues to serve me what I need.

Saturday 15 April
Mark 16:9–15

Now after he rose early on the first day of the week, he appeared first to Mary Magdalene, from whom he had cast out seven demons. She went out and told those who had been with him, while they were mourning and weeping. But when they heard that he was alive and had been seen by her, they would not believe it.

After this he appeared in another form to two of them, as they were walking into the country. And they went back and told the rest, but they did not believe them.

Later he appeared to the eleven themselves as they were sitting at the table; and he upbraided them for their lack of faith and stubbornness, because they had not believed those who saw him after he had risen. And he said to them, 'Go into all the world and proclaim the good news to the whole creation.'

- Sometimes outwardly confident yet harbouring doubts, at other times hesitant to proclaim what seems certain to me, I am like the disciples. Jesus invites me to a fullness of faith. He sees and understands my stubbornness and reluctance yet trusts me. Calmly and gently he sends me to 'go into all the world'.

The Second Week of Easter
16–22 April 2023

Something to think and pray about each day this week:

An Easter theme, and the main one that figures now in the Easter Vigil, is the acceptance of the risen Christ as a new light for humanity emerging out of the darkness of death. It can be impressive at the vigil service to see the candle flames springing up and spreading throughout the darkened congregation, as people share the 'light of Christ' by receiving it from the Paschal candle and passing it on to others; and to appreciate this as a living picture of the reality of people's shared faith in the risen Christ, the faith that they are meant to continue to live afterwards as they draw continued enlightenment from their Lord.

Jack Mahoney SJ, *Glimpses of the Gospels:*
Theological, Spiritual & Practical Reflections

The Presence of God

'Come to me, all you who are weary and are carrying heavy burdens, and I will give you rest' (Matthew 11:28). Here I am, Lord. I come to seek your presence. I long for your healing power.

Freedom

By God's grace I was born to live in freedom. Free to enjoy the pleasures he created for me. Dear Lord, grant that I may live as you intended, with complete confidence in your loving care.

Consciousness

Knowing that God loves me unconditionally, I look honestly over the past day, its events and my feelings. Do I have something to be grateful for? Then I give thanks. Is there something I am sorry for? Then I ask forgiveness.

The Word

God speaks to each of us individually. I listen attentively to hear what he is saying to me. Read the text a few times, then listen.
(Please turn to the Scripture on the following pages. Inspiration points are there, should you need them. When you are ready, return here to continue.)

Conversation

I know with certainty that there were times when you carried me, Lord. There were times when it was through your strength that I got through the dark times in my life.

Conclusion

Glory be to the Father, and to the Son, and to the Holy Spirit,
As it was in the beginning, is now and ever shall be,
World without end. Amen.

Sunday 16 April
Second Sunday of Easter
John 20:19–31

When it was evening on that day, the first day of the week, and the doors of the house where the disciples had met were locked for fear of the Jews, Jesus came and stood among them and said, 'Peace be with you.' After he said this, he showed them his hands and his side. Then the disciples rejoiced when they saw the Lord. Jesus said to them again, 'Peace be with you. As the Father has sent me, so I send you.' When he had said this, he breathed on them and said to them, 'Receive the Holy Spirit. If you forgive the sins of any, they are forgiven them; if you retain the sins of any, they are retained.'

But Thomas (who was called the Twin), one of the twelve, was not with them when Jesus came. So the other disciples told him, 'We have seen the Lord.' But he said to them, 'Unless I see the mark of the nails in his hands, and put my finger in the mark of the nails and my hand in his side, I will not believe.'

A week later his disciples were again in the house, and Thomas was with them. Although the doors were shut, Jesus came and stood among them and said, 'Peace be with you.' Then he said to Thomas, 'Put your finger here and see my hands. Reach out your hand and put it in my side. Do not doubt but believe.' Thomas answered him, 'My Lord and my God!' Jesus said to him, 'Have you believed because you have seen me? Blessed are those who have not seen and yet have come to believe.'

Now Jesus did many other signs in the presence of his disciples, which are not written in this book. But these are written so that you may come to believe that Jesus is the Messiah, the Son of God, and that through believing you may have life in his name.

- Here we are shown twice how Jesus breaks into the lives of his friends. Can he break in on me? Where am I in these scenes? Am I hesitant like Thomas? Am I looking for some sign before committing myself to the fact that I am living in a new world, the world of the Resurrection?

Monday 17 April
John 3:1–8

Now there was a Pharisee named Nicodemus, a leader of the Jews. He came to Jesus by night and said to him, 'Rabbi, we know that you are a teacher who has come from God; for no one can do these signs that you do apart from the presence of God.' Jesus answered him, 'Very truly, I tell you, no one can see the kingdom of God without being born from above.' Nicodemus said to him, 'How can anyone be born after having grown old? Can one enter a second time into the mother's womb and be born?' Jesus answered, 'Very truly, I tell you, no one can enter the kingdom of God without being born of water and Spirit. What is born of the flesh is flesh, and what is born of the Spirit is spirit. Do not be astonished that I said to you, "You must be born from above." The wind blows where it chooses, and you hear the sound of it, but you do not know where it comes from or where it goes. So it is with everyone who is born of the Spirit.'

- I too, like Nicodemus, find it difficult to imagine how I can change what is so clearly a part of me. I ask for the grace to know where Jesus is inviting me to be born anew, in things large or small, and to do my best to fulfil his will.

Tuesday 18 April
John 3:7b–15

Jesus said to Nicodemus, 'Do not be astonished that I said to you, "You must be born from above." The wind blows where it chooses, and you hear the sound of it, but you do not know where it comes from or where it goes. So it is with everyone who is born of the Spirit.' Nicodemus said to him, 'How can these things be?' Jesus answered him, 'Are you a teacher of Israel, and yet you do not understand these things?

'Very truly, I tell you, we speak of what we know and testify to what we have seen; yet you do not receive our testimony. If I have told you about earthly things and you do not believe, how can you believe if I tell you about heavenly things? No one has ascended into heaven except the one who descended from heaven, the Son of Man. And just as Moses lifted up the serpent in the wilderness, so must the Son of Man be lifted up, that whoever believes in him may have eternal life.'

- Jesus talks about 'heavenly things', but we spend most of our lives talking about 'earthly things'. Lord, keep me faithful to my daily prayer time so that you and I may chat about the divine dimension which pervades all earthly things.

Wednesday 19 April
John 3:16–21

Jesus said to Nicodemus, 'For God so loved the world that he gave his only Son, so that everyone who believes in him may not perish but may have eternal life.

'Indeed, God did not send the Son into the world to condemn the world, but in order that the world might be saved through him. Those who believe in him are not condemned; but those who do not believe are condemned already, because they have not believed in the name of the only Son of God. And this is the judgement, that the light has come into the world, and people loved darkness rather than light because their deeds were evil. For all who do evil hate the light and do not come to the light, so that their deeds may not be exposed. But those who do what is true come to the light, so that it may be clearly seen that their deeds have been done in God.'

- We live in the new world of God when we love; when we love others and love God. Prayer is relaxing into the mystery of being loved by God. Prayer moments like praying with Sacred Space bring us into the 'beyond', the world of love, of mystery and of endurance.

Thursday 20 April
John 3:31–36

John said, 'The one who comes from above is above all; the one who is of the earth belongs to the earth and speaks about earthly things. The one who comes from heaven is above all. He testifies to what he has seen and heard, yet no one accepts his testimony. Whoever has accepted his testimony has certified this, that God is true. He whom God has sent speaks the words of God, for he gives the Spirit without measure. The Father loves the Son and has placed all things in his hands. Whoever believes in the Son has eternal life; whoever disobeys the Son will not see life, but must endure God's wrath.'

- God's Word is spoken unceasingly in my soul. There is never an instant when he is not within me. With him, I make my own soul every day of my earthly life. I need have no fear of birth or rebirth, change of life or death. Instead, I see them for what they are – as thrilling stages along a transcendent journey home.

Friday 21 April

John 6:1–15

After this Jesus went to the other side of the Sea of Galilee, also called the Sea of Tiberias. A large crowd kept following him, because they saw the signs that he was doing for the sick. Jesus went up the mountain and sat down there with his disciples. Now the Passover, the festival of the Jews, was near. When he looked up and saw a large crowd coming towards him, Jesus said to Philip, 'Where are we to buy bread for these people to eat?' He said this to test him, for he himself knew what he was going to do. Philip answered him, 'Six months' wages would not buy enough bread for each of them to get a little.' One of his disciples, Andrew, Simon Peter's brother, said to him, 'There is a boy here who has five barley loaves and two fish. But what are they among so many people?' Jesus said, 'Make the people sit down.' Now there was a great deal of grass in the place; so they sat down, about five thousand in all. Then Jesus took the loaves, and when he had given thanks, he distributed them to those who were seated; so also the fish, as much as they wanted. When they were satisfied, he told his disciples, 'Gather up the fragments left over, so that nothing may be lost.' So they gathered them up, and from the fragments of the five barley loaves, left by those who had eaten, they filled twelve baskets. When the people saw the sign that he had done, they began to say, 'This is indeed the prophet who is to come into the world.'

When Jesus realised that they were about to come and take him by force to make him king, he withdrew again to the mountain by himself.

- What aspect of this story touches me – maybe the abundance of Jesus' concern for the people or the pathetic amount of food available to the disciples? Have I ever been surprised by the abundance of good that has come from my poverty?

- Who has fed me throughout my life? My body needs food and my spirit needs food too. How do I provide for my spirit's hunger?

Saturday 22 April

John 6:16–21

When evening came, his disciples went down to the lake, got into a boat, and started across the lake to Capernaum. It was now dark, and Jesus had not yet come to them. The lake became rough because a strong wind was blowing. When they had rowed about three or four miles, they saw Jesus walking on the lake and coming near the boat, and they were terrified. But he said to them, 'It is I; do not be afraid.' Then they wanted to take him into the boat, and immediately the boat reached the land towards which they were going.

- The disciples knew they were in difficulty and had work to do. They would have been keenly aware of Jesus' absence. Now, seeing him approach them, they had to ask what they meant to him. I consider how I sometimes struggle 'against the wind' and am slow to recognise that help Jesus offers to me.

Something to think and pray about each day this week:

We come to Easter faith by acknowledging the hungers of the heart ('our own hope had been'), by searching the scriptures ('our hearts burning within us'), by holding on to the story of the first disciples and witness of the women, by the Eucharist ('the breaking of the bread') and by sharing our faith ('they told their story'). Is there more? As the story starts, *he* stops *them*. Towards the end of the story, *they* stop *him* from walking out of their lives, perhaps for ever. Their choice to have him in their lives is what turns the story around. The moment of desire leads to the moment of recognition and a life-changing encounter.

Kieran O'Mahony OSA,
*Hearers of the Word: Praying and Exploring the
Readings for Easter & Pentecost*

The Presence of God

'Be still, and know that I am God!' Lord, your words lead us to the calmness and greatness of your presence.

Freedom

Leave me here freely all alone. / In cell where never sunlight shone. / Should no one ever speak to me. / This golden silence makes me free!
– Part of a poem by Bl. Titus Brandsma, written while he was a prisoner at Dachau concentration camp

Consciousness

Knowing that God loves me unconditionally, I can afford to be honest about how I am. How has the day been, and how do I feel now? I share my feelings openly with the Lord.

The Word

I take my time to read the word of God slowly, a few times, allowing myself to dwell on anything that strikes me.
(Please turn to the Scripture on the following pages. Inspiration points are there, should you need them. When you are ready, return here to continue.)

Conversation

Sometimes I wonder what I might say if I were to meet you in person, Lord. I think I might say, 'Thank you' because you are always there for me.

Conclusion

I thank God for these moments we have spent together and for any insights I have been given concerning the text.

Sunday 23 April
Third Sunday of Easter
Luke 24:13–35

Now on that same day two of them were going to a village called Emmaus, about seven miles from Jerusalem, and talking with each other about all these things that had happened. While they were talking and discussing, Jesus himself came near and went with them, but their eyes were kept from recognising him. And he said to them, 'What are you discussing with each other while you walk along?' They stood still, looking sad. Then one of them, whose name was Cleopas, answered him, 'Are you the only stranger in Jerusalem who does not know the things that have taken place there in these days?' He asked them, 'What things?' They replied, 'The things about Jesus of Nazareth, who was a prophet mighty in deed and word before God and all the people, and how our chief priests and leaders handed him over to be condemned to death and crucified him. But we had hoped that he was the one to redeem Israel. Yes, and besides all this, it is now the third day since these things took place. Moreover, some women of our group astounded us. They were at the tomb early this morning, and when they did not find his body there, they came back and told us that they had indeed seen a vision of angels who said that he was alive. Some of those who were with us went to the tomb and found it just as the women had said; but they did not see him.' Then he said to them, 'Oh, how foolish you are, and how slow of heart to believe all that the prophets have declared! Was it not necessary that the Messiah should suffer these things and then enter into his glory?' Then beginning with Moses and all the prophets, he interpreted to them the things about himself in all the scriptures.

As they came near the village to which they were going, he walked ahead as if he were going on. But they urged him strongly, saying, 'Stay with us, because it is almost evening and the day is now nearly over.' So he went in to stay with them. When he was at the table with them, he took bread, blessed and broke it, and gave it to them. Then their eyes were opened, and they recognised him; and he vanished from their sight. They said to each other, 'Were not our hearts burning within us while he was talking to us on the road, while he was opening the scriptures to us?'

That same hour they got up and returned to Jerusalem; and they found the eleven and their companions gathered together. They were saying, 'The Lord has risen indeed, and he has appeared to Simon!' Then they told what had happened on the road, and how he had been made known to them in the breaking of the bread.

- We feel so similar to the two disciples of Emmaus, full of disappointed hopes, which make us angry or even resentful. I let myself get in touch with the disappointments in my heart, and imagine Jesus walking with me as I struggle to regain hope and trust. I ask Jesus to enlighten me and to set my heart burning as he did for the two disciples.

Monday 24 April
John 6:22–29

The next day the crowd that had stayed on the other side of the lake saw that there had been only one boat there. They also saw that Jesus had not got into the boat with his disciples, but that his disciples had gone away alone. Then some boats from Tiberias came near the place where they had eaten the bread after the Lord had given thanks. So when the crowd saw that neither Jesus nor his disciples were there, they themselves got into the boats and went to Capernaum looking for Jesus.

When they found him on the other side of the lake, they said to him, 'Rabbi, when did you come here?' Jesus answered them, 'Very truly, I tell you, you are looking for me, not because you saw signs, but because you ate your fill of the loaves. Do not work for the food that perishes, but for the food that endures for eternal life, which the Son of Man will give you. For it is on him that God the Father has set his seal.' Then they said to him, 'What must we do to perform the works of God?' Jesus answered them, 'This is the work of God, that you believe in him whom he has sent.'

- 'Do not work for the food that perishes, but for the food that endures for eternal life.' Strong words from Jesus! Was it that Jesus knew that while many had enjoyed the food he provided for them, they had not listened to his message? Civilisations rise and fall. What is it that endures?

Tuesday 25 April
St Mark, Evangelist
Mark 16:15–20

And he said to them, 'Go into all the world and proclaim the good news to the whole creation. The one who believes and is baptised will be saved; but the one who does not believe will be condemned. And these signs will accompany those who believe: by using my name they will cast out demons; they will speak in new tongues; they will pick up snakes in their hands, and if they drink any deadly thing, it will not hurt them; they will lay their hands on the sick, and they will recover.'

So then the Lord Jesus, after he had spoken to them, was taken up into heaven and sat down at the right hand of God. And they went out and proclaimed the good news everywhere, while the Lord worked with them and confirmed the message by the signs that accompanied it.

- Each of us is called into the ministry of Jesus in some way. We are called to be 'other Christs', to be people who wish to make known and spread the love of God and his care for his people in the world. We may never know how much we have done this; it is sufficient that we do what we can. God has some work to do that can be done only through each person. In a time of prayer we ask that we use our gifts and talents as best we can in God's service.

Wednesday 26 April
John 6:35–40

Jesus said to them, 'I am the bread of life. Whoever comes to me will never be hungry, and whoever believes in me will never be thirsty. But I said to you that you have seen me and yet do not believe. Everything that the Father gives me will come to me, and anyone who comes to me I will never drive away; for I have come down from heaven, not to do my own will, but the will of him who sent me. And this is the will of him who sent me, that I should lose nothing of all that he has given me, but raise it up on the last day. This is indeed the will of my Father, that all who see the Son and believe in him may have eternal life; and I will raise them up on the last day.'

- It is the will of God that nothing should be lost; may I look on everything that is good as a gift from God and an invitation to embrace the life that God offers.

- So much is offered to God each day! I pray that all people who are blessed may realise that their identity and destiny lies in God.

Thursday 27 April
John 6:44–51

Jesus said to his disciples, 'No one can come to me unless drawn by the Father who sent me; and I will raise that person up on the last day. It is written in the prophets, "And they shall all be taught by God." Everyone who has heard and learned from the Father comes to me. Not that anyone has seen the Father except the one who is from God; he has seen the Father. Very truly, I tell you, whoever believes has eternal life. I am the bread of life. Your ancestors ate the manna in the wilderness, and they died. This is the bread that comes down from heaven, so that one may eat of it and not die. I am the living bread that came down from heaven. Whoever eats of this bread will live for ever; and the bread that I will give for the life of the world is my flesh.'

- In today's gospel, Jesus teaches that his Father draws one to believe and that those who believe in him (Jesus) have everlasting life. He reiterates the point that he is the bread of life from heaven, and that those who eat this bread (listen to and accept his word) will not die. How do you understand this?

- Our prayer is not our own initiative, but is itself a response to God who draws us to what is true, to what is life-giving, to what is loving.

Friday 28 April
John 6:52–59

The Jews then disputed among themselves, saying, 'How can this man give us his flesh to eat?' So Jesus said to them, 'Very truly, I tell you, unless you eat the flesh of the Son of Man and drink his blood, you have no life in you. Those who eat my flesh and drink my blood have eternal life, and I will raise them up on the last day; for my flesh is true food and my blood is true drink. Those who eat my flesh and drink my blood abide in me, and I in them. Just as the living Father sent me, and I live because of the Father, so whoever eats me will live because of me. This is the bread that came down from heaven, not like that which your ancestors ate, and they died. But the one who eats this bread will live for ever.' He said these things while he was teaching in the synagogue at Capernaum.

- Jesus did not want the people simply to agree with him, to assent to his ideas. He wanted them to be drawn fully into the life of God, just as he was. He invites us to be consumed by God, to let go of our reservations and hesitations and to trust in the one who gives life.

Saturday 29 April

John 6:60–69

When many of his disciples heard it, they said, 'This teaching is difficult; who can accept it?' But Jesus, being aware that his disciples were complaining about it, said to them, 'Does this offend you? Then what if you were to see the Son of Man ascending to where he was before? It is the spirit that gives life; the flesh is useless. The words that I have spoken to you are spirit and life. But among you there are some who do not believe.' For Jesus knew from the first who were the ones that did not believe, and who was the one that would betray him. And he said, 'For this reason I have told you that no one can come to me unless it is granted by the Father.'

Because of this many of his disciples turned back and no longer went about with him. So Jesus asked the twelve, 'Do you also wish to go away?' Simon Peter answered him, 'Lord, to whom can we go? You have the words of eternal life. We have come to believe and know that you are the Holy One of God.'

- We need the gifts of 'spirit and life', otherwise we will be like those disciples who no longer went about with Jesus. He was there in front of them but they could not recognise who he really was. We must not think that only some people are given the gift of faith: no, the Spirit is poured out on everyone, and Jesus' abiding desire is to give everyone life to the full.

- Lord, draw me close to you, and be spirit and life for me.

The Fourth Week of Easter
30 April–6 May 2023

Something to think and pray about each day this week:

The first big moment of vocation is baptism. The anointing of chrism at baptism might be called the anointing for vocation.

The baptismal vocation is for witness, love and service. This is expressed in ways in which people live out their baptism in married life, single life – and within the single life, maybe religious life or priesthood.

Our active witness is to the life and the values of Jesus in our lives. Teaching is not itself a vocation, for example, but the way we teach is a way of living out our vocation. It is the same with many of the helping professions and employments. Being a good neighbour can be a living out of our vocation.

We witness to love in marriage, in family, extended family, and in friendship. Any love is a sharing in the love of God. In the moments of unselfish love in any relationship we are living out our vocation. When we love, we are doing God's will!

Donal Neary SJ,
Gospel Reflections for Sundays of Year A

The Presence of God

'Come to me, all you who are weary and are carrying heavy burdens, and I will give you rest' (Matthew 11:28). Here I am, Lord. I come to seek your presence. I long for your healing power.

Freedom

By God's grace I was born to live in freedom. Free to enjoy the pleasures he created for me. Dear Lord, grant that I may live as you intended, with complete confidence in your loving care.

Consciousness

Knowing that God loves me unconditionally, I look honestly over the past day, its events and my feelings. Do I have something to be grateful for? Then I give thanks. Is there something I am sorry for? Then I ask forgiveness.

The Word

God speaks to each of us individually. I listen attentively to hear what he is saying to me. Read the text a few times, then listen.

(Please turn to the Scripture on the following pages. Inspiration points are there, should you need them. When you are ready, return here to continue.)

Conversation

I know with certainty that there were times when you carried me, Lord. There were times when it was through your strength that I got through the dark times in my life.

Conclusion

Glory be to the Father, and to the Son, and to the Holy Spirit,
As it was in the beginning, is now and ever shall be,
World without end. Amen.

Sunday 30 April
Fourth Sunday of Easter
John 10:1–10

Jesus said to them, 'Very truly, I tell you, anyone who does not enter the sheepfold by the gate but climbs in by another way is a thief and a bandit. The one who enters by the gate is the shepherd of the sheep. The gatekeeper opens the gate for him, and the sheep hear his voice. He calls his own sheep by name and leads them out. When he has brought out all his own, he goes ahead of them, and the sheep follow him because they know his voice. They will not follow a stranger, but they will run from him because they do not know the voice of strangers.' Jesus used this figure of speech with them, but they did not understand what he was saying to them.

So again Jesus said to them, 'Very truly, I tell you, I am the gate for the sheep. All who came before me are thieves and bandits; but the sheep did not listen to them. I am the gate. Whoever enters by me will be saved, and will come in and go out and find pasture. The thief comes only to steal and kill and destroy. I came that they may have life, and have it abundantly.'

- Jesus uses rich images from daily life to illustrate the depth of his desired relationship with us. On the one side, Jesus speaks of shepherd and sheep, gatekeeper and gate, pasture and life, recognition and salvation. The contrasting words are: strangers, thieves and bandits, killing and stealing, running away in fear instead of following, climbing in rather than walking through the open gate.

- The people do not understand the parable, so the Lord explains it: all must come through him to obtain true life. We could reflect on what it is or who it is that prevents us following the Lord.

Monday 1 May
Matthew 13:54–58

Jesus came to his home town and began to teach the people in their synagogue, so that they were astounded and said, 'Where did this man get this wisdom and these deeds of power? Is not this the carpenter's son? Is not his mother called Mary? And are not his brothers James and Joseph and Simon and Judas? And are not all his sisters with us? Where then did this man get all this?' And they took offence at him. But Jesus said to them, 'Prophets are not without honour except in their own country and in their own house.' And he did not do many deeds of power there, because of their unbelief.

- It is strange that nothing in the life of Jesus prepared his friends and relatives for his ministry and teaching. The point to reflect and pray about is: what makes one a disciple? A Jew is a Jew because their mother is a Jew but a Christian is a Christian because they believe in Jesus. Faith is the making of the Christian.
- Pray in thanksgiving for the gift of faith and for the deepening of your faith.

Tuesday 2 May
John 10:22–30

At that time the festival of the Dedication took place in Jerusalem. It was winter, and Jesus was walking in the temple, in the portico of Solomon. So the Jews gathered around him and said to him, 'How long will you keep us in suspense? If you are the Messiah, tell us plainly.' Jesus answered, 'I have told you, and you do not believe. The works that I do in my Father's name testify to me; but you do not believe, because you do not belong to my sheep. My sheep hear my voice. I know them, and they follow me. I give them eternal life, and they will never perish. No one will snatch them out of my hand. What my Father has given me is greater than all else, and no one can snatch it out of the Father's hand. The Father and I are one.'

- If my prayer and my Christian life are dull and lifeless, is it because I 'do not believe' all that Jesus has told me about his love for me? We Christians should be the happiest of people, no matter what our problems. Why? Because our future is fully secure and totally attractive. There are no terms and conditions.

Wednesday 3 May
Ss Philip and James, Apostles
John 14:6–14

Jesus said to him, 'I am the way, and the truth, and the life. No one comes to the Father except through me. If you know me, you will know my Father also. From now on you do know him and have seen him.'

Philip said to him, 'Lord, show us the Father, and we will be satisfied.' Jesus said to him, 'Have I been with you all this time, Philip, and you still do not know me? Whoever has seen me has seen the Father. How can you say, "Show us the Father"? Do you not believe that I am in the Father and the Father is in me? The words that I say to you I do not speak on my own; but the Father who dwells in me does his works. Believe me that I am in the Father and the Father is in me; but if you do not, then believe me because of the works themselves. Very truly, I tell you, the one who believes in me will also do the works that I do and, in fact, will do greater works than these, because I am going to the Father. I will do whatever you ask in my name, so that the Father may be glorified in the Son. If in my name you ask me for anything, I will do it.'

- We learn from the Gospels that it was the close relationship he had with his Father that led Jesus to behave in the ways that he did. The movement of God's spirit within me draws me into the life of Jesus and the Father. I take a few moments to recognise and appreciate where God is working around me.

Thursday 4 May
John 13:16–20

Jesus said to his disciples, 'Very truly, I tell you, servants are not greater than their master, nor are messengers greater than the one who sent them. If you know these things, you are blessed if you do them. I am not speaking of all of you; I know whom I have chosen. But it is to fulfil the scripture, "The one who ate my bread has lifted his heel against me." I tell you this now, before it occurs, so that when it does occur, you may believe that I am he. Very truly, I tell you, whoever receives one whom I send receives me; and whoever receives me receives him who sent me.'

- Jesus has no illusions about the group of inadequate, sinful men he is addressing. One will betray him, the others will scatter in the moment of testing. These men are also self-centred and ambitious, which is why Jesus has to demonstrate to them the attitude of service. But Jesus does not despair over these men. They are the ones he has 'chosen'. Even at this late hour he is showing them the way to happiness.

Friday 5 May
John 14:1–6

Jesus said to his disciples, 'Do not let your hearts be troubled. Believe in God, believe also in me. In my Father's house there are many dwelling-places. If it were not so, would I have told you that I go to prepare a place for you? And if I go and prepare a place for you, I will come again and will take you to myself, so that where I am, there you may be also. And you know the way to the place where I am going.' Thomas said to him, 'Lord, we do not know where you are going. How can we know the way?' Jesus said to him, 'I am the way, and the truth, and the life. No one comes to the Father except through me.'

• The words of Jesus are a source of consolation at funerals. It speaks powerfully to our fear of death, 'the undiscovered country', where we are all in the dark. Jesus, the Light, guides us on the most fearful and unknown journey of all.

Saturday 6 May
John 14:7–14

Jesus said to his disciples, 'If you know me, you will know my Father also. From now on you do know him and have seen him.'

Philip said to him, 'Lord, show us the Father, and we will be satisfied.' Jesus said to him, 'Have I been with you all this time, Philip, and you still do not know me? Whoever has seen me has seen the Father. How can you say, "Show us the Father"? Do you not believe that I am in the Father and the Father is in me? The words that I say to you I do not speak on my own; but the Father who dwells in me does his works. Believe me that I am in the Father and the Father is in me; but if you do not, then believe me because of the works themselves. Very truly, I tell you, the one who believes in me will also do the works that I do and, in fact, will do greater works than these, because I am going to the Father. I will do whatever you ask in my name, so that the Father may be glorified in the Son. If in my name you ask me for anything, I will do it.'

• The words of Jesus to Philip are astonishing. We could say that this is the high point of John's Gospel, and even of the New Testament as a whole. 'Whoever has seen me has seen the Father.' Jesus is not simply a holy man, or a prophet or a God-like angel – he is the image of the invisible God, God's self-portrait (God's 'selfie').

The Fifth Week of Easter
7–13 May 2023

Something to think and pray about each day this week:

A Christian writer went to visit a Vietnamese Buddhist. He was offered an orange by way of hospitality. While he was eating it, he became aware that his host was giving him a rather puzzled smile.

'Is something bothering you?' asked the visitor.

'It's the way you're eating that orange,' said the Buddhist, 'You're eating it so fast. You're thinking of the next piece all the time, not the piece you're eating. You're not living the present moment.'

The value of living the moment is recognised not only in the Buddhist tradition. I remember the rehearsal for the church wedding of someone dear to me. It was a complicated routine, and the couple felt that on the day they'd be lucky to remember half of what they'd been through. But the minister rounded off the rehearsal with heartening words.

'I will guide you. You must not worry about what bit comes next. That way you'll miss the moment that's happening, and you must enjoy every moment.'

Denis Tuohy,
Streets and Secret Places: Reflections of a News Reporter

The Presence of God

'I am standing at the door, knocking' (Revelation 3:20), says the Lord. What a wonderful privilege that the Lord of all creation desires to come to me. I welcome his presence.

Freedom

Everything has the potential to draw forth from me a fuller love and life. Yet my desires are often fixed, caught, on illusions of fulfilment. I ask that God, through my freedom, may orchestrate my desires in a vibrant loving melody rich in harmony.

Consciousness

To be conscious about something is to be aware of it.
Dear Lord, help me to remember that you gave me life.
Thank you for the gift of life.
Teach me to slow down, to be still and enjoy the pleasures created for me. To be aware of the beauty that surrounds me: the marvel of mountains, the calmness of lakes, the fragility of a flower petal. I need to remember that all these things come from you.

The Word

I read the word of God slowly, a few times over, and I listen to what God is saying to me.
(Please turn to the Scripture on the following pages. Inspiration points are there, should you need them. When you are ready, return here to continue.)

Conversation

What feelings are rising in me as I pray and reflect on God's word? I imagine Jesus himself sitting or standing near me, and I open my heart to him.

Conclusion

I thank God for these moments we have spent together and for any insights I have been given concerning the text.

Sunday 7 May
Fifth Sunday of Easter
John 14:1–12

Jesus said to his disciples, 'Do not let your hearts be troubled. Believe in God, believe also in me. In my Father's house there are many dwelling-places. If it were not so, would I have told you that I go to prepare a place for you? And if I go and prepare a place for you, I will come again and will take you to myself, so that where I am, there you may be also. And you know the way to the place where I am going.' Thomas said to him, 'Lord, we do not know where you are going. How can we know the way?' Jesus said to him, 'I am the way, and the truth, and the life. No one comes to the Father except through me. If you know me, you will know my Father also. From now on you do know him and have seen him.'

Philip said to him, 'Lord, show us the Father, and we will be satisfied.' Jesus said to him, 'Have I been with you all this time, Philip, and you still do not know me? Whoever has seen me has seen the Father. How can you say, "Show us the Father"? Do you not believe that I am in the Father and the Father is in me? The words that I say to you I do not speak on my own; but the Father who dwells in me does his works. Believe me that I am in the Father and the Father is in me; but if you do not, then believe me because of the works themselves. Very truly, I tell you, the one who believes in me will also do the works that I do and, in fact, will do greater works than these, because I am going to the Father.'

- We follow Jesus as one we know, not as we might follow a stranger. We have come to know him by studying his life and times, getting to know the places and events of his life, becoming familiar with the Gospels and getting to know him in the heart in prayer. This is the way of keeping our centre of conviction focused and our motivation strong. As this happens freedom grows and we begin to find him everywhere.

Monday 8 May
John 14:21–26

Jesus said to his disciples, 'They who have my commandments and keep them are those who love me; and those who love me will be loved by my Father, and I will love them and reveal myself to them.' Judas (not Iscariot) said to him, 'Lord, how is it that you will reveal yourself to us, and not to the world?' Jesus answered him, 'Those who love me will keep my word, and my Father will love them, and we will come to them and make our home with them. Whoever does not love me does not keep my words; and the word that you hear is not mine, but is from the Father who sent me.

'I have said these things to you while I am still with you. But the Advocate, the Holy Spirit, whom the Father will send in my name, will teach you everything, and remind you of all that I have said to you.'

• Do I think often enough about the Holy Spirit, that great gift from the Father to me, which Jesus talks about in today's gospel? Jesus promises that the Holy Spirit will teach me everything. This is a big promise! Do I rely on it? Do I turn to the Holy Spirit in moments of difficulty – especially difficulty in matters of faith – and ask the Spirit for guidance?

Tuesday 9 May
John 14:27–31

Jesus said to his disciples, 'Peace I leave with you; my peace I give to you. I do not give to you as the world gives. Do not let your hearts be troubled, and do not let them be afraid. You heard me say to you, "I am going away, and I am coming to you." If you loved me, you would rejoice that I am going to the Father, because the Father is greater than I. And now I have told you this before it occurs, so that when it does occur, you may believe. I will no longer talk much with you, for the ruler of this world is coming. He has no power over me; but I do as the Father has commanded me, so that the world may know that I love the Father. Rise, let us be on our way.'

• The peace that Jesus gives is available to me; I have to do nothing to receive it. But maybe that's the problem – I want to do something to earn what Jesus offers as a free gift. Lord, help me to do nothing in this time of prayer but to be ready to receive what you offer.

Wednesday 10 May
John 15:1–8

Jesus said to his disciples, 'I am the true vine, and my Father is the vine-grower. He removes every branch in me that bears no fruit. Every branch that bears fruit he prunes to make it bear more fruit. You have already been cleansed by the word that I have spoken to you. Abide in me as I abide in you. Just as the branch cannot bear fruit by itself unless it abides in the vine, neither can you unless you abide in me. I am the vine, you are the branches. Those who abide in me and I in them bear much fruit, because apart from me you can do nothing. Whoever does not abide in me is thrown away like a branch and withers; such branches are gathered, thrown into the fire, and burned. If you abide in me, and my words abide in you, ask for whatever you wish, and it will be done for you. My Father is glorified by this, that you bear much fruit and become my disciples.'

- 'Abide in me as I abide in you ... those who abide in me and I in them bear much fruit, because apart from me you can do nothing.' This is the advice Jesus gives us on the eve of his passion, his final message within the intimacy of the circle of his dearest friends. I let this invitation resound in my heart, asking for the grace to grow in my intimacy with Jesus my Saviour so that my life will bear much fruit.

Thursday 11 May
John 15:9–11

Jesus said to his disciples, 'As the Father has loved me, so I have loved you; abide in my love. If you keep my commandments, you will abide in my love, just as I have kept my Father's commandments and abide in his love. I have said these things to you so that my joy may be in you, and that your joy may be complete.'

- Today I am invited to recognise my close relationship with Jesus, which he compares to the relationship between a vine and the branches that grow on it. What does it mean for my life that the life of Jesus flows into me? What does it mean for me personally to know that I am as much a part of Jesus as the branch is a part of the vine? Are there things in my life that would be different if I consciously realised this? What are they? I reflect on these things, I talk to Jesus about them and I ask the Holy Spirit to guide and enlighten me.

Friday 12 May
John 15:12–17.

Jesus said to his disciples, 'This is my commandment, that you love one another as I have loved you. No one has greater love than this, to lay down one's life for one's friends. You are my friends if you do what I command you. I do not call you servants any longer, because the servant does not know what the master is doing; but I have called you friends, because I have made known to you everything that I have heard from my Father. You did not choose me but I chose you. And I appointed you to go and bear fruit, fruit that will last, so that the Father will give you whatever you ask him in my name. I am giving you these commands so that you may love one another.'

- 'Love one another as I have loved you.' This is not a burden, an impossible task, but an invitation to the fullness of love and life that Jesus lived. I ask for the grace to understand better how Jesus loved, so that my love can be modelled on his.

Saturday 13 May
John 15:18–21

Jesus said to his disciples, 'If the world hates you, be aware that it hated me before it hated you. If you belonged to the world, the world would love you as its own. Because you do not belong to the world, but I have chosen you out of the world – therefore the world hates you. Remember the word that I said to you, "Servants are not greater than their master." If they persecuted me, they will persecute you; if they kept my word, they will keep yours also. But they will do all these things to you on account of my name, because they do not know him who sent me.'

- Jesus grieves that the world does not know his Father who sent him to bring the good news of his endless love for us all. But whenever we pray our awareness of this love grows imperceptibly deeper. You can notice this only by reflection over a period of time. When you do notice that you have grown at least a little in love, thank God for it.

The Sixth Week of Easter
14–20 May 2023

Something to think and pray about each day this week:

Our faith, our entire hope, is based on the resurrection of Christ. Without the resurrection, Christ was a great man who lived a good life, did some extraordinary things, taught some extraordinary lessons and made some extraordinary claims, but if the resurrection is true, then the most extraordinary thing is true: that God really did become man 2,000 years ago, experienced our life, went through our death and rose for our salvation.

The evidence does not convince everyone: the testimony of a few frightened women, the claims of some apostles who ran away from the cross but saw him again in Galilee, the experiences of Paul and the other disciples that witness to his rising again and his ascension to the Father. If, as we believe, Paul is right that 'in fact Christ has been raised from the dead', then all of us have something to hope for.

Paul O'Reilly SJ,
Hope in All Things

The Presence of God

'Be still, and know that I am God!' (Psalm 46:10) Lord, your words lead us to the calmness and greatness of your presence.

Freedom

God is not foreign to my freedom. The Spirit breathes life into my most intimate desires, gently nudging me towards all that is good. I ask for the grace to let myself be enfolded by the Spirit.

Consciousness

Where do I sense hope, encouragement and growth in my life? By looking back over the past few months, I may be able to see which activities and occasions have produced rich fruit. If I do notice such areas, I will determine to give those areas both time and space in the future.

The Word

The word of God comes down to us through the Scriptures. May the Holy Spirit enlighten my mind and my heart to respond to the gospel teachings.

(Please turn to the Scripture on the following pages. Inspiration points are there, should you need them. When you are ready, return here to continue.)

Conversation

What is stirring in me as I pray? Am I consoled, troubled, left cold? I imagine Jesus standing or sitting at my side, and I share my feelings with him.

Conclusion

Glory be to the Father, and to the Son, and to the Holy Spirit,
As it was in the beginning, is now and ever shall be,
World without end. Amen.

Sunday 14 May
Sixth Sunday of Easter

John 14:15–21

Jesus said to his disciples, 'If you love me, you will keep my commandments. And I will ask the Father, and he will give you another Advocate, to be with you for ever. This is the Spirit of truth, whom the world cannot receive, because it neither sees him nor knows him. You know him, because he abides with you, and he will be in you.

'I will not leave you orphaned; I am coming to you. In a little while the world will no longer see me, but you will see me; because I live, you also will live. On that day you will know that I am in my Father, and you in me, and I in you. They who have my commandments and keep them are those who love me; and those who love me will be loved by my Father, and I will love them and reveal myself to them.'

- In our changing and increasingly secularised society, one can easily feel a sense of loss and abandonment, but the Holy Spirit continues to guide and inspire us into new and creative forms of communicating the Good News in ways that are relevant to today's world.

- I do not need to rely on my own resources but turn to God who promises to help me, ready to send the Holy Spirit. To be open to the Spirit, I must quieten first my body, then my heart. In this time of quiet God teaches me to see my world differently; I don't act in it alone but am accompanied by God's ever-present Spirit.

Monday 15 May

John 15:26–16:4

Jesus said to his disciples, 'When the Advocate comes, whom I will send to you from the Father, the Spirit of truth who comes from the Father, he will testify on my behalf. You also are to testify because you have been with me from the beginning.

'I have said these things to you to keep you from stumbling. They will put you out of the synagogues. Indeed, an hour is coming when those who kill you will think that by doing so they are offering worship to God. And they will do this because they have not known the Father or me. But I have said these things to you so that when their hour comes you may remember that I told you about them.

'I did not say these things to you from the beginning, because I was with you.'

- Jesus asks me to testify on his behalf, to announce the good news. Pope Francis has reminded us of this in his apostolic exhortation *The Joy of the Gospel*. He tells us that 'every Christian is challenged, here and now, to be actively engaged in evangelisation'. Am I engaged in spreading the Good News, either by my words or by my actions? If not, is there some way in which I can do this?

Tuesday 16 May
John 16:5–11

Jesus said to his disciples, 'But now I am going to him who sent me; yet none of you asks me, "Where are you going?" But because I have said these things to you, sorrow has filled your hearts. Nevertheless, I tell you the truth: it is to your advantage that I go away, for if I do not go away, the Advocate will not come to you; but if I go, I will send him to you. And when he comes, he will prove the world wrong about sin and righteousness and judgement: about sin, because they do not believe in me; about righteousness, because I am going to the Father and you will see me no longer; about judgement, because the ruler of this world has been condemned.'

- These words of Jesus at the Last Supper reflect some of the heavy sorrow of that meal, darkened by the disciples' awareness that they were losing Jesus. What he says to them applies to us also: Jesus remains with us through his Spirit, the Paraclete dwelling in us and linking us to the Father as he linked Jesus to the Father.

Wednesday 17 May
John 16:12–15

Jesus said to his disciples, 'I still have many things to say to you, but you cannot bear them now. When the Spirit of truth comes, he will guide you into all the truth; for he will not speak on his own, but will speak whatever he hears, and he will declare to you the things that are to come. He will glorify me, because he will take what is mine and declare it to you. All that the Father has is mine. For this reason I said that he will take what is mine and declare it to you.'

- I hear Jesus say that he has much more to say to me. How do I feel about that? Am I, perhaps, afraid of what Jesus might ask of me? Am I afraid to listen to him, in case I hear something I don't want to hear? I ask the Holy Spirit to guide me into the truth, and to help me to trust that what Jesus wants will always be life-giving for me.

- I let go of all resistance. What do you want to say to me, Lord? Speak, for I am listening. I sit quietly with Jesus and allow him to speak to my heart.

Thursday 18 May
John 16:16–20

Jesus said to his disciples, 'A little while, and you will no longer see me, and again a little while, and you will see me.' Then some of his disciples said to one another, 'What does he mean by saying to us, "A little while, and you will no longer see me, and again a little while, and you will see me"; and "Because I am going to the Father"?' They said, 'What does he mean by this "a little while"? We do not know what he is talking about.' Jesus knew that they wanted to ask him, so he said to them, 'Are you discussing among yourselves what I meant when I said, "A little while, and you will no longer see me, and again a little while, and you will see me"? Very truly, I tell you, you will weep and mourn, but the world will rejoice; you will have pain, but your pain will turn into joy.'

- Am I like the disciples in today's passage? Do I get irritated by some of Jesus' words because I don't understand them? Do I go over them again and again in my mind, discussing them with myself? Once again, I remind myself to move from my head to my heart, where the Holy Spirit will guide me into the truth of whatever Jesus has to say to me. I let go of my desire to understand intellectually, and I open my heart to the action of the Holy Spirit within me.

Friday 19 May
John 16:20–23

Jesus said to his disciples, 'Very truly, I tell you, you will weep and mourn, but the world will rejoice; you will have pain, but your pain will turn into joy. When a woman is in labour, she has pain, because her hour has come. But when her child is born, she no longer remembers the anguish because of the joy of having brought a human being into the world. So you have pain now; but I will see you again, and your hearts will rejoice, and no one will take your joy from you. On that day you will ask nothing of me. Very truly, I tell you, if you ask anything of the Father in my name, he will give it to you.'

- John's Gospel has much to say about God's love for us. To love is to give, to be with and for the one whom we love. May I have a sense of God loving me in my loving of the significant people in my life.

Saturday 20 May
John 16:23b–28

Jesus said to his disciples, 'On that day you will ask nothing of me. Very truly, I tell you, if you ask anything of the Father in my name, he will give it to you. Until now you have not asked for anything in my name. Ask and you will receive, so that your joy may be complete.

'I have said these things to you in figures of speech. The hour is coming when I will no longer speak to you in figures, but will tell you plainly of the Father. On that day you will ask in my name. I do not say to you that I will ask the Father on your behalf; for the Father himself loves you, because you have loved me and have believed that I came from God. I came from the Father and have come into the world; again, I am leaving the world and am going to the Father.'

- For John, love and faith are always closely linked, the two sides of our relationship with God. Like the Apostles, my faith and my love are not perfect, but I do try to do my best, and for the merciful Father that is enough. On the other hand, his love for me is without limits. I stay with this great mystery of the love the Father has for me, and I ask for more love and faith.

The Seventh Week of Easter
21–27 May 2023

Something to think and pray about each day this week:

Unexpectedly, very faraway worlds can seem familiar: an intense community, factions from within, pressures from outside, different 'versions' of the faith, not always reliable leadership, the departure of members, perhaps some significant. Questions arise. What has happened? Who are we? What do we hold on to? Where should we turn? What should we do? The faraway world of John's Gospel seems suddenly recognisable to us today. The message is simply: keep to the heart of the proclamation, Christ our life; keep loving each other; trust the Holy Spirit. After all, it is not *ours* but *God's project!*

Kieran J. O'Mahony OSA,
Hearers of the Word: Praying and Exploring the
Readings for Easter & Pentecost

The Presence of God
As I sit here, the beating of my heart,
the ebb and flow of my breathing, the movements of my mind
are all signs of God's ongoing creation of me.
I pause for a moment and become aware
of this presence of God within me.

Freedom
I will ask God's help
to be free from my own preoccupations,
to be open to God in this time of prayer,
to come to know, love and serve God more.

Consciousness
At this moment, Lord, I turn my thoughts to you.
I will leave aside my chores and preoccupations.
I will take rest and refreshment in your presence.

The Word
Now I turn to the Scripture set out for me this day. I read slowly over the
words and see if any sentence or sentiment appeals to me.
*(Please turn to the Scripture on the following pages. Inspiration points are there,
should you need them. When you are ready, return here to continue.)*

Conversation
Begin to talk to Jesus about the Scripture you have just read. What part
of it strikes a chord in you? Perhaps the words of a friend – or some story
you have heard recently – will slowly rise to the surface of your consciousness. If so, does the story throw light on what the Scripture passage may
be saying to you?

Conclusion
Glory be to the Father, and to the Son, and to the Holy Spirit,
As it was in the beginning, is now and ever shall be,
World without end. Amen.

Sunday 21 May
The Ascension of the Lord
Matthew 28:16–20

Now the eleven disciples went to Galilee, to the mountain to which Jesus had directed them. When they saw him, they worshipped him; but some doubted. And Jesus came and said to them, 'All authority in heaven and on earth has been given to me. Go therefore and make disciples of all nations, baptising them in the name of the Father and of the Son and of the Holy Spirit, and teaching them to obey everything that I have commanded you. And remember, I am with you always, to the end of the age.'

- Lord, you terrify me with this command to go and teach all nations. You were talking to eleven men, without education, money or influence, in a despised province of the Roman Empire. But they obeyed you, because they knew you were with them. And today Christians are the largest body of believers on this planet. Today's preaching is different. We are educated, sometimes too well. It is harder than ever to make our voice heard. Yet in Sacred Space your word goes out potentially to all nations, and you are still with us.

Monday 22 May
John 16:29–33

His disciples said, 'Yes, now you are speaking plainly, not in any figure of speech! Now we know that you know all things, and do not need to have anyone question you; by this we believe that you came from God.' Jesus answered them, 'Do you now believe? The hour is coming, indeed it has come, when you will be scattered, each one to his home, and you will leave me alone. Yet I am not alone because the Father is with me. I have said this to you, so that in me you may have peace. In the world you face persecution. But take courage; I have conquered the world!'

- Is faith a challenge for me? In what way? Do I feel in good company among the disciples who are 'slow learners'? Is there a sense in which faith is always beyond what I know, what I can imagine or even hope for?

- Do I have a sense of 'not being alone'? Can I ask God to not leave me alone? To always be with me? Have I ever experienced that 'peace' John speaks of? Can I ask for it?

Tuesday 23 May
John 17:1–11

After Jesus had spoken these words, he looked up to heaven and said, 'Father, the hour has come; glorify your Son so that the Son may glorify you, since you have given him authority over all people, to give eternal life to all whom you have given him. And this is eternal life, that they may know you, the only true God, and Jesus Christ whom you have sent. I glorified you on earth by finishing the work that you gave me to do. So now, Father, glorify me in your own presence with the glory that I had in your presence before the world existed.

'I have made your name known to those whom you gave me from the world. They were yours, and you gave them to me, and they have kept your word. Now they know that everything you have given me is from you; for the words that you gave to me I have given to them, and they have received them and know in truth that I came from you; and they have believed that you sent me. I am asking on their behalf; I am not asking on behalf of the world, but on behalf of those whom you gave me, because they are yours. All mine are yours, and yours are mine; and I have been glorified in them. And now I am no longer in the world, but they are in the world, and I am coming to you. Holy Father, protect them in your name that you have given me, so that they may be one, as we are one.'

- I have to work at this, Lord. The description of eternal life is stark. To know the only true God is beyond my imagination. Do we, in our glorified bodies, leave behind our senses of smell, taste, touch, hearing, vision, that delight us now and seem to be harbingers of better things to come? Somehow the knowledge of the one true God must bring all these joys to a new level.

Wednesday 24 May
John 17:11–19

Jesus said, 'And now I am no longer in the world, but they are in the world, and I am coming to you. Holy Father, protect them in your name that you have given me, so that they may be one, as we are one. While I was with them, I protected them in your name that you have given me. I guarded them, and not one of them was lost except the one destined to be lost, so that the scripture might be fulfilled. But now I am coming to you, and I speak these things in the world so that they may have my joy made complete in themselves. I have given them your word, and the world has hated them because they do not belong to the world, just as I do not belong to the world. I am not asking you to take them out of the world, but I ask you to protect them from the evil one. They do not belong to the world, just as I do not belong to the world. Sanctify them in the truth; your word is truth. As you have sent me into the world, so I have sent them into the world. And for their sakes I sanctify myself, so that they also may be sanctified in truth.'

- ' ... so that they may be one, as we are one'. As I look at our divided world, where not even those who believe in Christ are united, I join Jesus in this prayer, begging for the gift of unity among Christians. I bring to my prayer any situation that needs healing and the overcoming of division, as I am aware that I am joining my prayer to that of Jesus himself.

Thursday 25 May
John 17:20–26

Jesus said, 'I ask not only on behalf of these, but also on behalf of those who will believe in me through their word, that they may all be one. As you, Father, are in me and I am in you, may they also be in us, so that the world may believe that you have sent me. The glory that you have given me I have given them, so that they may be one, as we are one, I in them and you in me, that they may become completely one, so that the world may know that you have sent me and have loved them even as you have loved me. Father, I desire that those also, whom you have given me, may be with me where I am, to see my glory, which you have given me because you loved me before the foundation of the world.

'Righteous Father, the world does not know you, but I know you; and these know that you have sent me. I made your name known to them, and I will make it known, so that the love with which you have loved me may be in them, and I in them.'

- There are over 300 references to love in the New Testament. Love is God's greatest gift to us. By our mutual love we reveal God's love to the world. In the time of the early Church pagans said to one another: 'See how these Christians love one another!' They were impressed by this mystery and at least some came to believe in Jesus.

Friday 26 May
John 21:15–19

When they had finished breakfast, Jesus said to Simon Peter, 'Simon son of John, do you love me more than these?' He said to him, 'Yes, Lord; you know that I love you.' Jesus said to him, 'Feed my lambs.' A second time he said to him, 'Simon son of John, do you love me?' He said to him, 'Yes, Lord; you know that I love you.' Jesus said to him, 'Tend my sheep.' He said to him the third time, 'Simon son of John, do you love me?' Peter felt hurt because he said to him the third time, 'Do you love me?' And he said to him, 'Lord, you know everything; you know that I love you.' Jesus said to him, 'Feed my sheep. Very truly, I tell you, when you were younger, you used to fasten your own belt and to go wherever you wished. But when you grow old, you will stretch out your hands, and someone else will fasten a belt around you and take you where you do not wish to go.' (He said this to indicate the kind of death by which he would glorify God.) After this he said to him, 'Follow me.'

- Do you ever wonder do you really love the Lord? Did Peter? In the end he had no proof – he just knew the Lord knew. Jesus sees into the heart and knows love, and he also knows our efforts to love. We are called to feed his people in many ways, not because we are perfect, but because we do our best to share the best of our lives with others. When we wonder do we love God, we are better not answering, but just to offer the love of our hearts, imperfect as it is, and then we can say, 'Lord, you know I love you'. Leave the answer to him!

Saturday 27 May
John 21:20–25

Peter turned and saw the disciple whom Jesus loved following them; he was the one who had reclined next to Jesus at the supper and had said, 'Lord, who is it that is going to betray you?' When Peter saw him, he said to Jesus, 'Lord, what about him?' Jesus said to him, 'If it is my will that he remain until I come, what is that to you? Follow me!' So the rumour spread in the community that this disciple would not die. Yet Jesus did not say to him that he would not die, but, 'If it is my will that he remain until I come, what is that to you?'

This is the disciple who is testifying to these things and has written them, and we know that his testimony is true. But there are also many other things that Jesus did; if every one of them were written down, I suppose that the world itself could not contain the books that would be written.

- In my following of Jesus, do I ever take my focus off him and begin worrying about what others are doing or thinking or saying? Does the opinion of others matter too much to me? Does it cause me to turn away from following Jesus? Can I see where focus on other people or events has pulled me away from Jesus? I consider these questions honestly, and talk about them now with Jesus.

- Reflecting on a situation where I may have allowed myself to be pulled away from following Jesus, I listen to Jesus saying to me now, 'What is that to you? Follow me!' Lord, when I keep my focus on you, I cannot go astray. You are the Way and the Truth!

Something to think and pray about each day this week:

An image that helps me with the mystery of suffering and evil is the humble jigsaw puzzle. When I was young and the day was wet, I loved to pour out the bits of a puzzle on a large enamel tray. Slowly I would construct the outer frame of the picture, and when that was done, I'd get going on the inside parts. Mostly I'd finish the puzzle eventually, sometimes with a little adult help.

But not always. Not if the cover picture was fuzzy rather than clearly defined, nor if bits were missing or had got mixed up with other puzzles. And of course, if someone upset the tray – my elder brother or the cat were prime suspects! – I'd have to start all over again.

The jigsaw with its dependable outer frame can provide us with an image to help us see that there are *limits* to suffering and evil. *'And light shines in the darkness, and darkness could not overpower it'* (John 1:5). Not that we get *straight* lines, because evil is unpredictable and disorderly, but we are given an awareness of the boundaries which Christian faith provides for our *'mourning and weeping in this valley of tears'*. True, the cover picture of this cosmic jigsaw is fuzzy on detail, and is still being shaped by human history as it moves erratically along. The full picture will not be available for viewing until the history of this world is completed, but it does have a startling and encouraging outline, and sometimes we can see how even the dark elements of our own stories fit in surprisingly well with the outline provided for us.

Brian Grogan SJ,
God, You're Breaking my Heart

The Presence of God
At any time of the day or night we can call on Jesus.
He is always waiting, listening for our call.
What a wonderful blessing.
No phone needed, no e-mails, just a whisper.

Freedom
If God were trying to tell me something, would I know?
If God were reassuring me or challenging me, would I notice?
I ask for the grace to be free of my own preoccupations
and open to what God may be saying to me.

Consciousness
Help me, Lord, become more conscious of your presence. Teach me to recognise your presence in others. Fill my heart with gratitude for the times your love has been shown to me through the care of others.

The Word
In this expectant state of mind, please turn to the text for the day with confidence. Believe that the Holy Spirit is present and may reveal whatever the passage has to say to you. Read reflectively, listening with a third ear to what may be going on in your heart.
(Please turn to the Scripture on the following pages. Inspiration points are there, should you need them. When you are ready, return here to continue.)

Conversation
Conversation requires talking and listening.
As I talk to Jesus, may I also learn to pause and listen.
I picture the gentleness in his eyes and the love in his smile.
I can be totally honest with Jesus as I tell him my worries and cares.
I will open my heart to Jesus as I tell him my fears and doubts.
I will ask him to help me place myself fully in his care, knowing that he always desires good for me.

Conclusion
I thank God for these moments we have spent together and for any insights I have been given concerning the text.

Sunday 28 May
Pentecost Sunday
John 20:19–23

When it was evening on that day, the first day of the week, and the doors of the house where the disciples had met were locked for fear of the Jews, Jesus came and stood among them and said, 'Peace be with you.' After he said this, he showed them his hands and his side. Then the disciples rejoiced when they saw the Lord. Jesus said to them again, 'Peace be with you. As the Father has sent me, so I send you.' When he had said this, he breathed on them and said to them, 'Receive the Holy Spirit. If you forgive the sins of any, they are forgiven them; if you retain the sins of any, they are retained.'

• Thomas is an ordinary person, knotted up in his own fears and doubts. Perhaps we all carry something of his DNA? Here we are shown the transforming impact that his personal encounter with Jesus has on him. Pope Francis says: 'I invite all Christians to a renewed personal encounter with Jesus, or at least an openness to letting him encounter them. I ask all of you to do this unfailingly each day.'

Monday 29 May
Mark 10:17–27

As he was setting out on a journey, a man ran up and knelt before him, and asked him, 'Good Teacher, what must I do to inherit eternal life?' Jesus said to him, 'Why do you call me good? No one is good but God alone. You know the commandments: "You shall not murder; You shall not commit adultery; You shall not steal; You shall not bear false witness; You shall not defraud; Honour your father and mother."' He said to him, 'Teacher, I have kept all these since my youth.' Jesus, looking at him, loved him and said, 'You lack one thing; go, sell what you own, and give the money to the poor, and you will have treasure in heaven; then come, follow me.' When he heard this, he was shocked and went away grieving, for he had many possessions.

Then Jesus looked around and said to his disciples, 'How hard it will be for those who have wealth to enter the kingdom of God!' And the disciples were perplexed at these words. But Jesus said to them again,

'Children, how hard it is to enter the kingdom of God! It is easier for a camel to go through the eye of a needle than for someone who is rich to enter the kingdom of God.' They were greatly astounded and said to one another, 'Then who can be saved?' Jesus looked at them and said, 'For mortals it is impossible, but not for God; for God all things are possible.'

• We are living in times that seem pervaded by corruption, at all levels and in so many areas of public life: loyalty and truth are sold and bought for money. Jesus' strong words remind us how easily money can become an obstacle to entry into the kingdom! I ask for God's help, because for him nothing is impossible.

Tuesday 30 May
Mark 10:28–31

Peter began to say to him, 'Look, we have left everything and followed you.' Jesus said, 'Truly I tell you, there is no one who has left house or brothers or sisters or mother or father or children or fields, for my sake and for the sake of the good news, who will not receive a hundredfold now in this age – houses, brothers and sisters, mothers and children, and fields, with persecutions – and in the age to come eternal life. But many who are first will be last, and the last will be first.'

• Peter's experience as a fisherman told him that taking stock was neces-sary from time to time. Although he was often enthusiastic and spon-taneous, now he seems to panic as he suddenly realises that he may be left with nothing. I pray for a deeper trust and faith in the message of Jesus, in his presence to me. Aware of anything that causes me to be too cautious or calculating, I ask God's help.

Wednesday 31 May
The Visitation of the Blessed Virgin Mary
Luke 1:39–56

In those days Mary set out and went with haste to a Judean town in the hill country, where she entered the house of Zechariah and greeted Elizabeth. When Elizabeth heard Mary's greeting, the child leapt in her womb. And Elizabeth was filled with the Holy Spirit and exclaimed with a loud cry, 'Blessed are you among women, and blessed is the fruit of your womb. And why has this happened to me, that the mother of my Lord comes to me? For as soon as I heard the sound of your greeting, the child in my womb leapt for joy. And blessed is she who believed that there would be a fulfilment of what was spoken to her by the Lord.'

And Mary said,

'My soul magnifies the Lord,
    and my spirit rejoices in God my Saviour,
for he has looked with favour on the lowliness of his servant.
    Surely, from now on all generations will call me blessed;
for the Mighty One has done great things for me,
    and holy is his name.
His mercy is for those who fear him
    from generation to generation.
He has shown strength with his arm;
    he has scattered the proud in the thoughts of their hearts.
He has brought down the powerful from their thrones,
    and lifted up the lowly;
he has filled the hungry with good things,
    and sent the rich away empty.
He has helped his servant Israel,
    in remembrance of his mercy,
according to the promise he made to our ancestors,
    to Abraham and to his descendants for ever.'

And Mary remained with her for about three months and then returned to her home.

• On the feast of Mary's visitation to Elizabeth, I read the Magnificat prayerfully, dwelling on those words and phrases that touch my heart. It is a song of praise by someone who is deeply grateful for all she has received and for the insights about the way God acts in our world. I join my praise to hers.

Thursday 1 June
Mark 10:46–52

They came to Jericho. As he and his disciples and a large crowd were leaving Jericho, Bartimaeus son of Timaeus, a blind beggar, was sitting by the roadside. When he heard that it was Jesus of Nazareth, he began to shout out and say, 'Jesus, Son of David, have mercy on me!' Many sternly ordered him to be quiet, but he cried out even more loudly, 'Son of David, have mercy on me!' Jesus stood still and said, 'Call him here.' And they called the blind man, saying to him, 'Take heart; get up, he is calling you.' So throwing off his cloak, he sprang up and came to Jesus. Then Jesus said to him, 'What do you want me to do for you?' The blind man said to him, 'My teacher, let me see again.' Jesus said to him, 'Go; your faith has made you well.' Immediately he regained his sight and followed him on the way.

- Like the people who scolded Bartimaeus, telling him to be quiet and not to bring shame on them, I may sometimes prefer to keep the less presentable parts of my life out of Jesus' sight. Thinking of this scene, I realise that Jesus wants to stop, to listen to my plea for help and to cure me.

- Bartimaeus threw off his cloak – his only protection – and, being blind, risked not finding it again. I allow myself to be before Jesus, unshrouded, seen as I am, expressing my need in trust.

Friday 2 June
Mark 11:11–26

Then he entered Jerusalem and went into the temple; and when he had looked around at everything, as it was already late, he went out to Bethany with the twelve.

On the following day, when they came from Bethany, he was hungry. Seeing in the distance a fig tree in leaf, he went to see whether perhaps he would find anything on it. When he came to it, he found nothing but leaves, for it was not the season for figs. He said to it, 'May no one ever eat fruit from you again.' And his disciples heard it.

Then they came to Jerusalem. And he entered the temple and began to drive out those who were selling and those who were buying in the temple, and he overturned the tables of the money-changers and the seats of those who sold doves; and he would not allow anyone to carry anything through the temple. He was teaching and saying, 'Is it not written,

"My house shall be called a house of prayer for all the nations"?
But you have made it a den of robbers.'

And when the chief priests and the scribes heard it, they kept looking for a way to kill him; for they were afraid of him, because the whole crowd was spellbound by his teaching. And when evening came, Jesus and his disciples went out of the city.

In the morning as they passed by, they saw the fig tree withered away to its roots. Then Peter remembered and said to him, 'Rabbi, look! The fig tree that you cursed has withered.' Jesus answered them, 'Have faith in God. Truly I tell you, if you say to this mountain, "Be taken up and thrown into the sea", and if you do not doubt in your heart, but believe that what you say will come to pass, it will be done for you. So I tell you, whatever you ask for in prayer, believe that you have received it, and it will be yours.

'Whenever you stand praying, forgive, if you have anything against anyone; so that your Father in heaven may also forgive you your trespasses.'

- Jesus surprises us and perhaps even disturbs us, and this makes us think. He enters the temple and expels the sellers, using very strong language. The temple was the holiest place for the Jews, and Jesus is asserting his authority even on that place. No wonder the chief priests and the scribes were looking for a way to get rid of him, for he was very clearly challenging their authority, and winning the admiration and sympathy of the people.

Saturday 3 June
Mark 11:27–33

Again they came to Jerusalem. As he was walking in the temple, the chief priests, the scribes, and the elders came to him and said, 'By what authority are you doing these things? Who gave you this authority to do them?' Jesus said to them, 'I will ask you one question; answer me, and I will tell you by what authority I do these things. Did the baptism of John come from heaven, or was it of human origin? Answer me.' They argued with one another, 'If we say, "From heaven", he will say, "Why then did you not believe him?" But shall we say, "Of human origin"?' – they were afraid of the crowd, for all regarded John as truly a prophet. So they answered Jesus, 'We do not know.' And Jesus said to them, 'Neither will I tell you by what authority I am doing these things.'

- The chief priests were not seeking the truth but setting a trap for convicting Jesus. Jesus faces the high authorities of the temple, and his silence allows the truth to surface.

- Jesus knew that answering the Pharisees' question would lead only to further debate. I pray for the wisdom to know when, instead of trying to have the last word, it might be better for me to keep silent or to say less.

The Ninth Week in Ordinary Time
4–10 June 2023

Something to think and pray about each day this week:

Not everyone awakens to the spiritual journey. This might seem strange because the hungers of the heart are insistent. But we do live in a culture of distraction, filling up our time, busy with what Luke calls 'the cares of life' (Luke 21:34). These too are insistent but can become a narcotic, reducing the human adventure to sentient existence, our minds dulled and our hearts coarsened. We are constantly being asked to live on bread alone! The opium of the people is now a dull acceptance that this is all there is, inviting us to be satisfied with less. But surely we are not designed to sleepwalk through life? On the contrary!

As St Augustine noticed, the hungers of the heart are registered in restlessness, the vague – and sometimes not so vague – intuition that there is more. In acute cases, such as for Augustine himself, it can lead to emotional, existential and spiritual breakdown. Many in our day experience this unease but do not recognise what it is and do not know where to turn. In response, nothing can replace some kind of practice of meditation, quiet prayer, sitting with God. It *is* discipline, but we are at least engaging with the God in whom we live and move and have our being (Acts 17:28). And we are not alone. The classical spiritual tradition is alive and well and, nowadays, online. It continues to be nourished by the great spiritual guides from the past but is developing and growing in the present. Without this pool of stillness, how would any of us cope?

Kieran O'Mahony OSA,
Hearers of the Word: Praying and Exploring the
Readings for Easter & Pentecost

The Presence of God

Dear Jesus, as I call on you today, I realise that often I come asking for favours. Today I'd like just to be in your presence. Draw my heart in response to your love.

Freedom

It is so easy to get caught up
with the trappings of wealth in this life.
Grant, O Lord, that I may be free
from greed and selfishness.
Remind me that the best things in life are free:
Love, laughter, caring and sharing.

Consciousness

How am I really feeling? Lighthearted? Heavyhearted? I may be very much at peace, happy to be here.
Equally, I may be frustrated, worried or angry.
I acknowledge how I really am. It is the real me whom the Lord loves.

The Word

Lord Jesus, you became human to communicate with me.
You walked and worked on this earth.
You endured the heat and struggled with the cold.
All your time on this earth was spent in caring for humanity.
You healed the sick, you raised the dead.
Most important of all, you saved me from death.
(Please turn to the Scripture on the following pages. Inspiration points are there, should you need them. When you are ready, return here to continue.)

Conversation

Do I notice myself reacting as I pray with the word of God? Do I feel challenged, comforted, angry? Imagining Jesus sitting or standing by me, I speak out my feelings, as one trusted friend to another.

Conclusion

Glory be to the Father, and to the Son, and to the Holy Spirit,
As it was in the beginning, is now and ever shall be,
World without end. Amen.

Sunday 4 June
The Most Holy Trinity
John 3:16–18

Jesus said, 'For God so loved the world that he gave his only Son, so that everyone who believes in him may not perish but may have eternal life.

'Indeed, God did not send the Son into the world to condemn the world, but in order that the world might be saved through him. Those who believe in him are not condemned; but those who do not believe are condemned already, because they have not believed in the name of the only Son of God.'

• They looked down from heaven – the Father, Son and Holy Spirit – with love for their people – for all of us. They could see men and women of all races, colours, ages, faiths, holiness and sin. They knew help was needed for the human race and they waited a long time before the time was right. Prayer inserts us into our true space of belonging – into the community of the Trinity – and in that prayer we are called to bring this divine help to the human race.

Monday 5 June
Mark 12:1–12

Then he began to speak to them in parables. 'A man planted a vineyard, put a fence around it, dug a pit for the wine press, and built a watchtower; then he leased it to tenants and went to another country. When the season came, he sent a slave to the tenants to collect from them his share of the produce of the vineyard. But they seized him, and beat him, and sent him away empty-handed. And again he sent another slave to them; this one they beat over the head and insulted. Then he sent another, and that one they killed. And so it was with many others; some they beat, and others they killed. He had still one other, a beloved son. Finally he sent him to them, saying, "They will respect my son." But those tenants said to one another, "This is the heir; come, let us kill him, and the inheritance will be ours." So they seized him, killed him, and threw him out of the vineyard. What then will the owner of the vineyard do? He will come and destroy the tenants and give the vineyard to others. Have you not read this scripture:

"The stone that the builders rejected
    has become the cornerstone;
this was the Lord's doing,
    and it is amazing in our eyes"?'

When they realised that he had told this parable against them, they wanted to arrest him, but they feared the crowd. So they left him and went away.

• Jesus is the stone prophesied by Isaiah; he is the cornerstone, but the builders have rejected him. I may follow Jesus, but I must know that others will reject the one I trust, the one on whom I build my life. Have I ever felt others' rejection of my faith?

Tuesday 6 June
Mark 12:13–17

Then they sent to him some Pharisees and some Herodians to trap him in what he said. And they came and said to him, 'Teacher, we know that you are sincere, and show deference to no one; for you do not regard people with partiality, but teach the way of God in accordance with truth. Is it lawful to pay taxes to the emperor, or not? Should we pay them, or should we not?' But knowing their hypocrisy, he said to them, 'Why are you putting me to the test? Bring me a denarius and let me see it.' And they brought one. Then he said to them, 'Whose head is this, and whose title?' They answered, 'The emperor's.' Jesus said to them, 'Give to the emperor the things that are the emperor's, and to God the things that are God's.' And they were utterly amazed at him.

• Hypocrisy originally meant 'acting on a stage'. In the Bible it means falseness, sham, deceit. Here the lure of wealth distorts authentic relationships. Jesus' visitors are only trying to trap him: they are not interested in the truth.

• We have received everything from God – even life itself. What can we give back to God in gracious gratitude?

Wednesday 7 June
Mark 12:18–27

Some Sadducees, who say there is no resurrection, came to him and asked him a question, saying, 'Teacher, Moses wrote for us that if a man's brother dies, leaving a wife but no child, the man shall marry the widow and raise up children for his brother. There were seven brothers; the first married and, when he died, left no children; and the second married her and died, leaving no children; and the third likewise; none of the seven left children. Last of all the woman herself died. In the resurrection whose wife will she be? For the seven had married her.'

Jesus said to them, 'Is not this the reason you are wrong, that you know neither the scriptures nor the power of God? For when they rise from the dead, they neither marry nor are given in marriage, but are like angels in heaven. And as for the dead being raised, have you not read in the book of Moses, in the story about the bush, how God said to him, "I am the God of Abraham, the God of Isaac, and the God of Jacob"? He is God not of the dead, but of the living; you are quite wrong.'

• Chief priests, Sadducees, Herodians, scribes or Pharisees: they all have a challenge for Jesus and who would fancy being in their shoes!

• This challenge is a hypothetical hard case: just about the worst one they can think up. But Jesus knows his Scripture and he knows God.

• What is it like to prove somebody wrong when you are under attack?

Thursday 8 June
Mark 12:28–34

One of the scribes came near and heard them disputing with one another, and seeing that he answered them well, he asked him, 'Which commandment is the first of all?' Jesus answered, 'The first is, "Hear, O Israel: the Lord our God, the Lord is one; you shall love the Lord your God with all your heart, and with all your soul, and with all your mind, and with all your strength." The second is this, "You shall love your neighbour as yourself." There is no other commandment greater than these.' Then the scribe said to him, 'You are right, Teacher; you have truly said that "he is one, and besides him there is no other"; and "to love him with all the heart, and with all the understanding, and with all the strength", and "to love one's neighbour as oneself", – this is much more important than all whole burnt-offerings and sacrifices.' When Jesus saw that he answered wisely, he said to him, 'You are not far from the kingdom of God.' After that no one dared to ask him any question.

- Real prayer brings us into the kingdom of God; in prayer the kingdom or reign of God grows within us. Prayer that does not reach the heart can leave us dry, unenthusiastic about the things of God, and dissatisfied.

Friday 9 June
Mark 12:35–37

While Jesus was teaching in the temple, he said, 'How can the scribes say that the Messiah is the son of David? David himself, by the Holy Spirit, declared,

"The Lord said to my Lord,
'Sit at my right hand,
    until I put your enemies under your feet.'"

David himself calls him Lord; so how can he be his son?' And the large crowd was listening to him with delight.

- Jesus is more than the son of David. The arguments throughout the gospel about the identity of Jesus may not help or nourish prayer too much. It's enough to express our faith in prayer that Jesus is Lord, the beloved son 'in whom the Father was well pleased'. He is Son of God, human and divine. In his love and to him we pray.

- They listened 'with delight.' Lord, may I listen to you in this way, relish your goodness and insight, and nourish myself daily on your words.

Saturday 10 June
Mark 12:38–44

As he taught, he said, 'Beware of the scribes, who like to walk around in long robes, and to be greeted with respect in the market-places, and to have the best seats in the synagogues and places of honour at banquets! They devour widows' houses and for the sake of appearance say long prayers. They will receive the greater condemnation.'

He sat down opposite the treasury, and watched the crowd putting money into the treasury. Many rich people put in large sums. A poor widow came and put in two small copper coins, which are worth a penny. Then he called his disciples and said to them, 'Truly I tell you, this poor widow has put in more than all those who are contributing to the treasury. For all of them have contributed out of their abundance; but she out of her poverty has put in everything she had, all she had to live on.'

• Jesus proclaims that the woman who put in two small copper coins had given more than all the rich people. In a very real way it is a summary of the whole gospel, for God looks at the heart and its readiness to give generously. Do I measure my worth by my external success, or am I free to look at my heart and be ready to be generous even in my poverty? I ask God to help me look at myself and at others as he looks at us.

The Tenth Week in Ordinary Time
11–17 June 2023

Something to think and pray about each day this week:

The second Eucharistic Prayer has this marvellous line: 'Make us grow in love.' This, the Church tells us, is to be at the heart of our prayer. It's straight from the gospels: 'You shall love the Lord your God with all your heart and with all your soul and with all your mind, and you shall love your neighbour as yourself' (Matthew 22:37–39). This is to be our primary agenda – to become loving persons. But significantly, the Church asks God to make it his agenda for us. The text does not say '*May* we grown in love', but '*Make* us grow in love'. I like this bit because growing in love is not something we can do on our own – it doesn't just happen in us as ageing does. The daily news shows that many people are given more to hating rather than loving. So our growth in love is primarily God's agenda, but we are meant to collaborate actively and enthusiastically in its achievement.

Many people seem to go through life without ever asking 'What's it all about? What is meant to be happening to me? Is this all there is?' Imagine being at a meeting where no one knew what the agenda was! It is a huge help to know the divine agenda for ourselves: not growth in wealth or prestige or power, but *growth in love.*

The divine agenda is simple, dreadfully so. You don't have to be a theologian to grasp it. The divine agenda is to bring about a civilisation of love, a world of healthy and loving relationships from which no one is excluded. Each of us is needed to be a carrier of the divine agenda in our situation; each of us is to reveal God's creative love in a unique way.

Brian Grogan SJ,
To Grow in Love: A Spirituality of Ageing

The Presence of God

Dear Jesus, I come to you today longing for your presence. I desire to love you as you love me. May nothing ever separate me from you.

Freedom

Lord, grant me the grace to have freedom of the Spirit. Cleanse my heart and soul so that I may live joyously in your love.

Consciousness

Where am I with God? With others?
Do I have something to be grateful for? Then I give thanks.
Is there something I am sorry for? Then I ask forgiveness.

The Word

The word of God comes down to us through the Scriptures. May the Holy Spirit enlighten my mind and my heart to respond to the gospel teachings.

(Please turn to the Scripture on the following pages. Inspiration points are there, should you need them. When you are ready, return here to continue.)

Conversation

How has God's word moved me? Has it left me cold?
Has it consoled me or moved me to act in a new way?
I imagine Jesus standing or sitting beside me;
I turn and share my feelings with him.

Conclusion

I thank God for these moments we have spent together and for any insights I have been given concerning the text.

Sunday 11 June
The Most Holy Body and Blood of Christ
John 6:51–58

Jesus said to them, 'I am the living bread that came down from heaven. Whoever eats of this bread will live for ever; and the bread that I will give for the life of the world is my flesh.'

The Jews then disputed among themselves, saying, 'How can this man give us his flesh to eat?' So Jesus said to them, 'Very truly, I tell you, unless you eat the flesh of the Son of Man and drink his blood, you have no life in you. Those who eat my flesh and drink my blood have eternal life, and I will raise them up on the last day; for my flesh is true food and my blood is true drink. Those who eat my flesh and drink my blood abide in me, and I in them. Just as the living Father sent me, and I live because of the Father, so whoever eats me will live because of me. This is the bread that came down from heaven, not like that which your ancestors ate, and they died. But the one who eats this bread will live for ever.'

• In the Eucharist we deepen our relationship with Jesus, not mechanically but by becoming more and more like him over the years. We meet God in this mysterious and dramatic way: God gives himself to us, and we try to shape our lives into a loving gift for God. In heaven there will be no Eucharist as we know it, because our bonding with God will then be complete.

Monday 12 June
Matthew 5:1–12

When Jesus saw the crowds, he went up the mountain; and after he sat down, his disciples came to him. Then he began to speak, and taught them, saying:

'Blessed are the poor in spirit, for theirs is the kingdom of heaven.
'Blessed are those who mourn, for they will be comforted.
'Blessed are the meek, for they will inherit the earth.
'Blessed are those who hunger and thirst for righteousness, for they will be filled.
'Blessed are the merciful, for they will receive mercy.
'Blessed are the pure in heart, for they will see God.

'Blessed are the peacemakers, for they will be called children of God.

'Blessed are those who are persecuted for righteousness' sake, for theirs is the kingdom of heaven.

'Blessed are you when people revile you and persecute you and utter all kinds of evil against you falsely on my account. Rejoice and be glad, for your reward is great in heaven, for in the same way they persecuted the prophets who were before you.'

• In the Bible, poverty is an evil to be corrected; wealth is not an evil but a necessity for the well-being of the kingdom. However, the love of riches can lead to neglect of God and of the poor. The Christian community has always tried to make the care of the poor its priority, as it is God's priority. Is it mine?

Tuesday 13 June
Matthew 5:13–16

Jesus said to his disciples, 'You are the salt of the earth; but if salt has lost its taste, how can its saltiness be restored? It is no longer good for anything, but is thrown out and trampled under foot.

'You are the light of the world. A city built on a hill cannot be hidden. No one after lighting a lamp puts it under the bushel basket, but on the lampstand, and it gives light to all in the house. In the same way, let your light shine before others, so that they may see your good works and give glory to your Father in heaven.'

• In the Scriptures, just as light symbolises goodness, darkness symbolises evil. Jesus described himself as the 'light of the world'. Surprisingly, he then went further and said to his followers, 'You are the light of the world'. He is confident that we will contribute to the enlightenment of those around us to the extent that we are united with him.

Wednesday 14 June
Matthew 5:17–19

Jesus taught them, saying, 'Do not think that I have come to abolish the law or the prophets; I have come not to abolish but to fulfil. For truly I tell you, until heaven and earth pass away, not one letter, not one stroke of a letter, will pass from the law until all is accomplished. Therefore, whoever breaks one of the least of these commandments, and teaches others to do the same, will be called least in the kingdom of heaven; but whoever does them and teaches them will be called great in the kingdom of heaven.'

- Jesus is no destroyer of people's devotions and faith. He does not abolish the faith practice of a people or a person. All the goodness of our religion and our faith is precious to him. His grace is given to each personally; each of us prays differently, or in a variety of times, places and moods. 'Pray as you can, not as you can't', is one of the oldest and wisest recommendations for prayer. Prayer is entering and relaxing into the mystery of God's love, each in our own way.

Thursday 15 June
Matthew 5:20–26

Jesus said, 'For I tell you, unless your righteousness exceeds that of the scribes and Pharisees, you will never enter the kingdom of heaven.

'You have heard that it was said to those of ancient times, "You shall not murder"; and "whoever murders shall be liable to judgement." But I say to you that if you are angry with a brother or sister, you will be liable to judgement; and if you insult a brother or sister, you will be liable to the council; and if you say, "You fool", you will be liable to the hell of fire. So when you are offering your gift at the altar, if you remember that your brother or sister has something against you, leave your gift there before the altar and go; first be reconciled to your brother or sister, and then come and offer your gift. Come to terms quickly with your accuser while you are on the way to court with him, or your accuser may hand you over to the judge, and the judge to the guard, and you will be thrown into prison. Truly I tell you, you will never get out until you have paid the last penny.'

- The 'righteousness' of the scribes and Pharisees was all about rule-keeping. Do this, don't do that. But the righteousness that Jesus asks of his followers is not only greater, but different. It is about loving – loving God, and loving our fellow human beings, and showing that love in every way we can.

Friday 16 June
The Most Sacred Heart of Jesus
Matthew 11:25–30

At that time Jesus said, 'I thank you, Father, Lord of heaven and earth, because you have hidden these things from the wise and the intelligent and have revealed them to infants; yes, Father, for such was your gracious will. All things have been handed over to me by my Father; and no one knows the Son except the Father, and no one knows the Father except the Son and anyone to whom the Son chooses to reveal him.

'Come to me, all you that are weary and are carrying heavy burdens, and I will give you rest. Take my yoke upon you, and learn from me; for I am gentle and humble in heart, and you will find rest for your souls. For my yoke is easy, and my burden is light.'

- Here the curtain is drawn back on Jesus' prayer: we see that he prays directly to his Father and pours out his joy and desires before him. We sense that he is totally in love with his Father and loves the way the Father goes about things! His is a grateful heart, no matter what difficulties life throws at him. I pray for the rich relationship with God that he has.

Saturday 17 June
Luke 2:41–51

Now every year his parents went to Jerusalem for the festival of the Passover. And when he was twelve years old, they went up as usual for the festival. When the festival was ended and they started to return, the boy Jesus stayed behind in Jerusalem, but his parents did not know it. Assuming that he was in the group of travellers, they went a day's journey. Then they started to look for him among their relatives and friends. When they did not find him, they returned to Jerusalem to search for him. After three days they found him in the temple, sitting among the teachers, listening to them and asking them questions. And all who heard him were amazed at his understanding and his answers. When his parents saw him they were astonished; and his mother said to him, 'Child, why have you treated us like this? Look, your father and I have been searching for you in great anxiety.' He said to them, 'Why were you searching for me? Did you not know that I must be in my Father's house?' But they did not understand what he said to them. Then he went down with them and came to Nazareth, and was obedient to them. His mother treasured all these things in her heart.

- Isn't it consoling that even Mary did not understand everything fully? We so often do not understand why painful events happen in our lives. Like Mary, we can ask: Why? Where is God in this event? And again like Mary, we may not understand the answer. But Jesus goes with us, just as he went home with Mary and Joseph. And if, like Mary, we treasure what has happened in our heart, the day will come when all will be made clear to us.

- Lord, help me to trust you in the dark times, even when I don't understand.

The Eleventh Week in Ordinary Time
18–24 June 2023

Something to think and pray about each day this week:

The wilderness is a strong image. There are many different ways to imagine a wilderness. It could remind us, on the one hand, of walking in the countryside or in wide open spaces, with animals scurrying around about us in the sun or the rain. It could remind us of the silence of the many winding roads that don't seem to go any particular place, giving us time to think and pray. This is a positive experience of being in the wilderness. However, the wilderness can also be a place of desolation for us. It can be an internal landscape of worry, problems, sin and perceived distance from God. Being in the wilderness can be uncomfortable or worse.

Our job, it seems, is to bear with ourselves being in that wilderness. Wilderness times are inevitable parts of the story of life.

We see this in the Gospels when Jesus is driven into the wilderness. However, we are told that the wilderness was not the end of his journey. He emerged from that wilderness and came out the other side. Not only that, but he grew in the wilderness – he learned something about his life and his mission. We are told that he came out of the wilderness filled with the Spirit of God.

Emerging from the wilderness feels like a remote prospect when we are right in the middle of it. However, our emergence is as inevitable as the rising of the sun on a new day. We are invited to trust that God is with us in the wilderness and that we will emerge with deeper insights into ourselves, the world and our place in it. We need not worry or despair; it is God, after all, who ultimately straightens all paths out of the wilderness.

Brendan McManus SJ and Jim Deeds,
Deeper into the Mess: Praying Through Tough Times

The Presence of God
Dear Jesus, today I call on you, but not to ask for anything. I'd like only to dwell in your presence. May my heart respond to your love.

Freedom
God my creator, you gave me life and the gift of freedom. Through your love I exist in this world. May I never take the gift of life for granted. May I always respect others' right to life.

Consciousness
I ask how I am today. Am I particularly tired, stressed or anxious? If any of these characteristics apply, can I try to let go of the concerns that disturb me?

The Word
The word of God comes down to us through the Scriptures. May the Holy Spirit enlighten my mind and my heart to respond to the gospel teachings.
(Please turn to the Scripture on the following pages. Inspiration points are there, should you need them. When you are ready, return here to continue.)

Conversation
I begin to talk with Jesus about the Scripture I have just read. What part of it strikes a chord in me? Perhaps the words of a friend – or some story I have heard recently – will rise to the surface in my consciousness. If so, does the story throw light on what the Scripture passage may be saying to me?

Conclusion
Glory be to the Father, and to the Son, and to the Holy Spirit,
As it was in the beginning, is now and ever shall be,
World without end. Amen.

Sunday 18 June
Eleventh Sunday in Ordinary Time
Matthew 9:36–10:8

When he saw the crowds, he had compassion for them, because they were harassed and helpless, like sheep without a shepherd. Then he said to his disciples, 'The harvest is plentiful, but the labourers are few; therefore ask the Lord of the harvest to send out labourers into his harvest.'

Then Jesus summoned his twelve disciples and gave them authority over unclean spirits, to cast them out, and to cure every disease and every sickness. These are the names of the twelve apostles: first, Simon, also known as Peter, and his brother Andrew; James son of Zebedee, and his brother John; Philip and Bartholomew; Thomas and Matthew the tax-collector; James son of Alphaeus, and Thaddaeus; Simon the Cananaean, and Judas Iscariot, the one who betrayed him.

These twelve Jesus sent out with the following instructions: 'Go nowhere among the Gentiles, and enter no town of the Samaritans, but go rather to the lost sheep of the house of Israel. As you go, proclaim the good news, "The kingdom of heaven has come near." Cure the sick, raise the dead, cleanse the lepers, cast out demons. You received without payment; give without payment.'

- This seems to be a really outgoing gospel: we are to look at the big harvest, the sick, the dead, the outcasts; all the needs of people are part of prayer. It is in care and compassion that the kingdom of heaven comes near.

Monday 19 June
Matthew 5:38–42

Jesus said, 'You have heard that it was said, "An eye for an eye and a tooth for a tooth." But I say to you, Do not resist an evildoer. But if anyone strikes you on the right cheek, turn the other also; and if anyone wants to sue you and take your coat, give your cloak as well; and if anyone forces you to go one mile, go also the second mile. Give to everyone who begs from you, and do not refuse anyone who wants to borrow from you.'

- Jesus calls us to look beyond the limit of the law. We need to be generous and imaginative if we are to rise beyond the restrictions that life presents.

- I think of how I might be free from the constraints I find by acting from a generous spirit. I ask God to inspire and help me.

Tuesday 20 June
Matthew 5:43–48

Jesus said, 'You have heard that it was said, "You shall love your neighbour and hate your enemy." But I say to you, Love your enemies and pray for those who persecute you, so that you may be children of your Father in heaven; for he makes his sun rise on the evil and on the good, and sends rain on the righteous and on the unrighteous. For if you love those who love you, what reward do you have? Do not even the tax-collectors do the same? And if you greet only your brothers and sisters, what more are you doing than others? Do not even the Gentiles do the same? Be perfect, therefore, as your heavenly Father is perfect.'

- Inspired by the words of Jesus, I bring to mind those people I have learned to distrust. I place them before God. If I can, I ask God to bless them; if I cannot, I ask for the grace I need to wish them well.

Wednesday 21 June
Matthew 6:1–6, 16–18

Jesus said to them, 'Beware of practising your piety before others in order to be seen by them; for then you have no reward from your Father in heaven.

'So whenever you give alms, do not sound a trumpet before you, as the hypocrites do in the synagogues and in the streets, so that they may be praised by others. Truly I tell you, they have received their reward. But when you give alms, do not let your left hand know what your right hand is doing, so that your alms may be done in secret; and your Father who sees in secret will reward you.

'And whenever you pray, do not be like the hypocrites; for they love to stand and pray in the synagogues and at the street corners, so that they may be seen by others. Truly I tell you, they have received their reward. But whenever you pray, go into your room and shut the door and pray to your Father who is in secret; and your Father who sees in secret will reward you.

'And whenever you fast, do not look dismal, like the hypocrites, for they disfigure their faces so as to show others that they are fasting. Truly I tell you, they have received their reward. But when you fast, put oil on your head and wash your face, so that your fasting may be seen not by others but by your Father who is in secret; and your Father who sees in secret will reward you.'

- Today, Jesus reminds us of the three hallmarks of genuine religion: prayer, fasting and almsgiving. We need all three.

- Prayer without some element of fasting and almsgiving could become so heavenly, as someone has said, that it is no earthly use. Fasting without prayer and almsgiving might end up as self-preoccupied dieting. If we give alms but have no time for prayer or some self-denial, perhaps our motto is 'Do good and avoid God'!

Thursday 22 June
Matthew 6:7–15

Jesus said to his disciples, 'When you are praying, do not heap up empty phrases as the Gentiles do; for they think that they will be heard because of their many words. Do not be like them, for your Father knows what you need before you ask him.

'Pray then in this way:
Our Father in heaven,
    hallowed be your name.
Your kingdom come.
Your will be done,
    on earth as it is in heaven.
Give us this day our daily bread.
And forgive us our debts,
    as we also have forgiven our debtors.
And do not bring us to the time of trial,
    but rescue us from the evil one.

'For if you forgive others their trespasses, your heavenly Father will also forgive you; but if you do not forgive others, neither will your Father forgive your trespasses.'

- Are you having difficulty praying just now? Maybe you are confused, annoyed, daydreaming. Try to be still for a few moments. Do you not know what to say? Try the prayer that Jesus offers here, the Our Father, praying it slowly, or just be still and silent in the Lord's presence. Prayer is a time of relaxing into the mystery of God's love, letting go of tensions and worries for this period of time.

Friday 23 June
Matthew 6:19–23

Jesus said to them, 'Do not store up for yourselves treasures on earth, where moth and rust consume and where thieves break in and steal; but store up for yourselves treasures in heaven, where neither moth nor rust consumes and where thieves do not break in and steal. For where your treasure is, there your heart will be also.

'The eye is the lamp of the body. So, if your eye is healthy, your whole body will be full of light; but if your eye is unhealthy, your whole body will be full of darkness. If then the light in you is darkness, how great is the darkness!'

- Where is my treasure? Where does my heart gravitate towards when I am not busy? Is it to someone I love? Or is it to something trivial, prey to rust and moths?

Saturday 24 June
The Nativity of John the Baptist
Luke 1:57–66, 80

Now the time came for Elizabeth to give birth, and she bore a son. Her neighbours and relatives heard that the Lord had shown his great mercy to her, and they rejoiced with her.

On the eighth day they came to circumcise the child, and they were going to name him Zechariah after his father. But his mother said, 'No; he is to be called John.' They said to her, 'None of your relatives has this name.' Then they began motioning to his father to find out what name he wanted to give him. He asked for a writing-tablet and wrote, 'His name is John.' And all of them were amazed. Immediately his mouth was opened and his tongue freed, and he began to speak, praising God. Fear came over all their neighbours, and all these things were talked about throughout the entire hill country of Judea. All who heard them pondered them and said, 'What then will this child become?' For, indeed, the hand of the Lord was with him.

The child grew and became strong in spirit, and he was in the wilderness until the day he appeared publicly to Israel.

• The name 'John' in Hebrew means 'The Lord is gracious.' The Lord showed his kindness to Elizabeth and Zechariah, fulfilling their desire to have a child. I think of the ways he has been kind to me.

The Twelfth Week in Ordinary Time
25 June–1 July 2023

Something to think and pray about each day this week:

There is something special about the miracles of Jesus. Sometimes he manages to perform a miracle immediately, but there are also cases where he has to start again. Sometimes it doesn't work at all.

The reason for the latter is people's unbelief. Here is the heart of the matter. The miracles of Jesus ultimately have to do with faith in God. A miracle is a special sign in which the believer sees God's goodness and care for us at work. Whether it is about a healing or a special natural phenomenon, it is ultimately the faith that makes it that you can see a certain event as a sign of the greatness and the goodness of God. That is why Jesus, after a miracle, says several times 'Your faith has saved you' (Mark 5:34).

Nikolaas Sintobin SJ,
Did Jesus Really Exist? and 51 Other Questions

The Presence of God

Dear Lord, as I come to you today, fill my heart, my whole being, with the wonder of your presence. Help me remain receptive to you as I put aside the cares of this world. Fill my mind with your peace.

Freedom

Lord, grant me the grace to be free from the excesses of this life. Let me not get caught up with the desire for wealth. Keep my heart and mind free to love and serve you.

Consciousness

I exist in a web of relationships: links to nature, people, God.
I trace out these links, giving thanks for the life that flows through them.
Some links are twisted or broken; I may feel regret, anger, disappointment.
I pray for the gift of acceptance and forgiveness.

The Word

God speaks to each of us individually. I listen attentively to hear what he is saying to me. Read the text a few times, then listen.
(Please turn to the Scripture on the following pages. Inspiration points are there, should you need them. When you are ready, return here to continue.)

Conversation

Jesus, you speak to me through the words of the Gospels. May I respond to your call today. Teach me to recognise your hand at work in my daily living.

Conclusion

I thank God for these moments we have spent together and for any insights I have been given concerning the text.

Sunday 25 June
Twelfth Sunday in Ordinary Time
Matthew 10:26–33

Jesus said to his disciples, 'So have no fear of them; for nothing is covered up that will not be uncovered, and nothing secret that will not become known. What I say to you in the dark, tell in the light; and what you hear whispered, proclaim from the housetops. Do not fear those who kill the body but cannot kill the soul; rather fear him who can destroy both soul and body in hell. Are not two sparrows sold for a penny? Yet not one of them will fall to the ground unperceived by your Father. And even the hairs of your head are all counted. So do not be afraid; you are of more value than many sparrows.

'Everyone therefore who acknowledges me before others, I also will acknowledge before my Father in heaven; but whoever denies me before others, I also will deny before my Father in heaven.'

• Jesus mentions fear several times here: does fear sometimes make me betray the truth? Perhaps I may know what to do in a situation but I do nothing for fear of the reactions of others. I ask to believe that God knows me fully and values me limitlessly, so I need not fear.

Monday 26 June
Matthew 7:1–5

Jesus said to the crowds, 'Do not judge, so that you may not be judged. For with the judgement you make you will be judged, and the measure you give will be the measure you get. Why do you see the speck in your neighbour's eye, but do not notice the log in your own eye? Or how can you say to your neighbour, "Let me take the speck out of your eye", while the log is in your own eye? You hypocrite, first take the log out of your own eye, and then you will see clearly to take the speck out of your neighbour's eye.'

• Arrogance can make us believe that we are morally superior to others and can act as judges over them. As Jesus' imagery suggests, it is all too easy to see others' faults and remain blind to our own. Becoming obsessed with a small failing in another person can distract us from being aware of a much greater shortcoming in ourselves.

- Pray for an enlightened self-knowledge and a non-judgemental attitude (generosity of spirit) towards others.

Tuesday 27 June
Matthew 7:6, 12–14

Jesus said to them, 'Do not give what is holy to dogs; and do not throw your pearls before swine, or they will trample them under foot and turn and maul you.

'In everything do to others as you would have them do to you; for this is the law and the prophets.

'Enter through the narrow gate; for the gate is wide and the road is easy that leads to destruction, and there are many who take it. For the gate is narrow and the road is hard that leads to life, and there are few who find it.'

- 'Do not judge … '. What a difficult command! How many times do we judge without realising it – reading the newspaper, watching the news or walking down the street? Can I try to make allowances for people today?

Wednesday 28 June
Matthew 7:15–20

Jesus said, 'Beware of false prophets, who come to you in sheep's clothing but inwardly are ravenous wolves. You will know them by their fruits. Are grapes gathered from thorns, or figs from thistles? In the same way, every good tree bears good fruit, but the bad tree bears bad fruit. A good tree cannot bear bad fruit, nor can a bad tree bear good fruit. Every tree that does not bear good fruit is cut down and thrown into the fire. Thus you will know them by their fruits.'

- How does this passage touch me? Am I given to judging the book by the cover? Do I sometimes use this image to condemn others, as what would one expect from that family or that society or nation?
- Might this passage be inviting me to look again at the talents and gifts that I have been given and be grateful for them, asking that I might be able to use them for the good of others?

Thursday 29 June
Ss Peter and Paul, Apostles
Matthew 16:13–19

Now when Jesus came into the district of Caesarea Philippi, he asked his disciples, 'Who do people say that the Son of Man is?' And they said, 'Some say John the Baptist, but others Elijah, and still others Jeremiah or one of the prophets.' He said to them, 'But who do you say that I am?' Simon Peter answered, 'You are the Messiah, the Son of the living God.' And Jesus answered him, 'Blessed are you, Simon son of Jonah! For flesh and blood has not revealed this to you, but my Father in heaven. And I tell you, you are Peter, and on this rock I will build my church, and the gates of Hades will not prevail against it. I will give you the keys of the kingdom of heaven, and whatever you bind on earth will be bound in heaven, and whatever you loose on earth will be loosed in heaven.'

- If Peter is to be a rock, it is because he has found the rock that is Jesus. We all need strong and firm foundations for our faith and for our lives. We need strong stepping stones to guide us through life. Jesus is the way and the stepping stones. In him we need not fear for the future nor lose confidence in the present. To be able to say that Jesus is the living God is a grace to be treasured.

Friday 30 June
Matthew 8:1–4

When Jesus had come down from the mountain, great crowds followed him; and there was a leper who came to him and knelt before him, saying, 'Lord, if you choose, you can make me clean.' He stretched out his hand and touched him, saying, 'I do choose. Be made clean!' Immediately his leprosy was cleansed. Then Jesus said to him, 'See that you say nothing to anyone; but go, show yourself to the priest, and offer the gift that Moses commanded, as a testimony to them.'

- Miracle stories show that the world is not set in stone but is open to the power of God and his grace. What big or little miracle can I ask for?

Saturday 1 July
Matthew 8:5–17

When he entered Capernaum, a centurion came to him, appealing to him and saying, 'Lord, my servant is lying at home paralysed, in terrible distress.' And he said to him, 'I will come and cure him.' The centurion answered, 'Lord, I am not worthy to have you come under my roof; but only speak the word, and my servant will be healed. For I also am a man under authority, with soldiers under me; and I say to one, "Go", and he goes, and to another, "Come", and he comes, and to my slave, "Do this", and the slave does it.' When Jesus heard him, he was amazed and said to those who followed him, 'Truly I tell you, in no one in Israel have I found such faith. I tell you, many will come from east and west and will eat with Abraham and Isaac and Jacob in the kingdom of heaven, while the heirs of the kingdom will be thrown into the outer darkness, where there will be weeping and gnashing of teeth.' And to the centurion Jesus said, 'Go; let it be done for you according to your faith.' And the servant was healed in that hour.

When Jesus entered Peter's house, he saw his mother-in-law lying in bed with a fever; he touched her hand, and the fever left her, and she got up and began to serve him. That evening they brought to him many who were possessed by demons; and he cast out the spirits with a word, and cured all who were sick. This was to fulfil what had been spoken through the prophet Isaiah, 'He took our infirmities and bore our diseases.'

- The words of this pagan centurion have entered the liturgy of the Mass. There is goodness in everyone if I really take time to look for it. Is there someone in my life in whom I am struggling to see goodness? I bring this person into my prayer today.

- Let me go with Jesus into Peter's house. I will imagine the whole scene. Does the action of Jesus give me hope for what God can do for me?

Something to think and pray about each day this week:

Joy and happiness are two different things, although they are obviously related. There are things in our lives we feel happy doing or experiencing. For example, watching a good movie makes us feel happy for the time we're watching it. Happiness is very much in the moment, and it can be good. But joy is a different thing. Joy is a deeper sense than happiness. We feel happy watching a film, but feel joy when we see a good friend whom we haven't seen for a while. Joy is different.

Having that extra glass of wine, or that bigger slice of cake, might make us happy in the moment, but the next day (or sooner) we may be left feeling that it may not have been such a good idea. Joy is different here too. The things that give us joy do not come with the sense that they might not be a good thing. The things that make us joyful are the things that make us whole, or make us grow, or show us that life is good and precious.

Then there are things in life that might not make us very happy in the moment but leave us with joy. We think here of making a sacrifice for someone. In the moment, we might feel aggrieved or put out. After the fact, reflecting on the sacrifice we've made, we might feel joy at having done a good thing or the right thing.

To live lives of joy is not to depend on happiness or temporary experiences. It is to seek out the better path and walk it. It is to see the good and the better in all people and to love them. It is to know that we too are loved, held, cherished and special.

Jim Deeds and Brendan McManus SJ,
Finding God in the Mess: Meditations for Mindful Living

The Presence of God
God is with me, but even more astounding, God is within me.
Let me dwell for a moment on God's life-giving presence
in my body, in my mind, in my heart,
as I sit here, right now.

Freedom
Lord, may I never take the gift of freedom for granted. You gave me the
great blessing of freedom of spirit. Fill my spirit with your peace and joy.

Consciousness
I remind myself that I am in the presence of God, who is my strength in
times of weakness and my comforter in times of sorrow.

The Word
I take my time to read the word of God slowly, a few times, allowing
myself to dwell on anything that strikes me.
*(Please turn to the Scripture on the following pages. Inspiration points are there,
should you need them. When you are ready, return here to continue.)*

Conversation
Jesus, you always welcomed little children when you walked on this earth.
Teach me to have a childlike trust in you. Teach me to live in the knowl-
edge that you will never abandon me.

Conclusion
Glory be to the Father, and to the Son, and to the Holy Spirit,
As it was in the beginning, is now and ever shall be,
World without end. Amen.

Sunday 2 July
Thirteenth Sunday in Ordinary Time
Matthew 10:37–42

Jesus said to his disciples, 'Whoever loves father or mother more than me is not worthy of me; and whoever loves son or daughter more than me is not worthy of me; and whoever does not take up the cross and follow me is not worthy of me. Those who find their life will lose it, and those who lose their life for my sake will find it.

'Whoever welcomes you welcomes me, and whoever welcomes me welcomes the one who sent me. Whoever welcomes a prophet in the name of a prophet will receive a prophet's reward; and whoever welcomes a righteous person in the name of a righteous person will receive the reward of the righteous; and whoever gives even a cup of cold water to one of these little ones in the name of a disciple – truly I tell you, none of these will lose their reward.'

- The gospel of Jesus is not only about a way of life founded on love and mercy, but above all about the person of Jesus himself. Today he claims a special place in our lives, more important than our dearest ones. Being a disciple is not a marginal aspect of my life, it is central. I ask for the grace to be a real disciple of Jesus, capable of taking up my cross and following him.

Monday 3 July
St Thomas, Apostle
John 20:24–29

But Thomas (who was called the Twin), one of the twelve, was not with them when Jesus came. So the other disciples told him, 'We have seen the Lord.' But he said to them, 'Unless I see the mark of the nails in his hands, and put my finger in the mark of the nails and my hand in his side, I will not believe.'

A week later his disciples were again in the house, and Thomas was with them. Although the doors were shut, Jesus came and stood among them and said, 'Peace be with you.' Then he said to Thomas, 'Put your finger here and see my hands. Reach out your hand and put it in my side. Do not doubt but believe.' Thomas answered him, 'My Lord and my

God!' Jesus said to him, 'Have you believed because you have seen me? Blessed are those who have not seen and yet have come to believe.'

- We call Thomas 'doubting' and easily forget that he was also honest, acknowledging his hesitation and reluctance to believe. Because he was honest, Jesus was able to address him and he was able to respond to Jesus honestly and humbly. I take the opportunity of this time of prayer to speak to Jesus, not piously or in somebody else's formula, but from my heart. I too believe. Lord, help my unbelief!

Tuesday 4 July
Matthew 8:23–27

And when Jesus got into the boat, his disciples followed him. A gale arose on the lake, so great that the boat was being swamped by the waves; but he was asleep. And they went and woke him up, saying, 'Lord, save us! We are perishing!' And he said to them, 'Why are you afraid, you of little faith?' Then he got up and rebuked the winds and the sea; and there was a dead calm. They were amazed, saying, 'What sort of man is this, that even the winds and the sea obey him?'

- 'Lord, save us! We are perishing!' As with so many other prayers we find in the gospel, I may find that today this simple prayer resonates in my heart as I look at my family, my community, my country, our world. I stay with these words, pleading for Jesus' help.

Wednesday 5 July
Matthew 8:28–34

When he came to the other side, to the country of the Gadarenes, two demoniacs coming out of the tombs met him. They were so fierce that no one could pass that way. Suddenly they shouted, 'What have you to do with us, Son of God? Have you come here to torment us before the time?' Now a large herd of swine was feeding at some distance from them. The demons begged him, 'If you cast us out, send us into the herd of swine.' And he said to them, 'Go!' So they came out and entered the swine; and suddenly, the whole herd rushed down the steep bank into the lake and perished in the water. The swineherds ran off, and on going into the town, they told the whole story about what had happened to the demoniacs. Then the whole town came out to meet Jesus; and when they saw him, they begged him to leave their neighbourhood.

• Driving out demons was never straightforward, even for Jesus. Unlike in other, bigger, miracles, Jesus here encounters opposition and resistance, but at the end he prevails. Evil is a powerful force in our world, seemingly present everywhere, and is so difficult to eradicate. But as I look to Jesus who prevails against it, I ask for his help never to give up in my struggle against the evil around me.

Thursday 6 July
Matthew 9:1–8

And after getting into a boat he crossed the water and came to his own town.

And just then some people were carrying a paralysed man lying on a bed. When Jesus saw their faith, he said to the paralytic, 'Take heart, son; your sins are forgiven.' Then some of the scribes said to themselves, 'This man is blaspheming.' But Jesus, perceiving their thoughts, said, 'Why do you think evil in your hearts? For which is easier, to say, "Your sins are forgiven", or to say, "Stand up and walk"? But so that you may know that the Son of Man has authority on earth to forgive sins' – he then said to the paralytic – 'Stand up, take your bed and go to your home.' And he stood up and went to his home. When the crowds saw it, they were filled with awe, and they glorified God, who had given such authority to human beings.

• Jesus sees what is in the heart and helps each person to recognise their own motives and desires. Here, before God, I notice what is it like to have my heart known and I speak to Jesus about what is happening in my heart these days.

Friday 7 July
Matthew 9:9–13

As Jesus was walking along, he saw a man called Matthew sitting at the tax booth; and he said to him, 'Follow me.' And he got up and followed him.

And as he sat at dinner in the house, many tax-collectors and sinners came and were sitting with him and his disciples. When the Pharisees saw this, they said to his disciples, 'Why does your teacher eat with tax-collectors and sinners?' But when he heard this, he said, 'Those who are well have no need of a physician, but those who are sick. Go and learn what this means, "I desire mercy, not sacrifice." For I have come to call not the righteous but sinners.'

• We get so used to planning and arranging that we think God must surely agree with us! As I come into God's presence now, I realise that I am approaching tremendous mystery and ask, with awe and humility, for the help I need. I ask forgiveness for any way in which I have become self-satisfied, for thinking that I know all God's ways.

Saturday 8 July
Matthew 9:14–17

Then the disciples of John came to him, saying, 'Why do we and the Pharisees fast often, but your disciples do not fast?' And Jesus said to them, 'The wedding guests cannot mourn as long as the bridegroom is with them, can they? The days will come when the bridegroom is taken away from them, and then they will fast. No one sews a piece of unshrunk cloth on an old cloak, for the patch pulls away from the cloak, and a worse tear is made. Neither is new wine put into old wineskins; otherwise, the skins burst, and the wine is spilled, and the skins are destroyed; but new wine is put into fresh wineskins, and so both are preserved.'

• Jesus introduces us here to a radically new way of seeing him or to a vision of him that is beyond all our hopes and dreams. He is saying that he is drawing us into an intimacy with him that is imaged as that between a bridegroom and his bride. The environment he wants us to cultivate is that of a wedding where a celebratory atmosphere prevails. We are made for joy.

The Fourteenth Week in Ordinary Time
9–15 July 2023

Something to think and pray about each day this week:

Sometimes people don't pray because they feel they're not worthy of it. They think it's not for them. Mention the word 'contemplation' and they just run a mile. They think it's for monks and people who have all sorts of qualifications. Prayer and contemplation are nothing more than simply 'sitting with God'.

This world we live in can be very distracting. Everything gets broken down or torn apart, important concepts are shredded into little bits and pieces. Prayer, and particularly contemplation, allows you to enter into the heart of God, knowing that this world beats as one, that there's a harmony in the world. You are more than broken bits and pieces and individual parts. To be at peace you have to see the whole, get the picture of the whole, get the sense of the whole, and it is prayer and contemplation that helps you achieve this.

I find that when I pray in the morning I go out into my day with a greater sense of purpose. I'm not just fiddling with little bits and pieces and trying to fit them all together chaotically.

Alan Hilliard,
Dipping into Life: 40 Reflections for a Fragile Faith

The Presence of God
God is with me, but more,
God is within me, giving me existence.
Let me dwell for a moment on God's life-giving presence
in my body, my mind, my heart,
and in the whole of my life.

Freedom
Lord, you created me to live in freedom. May your Holy Spirit guide me
to follow you freely. Instil in my heart a desire to know and love you more
each day.

Consciousness
In God's loving presence I unwind the past day,
starting from now and looking back, moment by moment.
I gather in all the goodness and light, in gratitude.
I attend to the shadows and what they say to me,
seeking healing, courage, forgiveness.

The Word
God speaks to each of us individually. I listen attentively to hear what he
is saying to me. Read the text a few times, then listen.
*(Please turn to the Scripture on the following pages. Inspiration points are there,
should you need them. When you are ready, return here to continue.)*

Conversation
Jesus, you always welcomed little children when you walked on this earth.
Teach me to have a childlike trust in you. Teach me to live in the knowl-
edge that you will never abandon me.

Conclusion
I thank God for these moments we have spent together and for any insights I have been given concerning the text.

Sunday 9 July
Fourteenth Sunday in Ordinary Time
Matthew 11:25–30

At that time Jesus said, 'I thank you, Father, Lord of heaven and earth, because you have hidden these things from the wise and the intelligent and have revealed them to infants; yes, Father, for such was your gracious will. All things have been handed over to me by my Father; and no one knows the Son except the Father, and no one knows the Father except the Son and anyone to whom the Son chooses to reveal him.

'Come to me, all you that are weary and are carrying heavy burdens, and I will give you rest. Take my yoke upon you, and learn from me; for I am gentle and humble in heart, and you will find rest for your souls. For my yoke is easy, and my burden is light.'

• Think of a public figure who leaves a press conference and goes home to be greeted by her child: she is known and recognised in very different ways. Theologians can become scientists who are experts about God but, without prayer, God remains unknown. Here you are, drawn to prayer, called into relationship with your loving God: this gladdens Jesus' heart more than any library, thesis or ecclesiastical pronouncement. Listen for what God wants to reveal to you now.

Monday 10 July
Matthew 9:18–26

While he was saying these things to them, suddenly a leader of the synagogue came in and knelt before him, saying, 'My daughter has just died; but come and lay your hand on her, and she will live.' And Jesus got up and followed him, with his disciples. Then suddenly a woman who had been suffering from haemorrhages for twelve years came up behind him and touched the fringe of his cloak, for she said to herself, 'If I only touch his cloak, I will be made well.' Jesus turned, and seeing her he said, 'Take heart, daughter; your faith has made you well.' And instantly the woman was made well. When Jesus came to the leader's house and saw the flute-players and the crowd making a commotion, he said, 'Go away; for the girl is not dead but sleeping.' And they laughed at him. But when the crowd had been put outside, he went in and took her by the hand, and the girl got up. And the report of this spread throughout that district.

- Like the woman in today's text I may be suffering from some malady, physical or spiritual, that has become a permanent feature of my life, keeping me back from being my true self. Like her I might feel the urge to seek healing, to touch Jesus discreetly, believing in his power to heal me. I listen to Jesus' reply, affirming my move.

Tuesday 11 July
Matthew 9:32–38

After they had gone away, a demoniac who was mute was brought to him. And when the demon had been cast out, the one who had been mute spoke; and the crowds were amazed and said, 'Never has anything like this been seen in Israel.' But the Pharisees said, 'By the ruler of the demons he casts out the demons.'

Then Jesus went about all the cities and villages, teaching in their synagogues, and proclaiming the good news of the kingdom, and curing every disease and every sickness. When he saw the crowds, he had compassion for them, because they were harassed and helpless, like sheep without a shepherd. Then he said to his disciples, 'The harvest is plentiful, but the labourers are few; therefore ask the Lord of the harvest to send out labourers into his harvest.'

- The crowds were amazed after the demon was expelled, but the Pharisees said, 'By the ruler of the demons he casts out the demons.' How hard the human heart can be even in religious circles. I pray for peace and deep mutual respect in my Church and among all religious people.

Wednesday 12 July
Matthew 10:1–7

Then Jesus summoned his twelve disciples and gave them authority over unclean spirits, to cast them out, and to cure every disease and every sickness. These are the names of the twelve apostles: first, Simon, also known as Peter, and his brother Andrew; James son of Zebedee, and his brother John; Philip and Bartholomew; Thomas and Matthew the tax-collector; James son of Alphaeus, and Thaddaeus; Simon the Cananaean, and Judas Iscariot, the one who betrayed him.

These twelve Jesus sent out with the following instructions: 'Go nowhere among the Gentiles, and enter no town of the Samaritans, but go rather to the lost sheep of the house of Israel. As you go, proclaim the good news, "The kingdom of heaven has come near."'

- He trusted them so much that he sent them even at the beginning of his ministry, and gave them great power. He shared his own mission with them! I realise that Jesus calls me too by name, in spite of all my failings and limitations, and sends me to join him in combatting evil, healing hurts and proclaiming the kingdom. I thank Jesus for his trust in me and ask for the grace to be able to hear his call sending me to others.

Thursday 13 July
Matthew 10:7–15

And Jesus said to them, 'As you go, proclaim the good news, "The kingdom of heaven has come near." Cure the sick, raise the dead, cleanse the lepers, cast out demons. You received without payment; give without payment. Take no gold, or silver, or copper in your belts, no bag for your journey, or two tunics, or sandals, or a staff; for labourers deserve their food. Whatever town or village you enter, find out who in it is worthy, and stay there until you leave. As you enter the house, greet it. If the house is worthy, let your peace come upon it; but if it is not worthy, let your peace return to you. If anyone will not welcome you or listen to your words, shake off the dust from your feet as you leave that house or town. Truly I tell you, it will be more tolerable for the land of Sodom and Gomorrah on the day of judgement than for that town.'

- The followers of Jesus are sent out as messengers of peace, cautioned against keeping their attention on wounds or hurts. I take time to speak to Jesus about the dust I find difficult to shake off and humbly ask for healing.

Friday 14 July
Matthew 10:16–23

Jesus said to his disciples, 'See, I am sending you out like sheep into the midst of wolves; so be wise as serpents and innocent as doves. Beware of them, for they will hand you over to councils and flog you in their synagogues; and you will be dragged before governors and kings because of me, as a testimony to them and the Gentiles. When they hand you over, do not worry about how you are to speak or what you are to say; for what you are to say will be given to you at that time; for it is not you who speak, but the Spirit of your Father speaking through you. Brother will betray brother to death, and a father his child, and children will rise against parents and have them put to death; and you will be hated by all because of my name. But the one who endures to the end will be saved. When they persecute you in one town, flee to the next; for truly I tell you, you will not have gone through all the towns of Israel before the Son of Man comes.'

- Jesus does not allow us to romanticise or idealise the life of the disciple; he tells us that it will be difficult, challenging us by his words and by his example. I pray for the wisdom to listen to the fullness of Jesus' words, cherishing their comfort and promise and being called to be alert as I follow him.

Saturday 15 July
Matthew 10:24–33

Jesus said to his disciples, 'A disciple is not above the teacher, nor a slave above the master; it is enough for the disciple to be like the teacher, and the slave like the master. If they have called the master of the house Beelzebul, how much more will they malign those of his household!

'So have no fear of them; for nothing is covered up that will not be uncovered, and nothing secret that will not become known. What I say to you in the dark, tell in the light; and what you hear whispered, proclaim from the housetops. Do not fear those who kill the body but cannot kill the soul; rather fear him who can destroy both soul and body in hell. Are not two sparrows sold for a penny? Yet not one of them will fall to the ground unperceived by your Father. And even the hairs of your head are all counted. So do not be afraid; you are of more value than many sparrows.

'Everyone therefore who acknowledges me before others, I also will acknowledge before my Father in heaven; but whoever denies me before others, I also will deny before my Father in heaven.'

- In an age when we incline to see everything in material, monetary and functional terms it is good to talk to Jesus about how nothing 'falls to the ground unperceived', much less you who 'are of more value than many sparrows'.

The Fifteenth Sunday in Ordinary Time
16–22 July 2023

Something to think and pray about each day this week:

At the start of an academic year recently a friend was working through the mess that was her room. Covered in dust after some interior construction, it took some time to shape everything up, separate the rubbish from the things worth keeping, put aside clothes and stuff for recycling (the 'not used in one year' rule) and trim down to the basics. It was a whole day's work but well worth it for the energy and enthusiasm of a new start. She was commenting how much it helped her emotionally and spiritually to clear some space, get rid of old things that are no longer needed and to be open to something new. She said it was a prayer for her, a kind of retreat into the past, in order to go forward.

Of course, the practical stuff is easy to sort out, but the spiritual, the deepest part of us, is much more tricky. An essential part is a recommitment to prayer and reflection, but what is not immediately obvious is enlisting God's help with those trickier messes: resentment, anger against another, wounds of grief or betrayal. This is what St Ignatius Loyola recommends: pray with the difficulties and 'the mess' in order that we may be free from unnecessary weights and travel light. Paradoxically it is about trying to understand it from God's point of view and God's desire to heal us, not just our point of view. This change of focus helps to break old ways of thinking and praying and move into some new beginnings, the real fresh start we long for.

Brendan McManus SJ and Jim Deeds,
Deeper into the Mess: Praying Through Tough Times

The Presence of God
I pause for a moment and think of the love and the grace that God showers on me. I am created in the image and likeness of God; I am God's dwelling place.

Freedom
I am free. When I look at these words in writing, they seem to create in me a feeling of awe. Yes, a wonderful feeling of freedom. Thank you, God.

Consciousness
In the presence of my loving Creator, I look honestly at my feelings over the past day: the highs, the lows, and the level ground. Can I see where the Lord has been present?

The Word
I read the word of God slowly, a few times over, and I listen to what God is saying to me.
(Please turn to the Scripture on the following pages. Inspiration points are there, should you need them. When you are ready, return here to continue.)

Conversation
Remembering that I am still in God's presence,
I imagine Jesus standing or sitting beside me,
and I say whatever is on my mind, whatever is in my heart,
speaking as one friend to another.

Conclusion
Glory be to the Father, and to the Son, and to the Holy Spirit,
As it was in the beginning, is now and ever shall be,
World without end. Amen.

Sunday 16 July
Fifteenth Sunday in Ordinary Time
Matthew 13:1–23

That same day Jesus went out of the house and sat beside the lake. Such great crowds gathered around him that he got into a boat and sat there, while the whole crowd stood on the beach. And he told them many things in parables, saying: 'Listen! A sower went out to sow. And as he sowed, some seeds fell on the path, and the birds came and ate them up. Other seeds fell on rocky ground, where they did not have much soil, and they sprang up quickly, since they had no depth of soil. But when the sun rose, they were scorched; and since they had no root, they withered away. Other seeds fell among thorns, and the thorns grew up and choked them. Other seeds fell on good soil and brought forth grain, some a hundred-fold, some sixty, some thirty. Let anyone with ears listen!'

Then the disciples came and asked him, 'Why do you speak to them in parables?' He answered, 'To you it has been given to know the secrets of the kingdom of heaven, but to them it has not been given. For to those who have, more will be given, and they will have an abundance; but from those who have nothing, even what they have will be taken away. The reason I speak to them in parables is that "seeing they do not perceive, and hearing they do not listen, nor do they understand." With them indeed is fulfilled the prophecy of Isaiah that says:

"You will indeed listen, but never understand,
   and you will indeed look, but never perceive.
For this people's heart has grown dull,
   and their ears are hard of hearing,
      and they have shut their eyes;
         so that they might not look with their eyes,
   and listen with their ears,
and understand with their heart and turn –
   and I would heal them."

But blessed are your eyes, for they see, and your ears, for they hear. Truly I tell you, many prophets and righteous people longed to see what you see, but did not see it, and to hear what you hear, but did not hear it.

'Hear then the parable of the sower. When anyone hears the word of the kingdom and does not understand it, the evil one comes and snatches away what is sown in the heart; this is what was sown on the path. As for what was sown on rocky ground, this is the one who hears the word and immediately receives it with joy; yet such a person has no root, but endures only for a while, and when trouble or persecution arises on account of the word, that person immediately falls away. As for what was sown among thorns, this is the one who hears the word, but the cares of the world and the lure of wealth choke the word, and it yields nothing. But as for what was sown on good soil, this is the one who hears the word and understands it, who indeed bears fruit and yields, in one case a hundredfold, in another sixty, and in another thirty.'

- This is certainly the parable for the optimists. However much seed fell elsewhere, the sower would make sure that most of the seed would fall on good ground. Even the poorest yield is thirtyfold! In the gospel Jesus often uses the metaphor of the seed to describe the kingdom and its innate energy. Do I share his optimism, or am I a prophet of doom about the future of the kingdom in our world?

Monday 17 July
Matthew 10:34–11:1

Jesus said to his disciples, 'Do not think that I have come to bring peace to the earth; I have not come to bring peace, but a sword.

> For I have come to set a man against his father,
> and a daughter against her mother,
> and a daughter-in-law against her mother-in-law;
> and one's foes will be members of one's own household.

'Whoever loves father or mother more than me is not worthy of me; and whoever loves son or daughter more than me is not worthy of me; and whoever does not take up the cross and follow me is not worthy of me. Those who find their life will lose it, and those who lose their life for my sake will find it.

'Whoever welcomes you welcomes me, and whoever welcomes me welcomes the one who sent me. Whoever welcomes a prophet in the name of a prophet will receive a prophet's reward; and whoever welcomes a righteous person in the name of a righteous person will receive the reward of the righteous; and whoever gives even a cup of cold water to one of these little ones in the name of a disciple – truly I tell you, none of these will lose their reward.'

Now when Jesus had finished instructing his twelve disciples, he went on from there to teach and proclaim his message in their cities.

- The words of Jesus will be a scandal, a stumbling block, to us if we try to understand them on their own. As we keep our eyes on Jesus and see the fullness of his sacred heart, his personality and vision, we understand how he is inviting us to take good care. Help me now, Jesus, to receive your word that saves me and not focus on what might trip me up.

Tuesday 18 July
Matthew 11:20–24

Then he began to reproach the cities in which most of his deeds of power had been done, because they did not repent. 'Woe to you, Chorazin! Woe to you, Bethsaida! For if the deeds of power done in you had been done in Tyre and Sidon, they would have repented long ago in sackcloth and ashes. But I tell you, on the day of judgement it will be more tolerable for Tyre and Sidon than for you. And you, Capernaum,

will you be exalted to heaven?
No, you will be brought down to Hades.

'For if the deeds of power done in you had been done in Sodom, it would have remained until this day. But I tell you that on the day of judgement it will be more tolerable for the land of Sodom than for you.'

- These verses hint at the mass of unrecorded history that the Gospels omit: the deeds of power performed by Jesus in the towns at the northern end of the Sea of Tiberias. Here were communities that listened to Jesus, and saw his miracles, but shrugged their shoulders and sent him on his way.

- Lord, open my eyes and my heart to the signs of your grace around me. Help me to hear your message, even if it upsets my habits.

Wednesday 19 July
Matthew 11:25–27

At that time Jesus said, 'I thank you, Father, Lord of heaven and earth, because you have hidden these things from the wise and the intelligent and have revealed them to infants; yes, Father, for such was your gracious will. All things have been handed over to me by my Father; and no one knows the Son except the Father, and no one knows the Father except the Son and anyone to whom the Son chooses to reveal him.'

- The best way to know God is through humility, and the greatest obstacle is pride. Jesus rejoices that the Father has decided to reveal himself to the little ones and not to the proud. I ask for help in the battle against my pride.

Thursday 20 July
Matthew 11:28–30

Jesus said to his disciples, 'Come to me, all you that are weary and are carrying heavy burdens, and I will give you rest. Take my yoke upon you, and learn from me; for I am gentle and humble in heart, and you will find rest for your souls. For my yoke is easy, and my burden is light.'

- Do I hear the Lord's invitation to me as life-giving and liberating? Where do I feel burdened or enslaved, knowing the Lord desires freedom in service of him and others? I turn to the Lord for what I need to travel more lightly in life.

Friday 21 July
Matthew 12:1–8

At that time Jesus went through the cornfields on the sabbath; his disciples were hungry, and they began to pluck heads of grain and to eat. When the Pharisees saw it, they said to him, 'Look, your disciples are doing what is not lawful to do on the sabbath.' He said to them, 'Have you not read what David did when he and his companions were hungry? He entered the house of God and ate the bread of the Presence, which it was not lawful for him or his companions to eat, but only for the priests. Or have you not read in the law that on the sabbath the priests in the temple break the sabbath and yet are guiltless? I tell you, something greater than the temple is here. But if you had known what this means, "I desire mercy and not sacrifice", you would not have condemned the guiltless. For the Son of Man is lord of the sabbath.'

- Jesus was not preoccupied by what limited the Pharisees but trusted his understanding of God's heart. I ask for the wisdom I need to be guided by ordinary rules and regulations while being formed and motivated by a more lasting truth.

Saturday 22 July
St Mary Magdalene
John 20:1–2, 11–18

Early on the first day of the week, while it was still dark, Mary Magdalene came to the tomb and saw that the stone had been removed from the tomb. So she ran and went to Simon Peter and the other disciple, the one whom Jesus loved, and said to them, 'They have taken the Lord out of the tomb, and we do not know where they have laid him.'

But Mary stood weeping outside the tomb. As she wept, she bent over to look into the tomb; and she saw two angels in white, sitting where the body of Jesus had been lying, one at the head and the other at the feet. They said to her, 'Woman, why are you weeping?' She said to them, 'They have taken away my Lord, and I do not know where they have laid him.' When she had said this, she turned round and saw Jesus standing there, but she did not know that it was Jesus. Jesus said to her, 'Woman, why are you weeping? For whom are you looking?' Supposing him to be the gardener, she said to him, 'Sir, if you have carried him away, tell me where you have laid him, and I will take him away.' Jesus said to her, 'Mary!' She turned and said to him in Hebrew, 'Rabbouni!' (which means Teacher). Jesus said to her, 'Do not hold on to me, because I have not yet ascended to the Father. But go to my brothers and say to them, "I am ascending to my Father and your Father, to my God and your God."' Mary Magdalene went and announced to the disciples, 'I have seen the Lord'; and she told them that he had said these things to her.

- The Risen Jesus does not let Mary cling to him but sends her on a mission, telling others he is risen. What do I feel Jesus sending me to do, after my personal encounter with him after his resurrection? I pray for the grace not to be deaf to this call, but ready to respond to it with generosity.

The Sixteenth Week in Ordinary Time
23–29 July 2023

Something to think and pray about each day this week:

In the Christian vision of things each of us is completed as a work of art, not on our birth-day, but on our death-day. In the emptiness of our dying God adds the final creative touch which completes us. A non-believer attending someone who has just died can say, 'He's finished!' or 'She didn't make it!' A believer will say instead: 'God has completed his work.'

Death, then, is not a total dissolution but rather the final stitch which completes a tapestry, or the last dab of paint that makes a great portrait. We become 'a new creation' (Galatians 6:15).

I stood early one morning in a town in Pakistan outside a dim and smelly shed while I waited for the local bank to open. To my amazement, out of the dark shed were brought beautiful wooden sculptures, shining in the morning sun. This gave me a hint of what is going on in the world – that despite all the chaos of human lives, something beautiful for God is being crafted out of every life. From the chaotic materials of human history the beauty and richness of God's images are drawn, each one revealing something of the genius of the divine artist.

Brian Grogan SJ,
To Grow in Love: A Spirituality of Ageing

The Presence of God

I pause for a moment and think of the love and the grace that God showers on me. I am created in the image and likeness of God; I am God's dwelling place.

Freedom

Lord, you granted me the great gift of freedom. In these times, O Lord, grant that I may be free from any form of racism or intolerance. Remind me that we are all equal in your loving eyes.

Consciousness

Knowing that God loves me unconditionally, I can afford to be honest about how I am. How has the day been, and how do I feel now? I share my feelings openly with the Lord.

The Word

I take my time to read the word of God slowly, a few times, allowing myself to dwell on anything that strikes me.

(Please turn to the Scripture on the following pages. Inspiration points are there, should you need them. When you are ready, return here to continue.)

Conversation

Sometimes I wonder what I might say if I were to meet you in person, Lord. I think I might say, 'Thank you' because you are always there for me.

Conclusion

I thank God for these moments we have spent together and for any insights I have been given concerning the text.

Sunday 23 July
Sixteenth Sunday in Ordinary Time
Matthew 13:24–43

He put before them another parable: 'The kingdom of heaven may be compared to someone who sowed good seed in his field; but while everybody was asleep, an enemy came and sowed weeds among the wheat, and then went away. So when the plants came up and bore grain, then the weeds appeared as well. And the slaves of the householder came and said to him, "Master, did you not sow good seed in your field? Where, then, did these weeds come from?" He answered, "An enemy has done this." The slaves said to him, "Then do you want us to go and gather them?" But he replied, "No; for in gathering the weeds you would uproot the wheat along with them. Let both of them grow together until the harvest; and at harvest time I will tell the reapers, Collect the weeds first and bind them in bundles to be burned, but gather the wheat into my barn."'

He put before them another parable: 'The kingdom of heaven is like a mustard seed that someone took and sowed in his field; it is the smallest of all the seeds, but when it has grown it is the greatest of shrubs and becomes a tree, so that the birds of the air come and make nests in its branches.'

He told them another parable: 'The kingdom of heaven is like yeast that a woman took and mixed in with three measures of flour until all of it was leavened.'

Jesus told the crowds all these things in parables; without a parable he told them nothing. This was to fulfil what had been spoken through the prophet:

> 'I will open my mouth to speak in parables;
>   I will proclaim what has been hidden from the foundation of
>   the world.'

Then he left the crowds and went into the house. And his disciples approached him, saying, 'Explain to us the parable of the weeds of the field.' He answered, 'The one who sows the good seed is the Son of Man; the field is the world, and the good seed are the children of the kingdom; the weeds are the children of the evil one, and the enemy who sowed them is the devil; the harvest is the end of the age, and the reapers are angels.

Just as the weeds are collected and burned up with fire, so will it be at the end of the age. The Son of Man will send his angels, and they will collect out of his kingdom all causes of sin and all evildoers, and they will throw them into the furnace of fire, where there will be weeping and gnashing of teeth. Then the righteous will shine like the sun in the kingdom of their Father. Let anyone with ears listen!'

• The master in the story recognised the work of the enemy but did not let it alter his course or define his life; his concern remained with his field of wheat, his eye on the harvest it could yield. Help me, God, to be able to know and to name what impoverishes me but to keep my eye and heart on what you are doing and what you desire for me.

Monday 24 July
Matthew 12:38–42

Then some of the scribes and Pharisees said to him, 'Teacher, we wish to see a sign from you.' But he answered them, 'An evil and adulterous generation asks for a sign, but no sign will be given to it except the sign of the prophet Jonah. For just as Jonah was for three days and three nights in the belly of the sea monster, so for three days and three nights the Son of Man will be in the heart of the earth. The people of Nineveh will rise up at the judgement with this generation and condemn it, because they repented at the proclamation of Jonah, and see, something greater than Jonah is here! The queen of the South will rise up at the judgement with this generation and condemn it, because she came from the ends of the earth to listen to the wisdom of Solomon, and see, something greater than Solomon is here!'

• It often surprises us how, even in this sophisticated world we live in, people look for external signs that apparently do away with the need for personal decisions. Life can seem so complicated that real decisions appear impossible, so that instead of looking inside us we look for signs from the outside. But Jesus insists that God only gave us one sign – Jesus himself – who was proved right by rising from the dead. I thank God for this unique sign, as I ask myself how important is my faith in the risen Jesus.

Tuesday 25 July
St James, Apostle
Matthew 20:20–28

Then the mother of the sons of Zebedee came to him with her sons, and kneeling before him, she asked a favour of him. And he said to her, 'What do you want?' She said to him, 'Declare that these two sons of mine will sit, one at your right hand and one at your left, in your kingdom.' But Jesus answered, 'You do not know what you are asking. Are you able to drink the cup that I am about to drink?' They said to him, 'We are able.' He said to them, 'You will indeed drink my cup, but to sit at my right hand and at my left, this is not mine to grant, but it is for those for whom it has been prepared by my Father.'

When the ten heard it, they were angry with the two brothers. But Jesus called them to him and said, 'You know that the rulers of the Gentiles lord it over them, and their great ones are tyrants over them. It will not be so among you; but whoever wishes to be great among you must be your servant, and whoever wishes to be first among you must be your slave; just as the Son of Man came not to be served but to serve, and to give his life a ransom for many.'

• James and John were two of the three apostles who were closest to Jesus. Yet they too seem to have misunderstood his message, and asked to be given the highest posts in the future kingdom. No wonder I too feel so attracted to power and prestige, and that even the Church nowadays seems not to be exempt from power struggles. I ask for a deeper understanding of the gospel and its radical message of service. I ask Jesus to make me a real disciple of his, able to drink the same cup he drank.

Wednesday 26 July
Matthew 13:1–9

That same day Jesus went out of the house and sat beside the lake. Such great crowds gathered around him that he got into a boat and sat there, while the whole crowd stood on the beach. And he told them many things in parables, saying: 'Listen! A sower went out to sow. And as he sowed, some seeds fell on the path, and the birds came and ate them up. Other seeds fell on rocky ground, where they did not have much soil, and they sprang up quickly, since they had no depth of soil. But when the sun rose, they were scorched; and since they had no root, they withered away. Other seeds fell among thorns, and the thorns grew up and choked them. Other seeds fell on good soil and brought forth grain, some a hundred-fold, some sixty, some thirty. Let anyone with ears listen!'

• To tell a parable like this, Jesus must have spent much time observing, noticing and reflecting on simple events. The truth of how God is was revealed in how God works. Thinking of what you like to notice and reflect on, what speaks to you about the way God is at work in your life?

Thursday 27 July
Matthew 13:10–17

Then the disciples came and asked him, 'Why do you speak to them in parables?' He answered, 'To you it has been given to know the secrets of the kingdom of heaven, but to them it has not been given. For to those who have, more will be given, and they will have an abundance; but from those who have nothing, even what they have will be taken away. The reason I speak to them in parables is that "seeing they do not perceive, and hearing they do not listen, nor do they understand." With them indeed is fulfilled the prophecy of Isaiah that says:

"You will indeed listen, but never understand,
    and you will indeed look, but never perceive.
For this people's heart has grown dull,
    and their ears are hard of hearing,
        and they have shut their eyes;
        so that they might not look with their eyes,
    and listen with their ears,
and understand with their heart and turn –
    and I would heal them."

But blessed are your eyes, for they see, and your ears, for they hear. Truly I tell you, many prophets and righteous people longed to see what you see, but did not see it, and to hear what you hear, but did not hear it.'

• Am I one of those who look without seeing, or hear without understanding? Jesus speaks in parables to challenge us out of our laziness, seeking the deeper meaning of things. How easy to be distracted, especially nowadays when we feel overwhelmed by too much information and images without any insight.

Friday 28 July
Matthew 13:18–23

He said to the disciples, 'Hear then the parable of the sower. When anyone hears the word of the kingdom and does not understand it, the evil one comes and snatches away what is sown in the heart; this is what was sown on the path. As for what was sown on rocky ground, this is the one who hears the word and immediately receives it with joy; yet such a person has no root, but endures only for a while, and when trouble or persecution arises on account of the word, that person immediately falls away. As for what was sown among thorns, this is the one who hears the word, but the cares of the world and the lure of wealth choke the word, and it yields nothing. But as for what was sown on good soil, this is the one who hears the word and understands it, who indeed bears fruit and yields, in one case a hundredfold, in another sixty, and in another thirty.'

• Jesus tells me here that 'understanding' is essential for the word to take root in my heart and to be effective in my life. Reflective and unhurried listening enables it to speak to my heart. Lord Jesus, may your living and life-giving word always be a priority for me. May I put aside some time each day – like now! – to listen to it and to put it into practice.

Saturday 29 July
Luke 10:38–42

Now as they went on their way, he entered a certain village, where a woman named Martha welcomed him into her home. She had a sister named Mary, who sat at the Lord's feet and listened to what he was saying. But Martha was distracted by her many tasks; so she came to him and asked, 'Lord, do you not care that my sister has left me to do all the work by myself? Tell her then to help me.' But the Lord answered her, 'Martha, Martha, you are worried and distracted by many things; there is need of only one thing. Mary has chosen the better part, which will not be taken away from her.'

• What is the meaning of Jesus' words to Martha? Certainly not that listening is better than doing, for throughout the gospel Jesus insists that listening without doing is worthless. He gently chides Martha about being too distracted and fretting about so many things that she risks losing sight of what is really important. We live in a world that is always so full of distractions. I ask the Lord to grant me insight into my own lifestyle, to know how to choose the better part that will not be taken from me.

The Seventeenth Week in Ordinary Time
30 July–5 August 2023

Something to think and pray about each day this week:

Whenever we set out on a worthwhile personal or communal journey, there will often be times when we wonder if we might have been better off just staying where we had been. Such moments of questioning, of self-doubt, are not necessarily a sign that we should never have set out in the first place. Any worthwhile journey will bring us face to face with our limitations. Whenever we set out on some journey in response to what we consider to be the Lord's call we will find ourselves being tested. Our faith in the Lord will often be put to the test. We will find ourselves asking, 'Why?' Jesus set out on a very significant journey at the moment of his baptism in response to God's call. He was certainly put to the test many times along the way. Yet he could say, 'He who sent me is with me, and has not left me to myself.' We can each make our own those words of Jesus. The Lord who prompts us to keep setting out anew on the journey of discipleship is always with us. He does not leave us to ourselves, but sustains us along the way.

Martin Hogan, *My Words Will Not Pass Away:*
Reflections on the Weekday Readings

The Presence of God
I pause for a moment
and reflect on God's life-giving presence
in every part of my body,
in everything around me,
in the whole of my life.

Freedom
Many countries are at this moment suffering the agonies of war. I bow my head in thanksgiving for my freedom. I pray for all prisoners and captives.

Consciousness
Knowing that God loves me unconditionally, I look honestly over the past day, its events and my feelings. Do I have something to be grateful for? Then I give thanks. Is there something I am sorry for? Then I ask forgiveness.

The Word
Now I turn to the Scripture set out for me this day. I read slowly over the words and see if any sentence or sentiment appeals to me.
(Please turn to the Scripture on the following pages. Inspiration points are there, should you need them. When you are ready, return here to continue.)

Conversation
I know with certainty that there were times when you carried me, Lord. There were times when it was through your strength that I got through the dark times in my life.

Conclusion
Glory be to the Father, and to the Son, and to the Holy Spirit,
As it was in the beginning, is now and ever shall be,
World without end. Amen.

Sunday 30 July
Seventeenth Sunday in Ordinary Time
Matthew 13:44–52

He put before them a parable: 'The kingdom of heaven is like treasure hidden in a field, which someone found and hid; then in his joy he goes and sells all that he has and buys that field.

'Again, the kingdom of heaven is like a merchant in search of fine pearls; on finding one pearl of great value, he went and sold all that he had and bought it.

'Again, the kingdom of heaven is like a net that was thrown into the sea and caught fish of every kind; when it was full, they drew it ashore, sat down, and put the good into baskets but threw out the bad. So it will be at the end of the age. The angels will come out and separate the evil from the righteous and throw them into the furnace of fire, where there will be weeping and gnashing of teeth.

'Have you understood all this?' They answered, 'Yes.' And he said to them, 'Therefore every scribe who has been trained for the kingdom of heaven is like the master of a household who brings out of his treasure what is new and what is old.'

- Selling everything to obtain what they really desired so deeply filled both men in the parables with deep joy. This seems a contradiction, but this is what our experience tells us. As the prayer of St Francis puts it, it is in giving that we receive. I ask for a heart full of freedom, freedom to give all and to receive all.

Monday 31 July
Matthew 13:31–35

He put before them another parable: 'The kingdom of heaven is like a mustard seed that someone took and sowed in his field; it is the smallest of all the seeds, but when it has grown it is the greatest of shrubs and becomes a tree, so that the birds of the air come and make nests in its branches.'

He told them another parable: 'The kingdom of heaven is like yeast that a woman took and mixed in with three measures of flour until all of it was leavened.'

Jesus told the crowds all these things in parables; without a parable he told them nothing. This was to fulfil what had been spoken through the prophet:

'I will open my mouth to speak in parables;
I will proclaim what has been hidden from the foundation of
the world.'

- The mustard seed and the yeast symbolise the growth brought about by Jesus' ministry. We are meant to be struck with wonder that one man, Jesus, could bring about the salvation of the world. I ask that I may never try to domesticate God, nor reduce his greatness to what is small and manageable. God is overflowing goodness: let me trust that and rejoice in it.

Tuesday 1 August
Matthew 13:36–43

Then he left the crowds and went into the house. And his disciples approached him, saying, 'Explain to us the parable of the weeds of the field.' He answered, 'The one who sows the good seed is the Son of Man; the field is the world, and the good seed are the children of the kingdom; the weeds are the children of the evil one, and the enemy who sowed them is the devil; the harvest is the end of the age, and the reapers are angels. Just as the weeds are collected and burned up with fire, so will it be at the end of the age. The Son of Man will send his angels, and they will collect out of his kingdom all causes of sin and all evildoers, and they will throw them into the furnace of fire, where there will be weeping and gnashing of teeth. Then the righteous will shine like the sun in the kingdom of their Father. Let anyone with ears listen!'

- I sit with the disciples as Jesus explains the parable. He sows good seed in an evil world. The disciples are told not to pass judgement on bad people, but to leave judgement to God. Am I judgemental? Do I condemn the faults of others? If I do, do I think I am faultless?

Wednesday 2 August
Matthew 13:44–46

Jesus said to his disciples, 'The kingdom of heaven is like treasure hidden in a field, which someone found and hid; then in his joy he goes and sells all that he has and buys that field.

'Again, the kingdom of heaven is like a merchant in search of fine pearls; on finding one pearl of great value, he went and sold all that he had and bought it.'

- Imagine the reaction of the person who finds the hidden treasure in this parable, how their heart must have leapt to find it! Their whole life is turned around; for the first time in their life they have hope that things will be better. They can't wait to tell their family, but they know they have to keep the treasure a secret until they have bought the field. But the person's family will notice the change in them and wonder what good news has got hold of them.
- Lord, let your presence in my heart transform everything for me.

Thursday 3 August
Matthew 13:47–53

Jesus said to his disciples, 'Again, the kingdom of heaven is like a net that was thrown into the sea and caught fish of every kind; when it was full, they drew it ashore, sat down, and put the good into baskets but threw out the bad. So it will be at the end of the age. The angels will come out and separate the evil from the righteous and throw them into the furnace of fire, where there will be weeping and gnashing of teeth.

'Have you understood all this?' They answered, 'Yes.' And he said to them, 'Therefore every scribe who has been trained for the kingdom of heaven is like the master of a household who brings out of his treasure what is new and what is old.' When Jesus had finished these parables, he left that place.

- Jesus says the member of the kingdom is the wise householder who from his treasury brings out what is new and what is old. The Church is in many places tormented by deep conflicts between liberals and conservatives, traditionalists and innovators. Jesus invites us to be wise, able to discern what is of value, whether new or old. I pray for this wisdom, and for peace and respect within the Church.

Friday 4 August
Matthew 13:54–58

He came to his home town and began to teach the people in their synagogue, so that they were astounded and said, 'Where did this man get this wisdom and these deeds of power? Is not this the carpenter's son? Is not his mother called Mary? And are not his brothers James and Joseph and Simon and Judas? And are not all his sisters with us? Where then did this man get all this?' And they took offence at him. But Jesus said to them, 'Prophets are not without honour except in their own country and in their own house.' And he did not do many deeds of power there, because of their unbelief.

- The unbelief of the people created a forbidding climate, causing Jesus to go elsewhere. Lord, help my unbelief. I take a moment to invite the Spirit of God to bless me with trust, hope and readiness to receive what God is offering.

Saturday 5 August
Matthew 14:1–12

At that time Herod the ruler heard reports about Jesus; and he said to his servants, 'This is John the Baptist; he has been raised from the dead, and for this reason these powers are at work in him.' For Herod had arrested John, bound him, and put him in prison on account of Herodias, his brother Philip's wife, because John had been telling him, 'It is not lawful for you to have her.' Though Herod wanted to put him to death, he feared the crowd, because they regarded him as a prophet. But when Herod's birthday came, the daughter of Herodias danced before the company, and she pleased Herod so much that he promised on oath to grant her whatever she might ask. Prompted by her mother, she said, 'Give me the head of John the Baptist here on a platter.' The king was grieved, yet out of regard for his oaths and for the guests, he commanded it to be given; he sent and had John beheaded in the prison. The head was brought on a platter and given to the girl, who brought it to her mother. His disciples came and took the body and buried it; then they went and told Jesus.

- If I had been one of Herod's guests then, would I have protested or stayed silent? Today, what do I do when I see others suffering injustice? If, like Herod, I make a bad decision, have I the courage to reverse it, even at cost to myself?

- Lord, strengthen my weak heart so that I may truly witness to your values.

6–12 August 2023

Something to think and pray about each day this week:

We talk easily about what's happening on the surface of our lives. But what's really going on? Beneath the surface level of life on earth lies a strategy, backed by divine power and artistry, that is sweeping everything up into one infinitely complex whole, so that finally God may become all in all. Even to glimpse occasionally that this is what's really going on gives hope, and is an antidote to the view that our common home can never be put to rights, and that human history will end in tragic burnout. We are to live and work in hope, 'with the eyes of our hearts enlightened'. This is what mysticism is about.

The insights of science about the cosmos are coming to us thick and fast. Our generation is being showered with insights about the history and structure of creation which were hidden from our predecessors. This new knowledge helps us to understand God's artistic work, appreciate it properly and relate lovingly to its creator. Creation is God's self-revelation, and we have so much to learn from it. Then we can participate more effectively in co-creating and restoring the divine masterpiece.

Brian Grogan SJ,
Finding God in a Leaf: The Mysticism of Laudato Si'

The Presence of God
I remind myself that I am in the presence of God, who is my strength in times of weakness and my comforter in times of sorrow.

Freedom
Saint Ignatius thought that a thick and shapeless tree trunk would never believe that it could become a statue, admired as a miracle of sculpture, and would never submit itself to the chisel of the sculptor, who sees by her genius what she can make of it. I ask for the grace to let myself be shaped by my loving Creator.

Consciousness
Dear Lord, help me to remember that you gave me life. Teach me to slow down, to be still and enjoy the pleasures created for me. To be aware of the beauty that surrounds me: the marvel of mountains, the calmness of lakes, the fragility of a flower petal. I need to remember that all these things come from you.

The Word
In this expectant state of mind, please turn to the text for the day with confidence. Believe that the Holy Spirit is present and may reveal whatever the passage has to say to you. Read reflectively, listening with a third ear to what may be going on in your heart.
(Please turn to the Scripture on the following pages. Inspiration points are there, should you need them. When you are ready, return here to continue.)

Conversation
What feelings are rising in me as I pray and reflect on God's word? I imagine Jesus himself sitting or standing near me, and I open my heart to him.

Conclusion
I thank God for these moments we have spent together and for any insights I have been given concerning the text.

Sunday 6 August
The Transfiguration of the Lord
Matthew 17:1–9

Six days later, Jesus took with him Peter and James and his brother John and led them up a high mountain, by themselves. And he was transfigured before them, and his face shone like the sun, and his clothes became dazzling white. Suddenly there appeared to them Moses and Elijah, talking with him. Then Peter said to Jesus, 'Lord, it is good for us to be here; if you wish, I will make three dwellings here, one for you, one for Moses, and one for Elijah.' While he was still speaking, suddenly a bright cloud overshadowed them, and from the cloud a voice said, 'This is my Son, the Beloved; with him I am well pleased; listen to him!' When the disciples heard this, they fell to the ground and were overcome by fear. But Jesus came and touched them, saying, 'Get up and do not be afraid.' And when they looked up, they saw no one except Jesus himself alone.

As they were coming down the mountain, Jesus ordered them, 'Tell no one about the vision until after the Son of Man has been raised from the dead.'

• At the sound of God's voice, the disciples prostrate themselves on the ground, terrified. They hear the gentle voice of Jesus: 'Get up [rise up] and do not be afraid.' Jesus' words point to resurrection to a new life and the abolition of fear and anxiety. Imagine this scene during this time of prayer – can you hear the gentle voice of Jesus speaking to you now?

Monday 7 August
Matthew 14:13–21

Now when Jesus heard this, he withdrew from there in a boat to a deserted place by himself. But when the crowds heard it, they followed him on foot from the towns. When he went ashore, he saw a great crowd; and he had compassion for them and cured their sick. When it was evening, the disciples came to him and said, 'This is a deserted place, and the hour is now late; send the crowds away so that they may go into the villages and buy food for themselves.' Jesus said to them, 'They need not go away; you give them something to eat.' They replied, 'We have nothing here but five loaves and two fish.' And he said, 'Bring them here to me.' Then he ordered the crowds to sit down on the grass. Taking the five loaves and the two fish, he looked up to heaven, and blessed and broke the loaves, and gave them to the disciples, and the disciples gave them to the crowds. And all ate and were filled; and they took up what was left over of the broken pieces, twelve baskets full. And those who ate were about five thousand men, besides women and children.

• This reminds us of the abundance of wine at the wedding of Cana, and of so much of God's dealing with us, with me. He always beats us at generosity; he promises us a hundredfold.

• Where in my life are there opportunities to 'share my food' so others will have enough?

Tuesday 8 August
Matthew 15:1–2, 10–14

Then Pharisees and scribes came to Jesus from Jerusalem and said, 'Why do your disciples break the tradition of the elders? For they do not wash their hands before they eat.'

Then he called the crowd to him and said to them, 'Listen and understand: it is not what goes into the mouth that defiles a person, but it is what comes out of the mouth that defiles.' Then the disciples approached and said to him, 'Do you know that the Pharisees took offence when they heard what you said?' He answered, 'Every plant that my heavenly Father has not planted will be uprooted. Let them alone; they are blind guides of the blind. And if one blind person guides another, both will fall into a pit.'

• These are harsh words about the Pharisees, who were, after all, the upholders of religion and law. They were not 'bad people'! Somehow they were righteous, moral, people of high standards. But Jesus always seems to look further than people do – he looks to the heart. He looks to see if we nourish what his Father plants in us – care, compassion, openness and union with the Father. On this we judge ourselves and others, if we judge at all.

Wednesday 9 August
Matthew 15:21–28

Jesus left that place and went away to the district of Tyre and Sidon. Just then a Canaanite woman from that region came out and started shouting,

'Have mercy on me, Lord, Son of David; my daughter is tormented by a demon.' But he did not answer her at all. And his disciples came and urged him, saying, 'Send her away, for she keeps shouting after us.' He answered, 'I was sent only to the lost sheep of the house of Israel.' But she came and knelt before him, saying, 'Lord, help me.' He answered, 'It is not fair to take the children's food and throw it to the dogs.' She said, 'Yes, Lord, yet even the dogs eat the crumbs that fall from their masters' table.' Then Jesus answered her, 'Woman, great is your faith! Let it be done for you as you wish.' And her daughter was healed instantly.

- In a way this pagan woman can give us a lesson in prayer. We are not always happy with our lot or the lot of others, and we should express our real feelings to Christ, not just our sanitised ones. Jesus hears my prayer.

Thursday 10 August
John 12:24–26

Jesus said to his disciples, 'Very truly, I tell you, unless a grain of wheat falls into the earth and dies, it remains just a single grain; but if it dies, it bears much fruit. Those who love their life lose it, and those who hate their life in this world will keep it for eternal life. Whoever serves me must follow me, and where I am, there will my servant be also. Whoever serves me, the Father will honour.'

- Jesus cannot be seen or understood unless one grasps the purpose and meaning of his death and resurrection. In order for it to be fruitful, a grain of wheat has to fall into the ground and die so that it will be transformed into a new plant which in time will reproduce itself many times over.

- This is exactly what Jesus will do. He will surrender his life through his suffering and death on the cross only to rise again in new life. Where is 'new life' possible in my life today?

Friday 11 August
Matthew 16:24–28

Then Jesus told his disciples, 'If any want to become my followers, let them deny themselves and take up their cross and follow me. For those who want to save their life will lose it, and those who lose their life for my sake will find it. For what will it profit them if they gain the whole world but forfeit their life? Or what will they give in return for their life?

'For the Son of Man is to come with his angels in the glory of his Father, and then he will repay everyone for what has been done. Truly I tell you, there are some standing here who will not taste death before they see the Son of Man coming in his kingdom.'

- To share the glory of Christ we have to share his suffering; this makes no sense except through faith in Christ.

- I pray for the freedom I need to be able to let go, to realise that my life is not mine to save; it comes from God and its fullness lies in God.

Saturday 12 August
Matthew 17:14–20

When they came to the crowd, a man came to him, knelt before him, and said, 'Lord, have mercy on my son, for he is an epileptic and he suffers terribly; he often falls into the fire and often into the water. And I brought him to your disciples, but they could not cure him.' Jesus answered, 'You faithless and perverse generation, how much longer must I be with you? How much longer must I put up with you? Bring him here to me.' And Jesus rebuked the demon, and it came out of him, and the boy was cured instantly. Then the disciples came to Jesus privately and said, 'Why could we not cast it out?' He said to them, 'Because of your little faith. For truly I tell you, if you have faith the size of a mustard seed, you will say to this mountain, "Move from here to there", and it will move; and nothing will be impossible for you.'

- 'Lord, have mercy on my son, for … he suffers terribly.' Like the father in this episode, I bring someone I love to Jesus, asking insistently for their cure.

- The apostles were upset that they failed to cure this boy and wanted to know why. 'Because of your little faith.' Jesus is no wonder worker, but one who builds on our faith, even if it is as little as a mustard seed. I pray insistently to grow in my small faith, believing that nothing will be impossible for me.

Something to think and pray about each day this week:

Mary always remained a child, totally dependent upon God, gladly receiving everything from God's hands, and never wanting to be apart from him. Mary's spirit is the spirit of childhood, a combination of utter powerlessness and immense confidence. A child is small and helpless, yet isn't closed in on itself but delights in the world around it, full of a sense of wonder and trust. A child walks along the road of life with a spirit of astonishment, and with enough confidence to believe that God may appear at any turn. Mary looked at the path of life with the eyes of a child.

We could all gain a lot by recovering this spirit of childhood, by becoming again faithful to the children we once were. One of Pope Francis's favourite poems puts this well. It is by Friedrich Hölderlin, and is dedicated to his grandmother. It finishes with the line; 'May the man hold fast to what the child has promised.' The child is filled with hope because it sees beauty everywhere, a beauty that is invisible to sceptics and cynics. Mary had that childlike spirit, that transparency and that simplicity, because she surrendered herself completely to God.

Thomas Casey SJ,
Smile of Joy: Mary of Nazareth

The Presence of God
I remind myself that, as I sit here now,
God is gazing on me with love and holding me in being.
I pause for a moment and think of this.

Freedom
'There are very few people who realise what God would make of them
if they abandoned themselves into his hands, and let themselves be
formed by his grace' (St Ignatius). I ask for the grace to trust myself totally to God's love.

Consciousness
Where do I sense hope, encouragement and growth in my life? By looking
back over the past few months, I may be able to see which activities and
occasions have produced rich fruit. If I do notice such areas, I will determine to give those areas both time and space in the future.

The Word
Lord Jesus, you became human to communicate with me.
You walked and worked on this earth.
You endured the heat and struggled with the cold.
All your time on this earth was spent in caring for humanity.
You healed the sick, you raised the dead.
Most important of all, you saved me from death.
*(Please turn to the Scripture on the following pages. Inspiration points are there,
should you need them. When you are ready, return here to continue.)*

Conversation
What is stirring in me as I pray? Am I consoled, troubled, left cold? I
imagine Jesus standing or sitting at my side, and I share my feelings with
him.

Conclusion
Glory be to the Father, and to the Son, and to the Holy Spirit,
As it was in the beginning, is now and ever shall be,
World without end. Amen.

Sunday 13 August
Nineteenth Sunday in Ordinary Time
Matthew 14:22–33

Immediately he made the disciples get into the boat and go on ahead to the other side, while he dismissed the crowds. And after he had dismissed the crowds, he went up the mountain by himself to pray. When evening came, he was there alone, but by this time the boat, battered by the waves, was far from the land, for the wind was against them. And early in the morning he came walking towards them on the lake. But when the disciples saw him walking on the lake, they were terrified, saying, 'It is a ghost!' And they cried out in fear. But immediately Jesus spoke to them and said, 'Take heart, it is I; do not be afraid.'

Peter answered him, 'Lord, if it is you, command me to come to you on the water.' He said, 'Come.' So Peter got out of the boat, started walking on the water, and came towards Jesus. But when he noticed the strong wind, he became frightened, and beginning to sink, he cried out, 'Lord, save me!' Jesus immediately reached out his hand and caught him, saying to him, 'You of little faith, why did you doubt?' When they got into the boat, the wind ceased. And those in the boat worshipped him, saying, 'Truly you are the Son of God.'

- I can rely too much on myself and, like Peter, lose sight of where I am going. Help me, Jesus, to keep my eyes fixed on you and to trust that you reach out to me, offering me loving help.

Monday 14 August
Matthew 17:22–27

As they were gathering in Galilee, Jesus said to them, 'The Son of Man is going to be betrayed into human hands, and they will kill him, and on the third day he will be raised.' And they were greatly distressed.

When they reached Capernaum, the collectors of the temple tax came to Peter and said, 'Does your teacher not pay the temple tax?' He said, 'Yes, he does.' And when he came home, Jesus spoke of it first, asking, 'What do you think, Simon? From whom do kings of the earth take toll or tribute? From their children or from others?' When Peter said, 'From others', Jesus said to him, 'Then the children are free. However, so that we do not give offence to them, go to the lake and cast a hook; take the first fish that comes up; and when you open its mouth, you will find a coin; take that and give it to them for you and me.'

- Jesus wanted people to be free to live their lives to the full, and that is his desire for you too. I ask him to free me from the fixations, irritations and trivialities that distract me from the fundamental task of growing in love and of playing my part in advancing the kingdom of God.

Tuesday 15 August
The Assumption of the Blessed Virgin Mary
Luke 1:39–56

In those days Mary set out and went with haste to a Judean town in the hill country, where she entered the house of Zechariah and greeted Elizabeth. When Elizabeth heard Mary's greeting, the child leapt in her womb. And Elizabeth was filled with the Holy Spirit and exclaimed with a loud cry, 'Blessed are you among women, and blessed is the fruit of your womb. And why has this happened to me, that the mother of my Lord comes to me? For as soon as I heard the sound of your greeting, the child in my womb leapt for joy. And blessed is she who believed that there would be a fulfilment of what was spoken to her by the Lord.'

And Mary said,

'My soul magnifies the Lord,
    and my spirit rejoices in God my Saviour,
for he has looked with favour on the lowliness of his servant.
    Surely, from now on all generations will call me blessed;
for the Mighty One has done great things for me,
    and holy is his name.
His mercy is for those who fear him
    from generation to generation.
He has shown strength with his arm;
    he has scattered the proud in the thoughts of their hearts.
He has brought down the powerful from their thrones,
    and lifted up the lowly;
he has filled the hungry with good things,
    and sent the rich away empty.

> He has helped his servant Israel,
>> in remembrance of his mercy,
> according to the promise he made to our ancestors,
>> to Abraham and to his descendants for ever.'

And Mary remained with her for about three months and then returned to her home.

- The Visitation is the primordial encounter, where two people meet. Mary was carrying God within her and they brought joy to Elizabeth and John within her. Every time we meet another person, we bring God to each other; let us also bring joy.

Wednesday 16 August
Matthew 18:15–20

Jesus said, 'If another member of the church sins against you, go and point out the fault when the two of you are alone. If the member listens to you, you have regained that one. But if you are not listened to, take one or two others along with you, so that every word may be confirmed by the evidence of two or three witnesses. If the member refuses to listen to them, tell it to the church; and if the offender refuses to listen even to the church, let such a one be to you as a Gentile and a tax-collector. Truly I tell you, whatever you bind on earth will be bound in heaven, and whatever you loose on earth will be loosed in heaven. Again, truly I tell you, if two of you agree on earth about anything you ask, it will be done for you by my Father in heaven. For where two or three are gathered in my name, I am there among them.'

- To what extent do we feel responsible for the wrongdoings of our fellow Christians? To what extent do we realise that our behaviour both as individuals and groups reflects on the overall witness that the Church is called to give?
- 'Where two or three are gathered in my name, I am there among them.' Let us pray today for a greater awareness and understanding of these words of Jesus. Let us pray for eyes to see and ears to hear Jesus among us.

Thursday 17 August
Matthew 18:21–19:1

Then Peter came and said to him, 'Lord, if another member of the church sins against me, how often should I forgive? As many as seven times?' Jesus said to him, 'Not seven times, but, I tell you, seventy-seven times.

'For this reason the kingdom of heaven may be compared to a king who wished to settle accounts with his slaves. When he began the reckoning, one who owed him ten thousand talents was brought to him; and, as he could not pay, his lord ordered him to be sold, together with his wife and children and all his possessions, and payment to be made. So the slave fell on his knees before him, saying, "Have patience with me, and I will pay you everything." And out of pity for him, the lord of that slave released him and forgave him the debt. But that same slave, as he went out, came upon one of his fellow-slaves who owed him a hundred denarii; and seizing him by the throat, he said, "Pay what you owe." Then his fellow-slave fell down and pleaded with him, "Have patience with me, and I will pay you." But he refused; then he went and threw him into prison until he should pay the debt. When his fellow-slaves saw what had happened, they were greatly distressed, and they went and reported to their lord all that had taken place. Then his lord summoned him and said to him, "You wicked slave! I forgave you all that debt because you pleaded with me. Should you not have had mercy on your fellow-slave, as I had mercy on you?" And in anger his lord handed him over to be tortured until he should pay his entire debt. So my heavenly Father will also do to every one of you, if you do not forgive your brother or sister from your heart.'

When Jesus had finished saying these things, he left Galilee and went to the region of Judea beyond the Jordan.

- We do not expect God to forgive us once or twice or any limited number of times but every time. It isn't written that we have, for example, only ten chances of going to confession, and once our quota is used up, there is nothing left.

- If that is true of our relationship with God, it also has to be true in our relationships with others. We should always strive never to refuse an offer of reconciliation. As I reflect on this gospel today is there someone I need to be reconciled with? I bring this relationship to Jesus in this time of prayer.

Friday 18 August
Matthew 19:3–12

Some Pharisees came to him, and to test him they asked, 'Is it lawful for a man to divorce his wife for any cause?' He answered, 'Have you not read that the one who made them at the beginning "made them male and female", and said, "For this reason a man shall leave his father and mother and be joined to his wife, and the two shall become one flesh"? So they are no longer two, but one flesh. Therefore what God has joined together, let no one separate.' They said to him, 'Why then did Moses command us to give a certificate of dismissal and to divorce her?' He said to them, 'It was because you were so hard-hearted that Moses allowed you to divorce your wives, but at the beginning it was not so. And I say to you, whoever divorces his wife, except for unchastity, and marries another commits adultery.'

His disciples said to him, 'If such is the case of a man with his wife, it is better not to marry.' But he said to them, 'Not everyone can accept this teaching, but only those to whom it is given. For there are eunuchs who have been so from birth, and there are eunuchs who have been made eunuchs by others, and there are eunuchs who have made themselves eunuchs for the sake of the kingdom of heaven. Let anyone accept this who can.'

• I pray with thanks for all the people I know who have been able to live out their desires and dreams through marriage. I pray for those whose marriages are in difficulty. Keep love burning in their hearts, and in mine.

Saturday 19 August
Matthew 19:13–15

Then little children were being brought to him in order that he might lay his hands on them and pray. The disciples spoke sternly to those who brought them; but Jesus said, 'Let the little children come to me, and do not stop them; for it is to such as these that the kingdom of heaven belongs.' And he laid his hands on them and went on his way.

- Children are always a challenge to us. Am I one of those who bring children to Jesus, or like the disciples who turn them away, for one reason or another? Do I believe it is good for children to be near Jesus, to know him better and love him as a friend and benefactor? In prayer, I bring some children I know to Jesus, to lay his hands on them and say a prayer.

- I thank Jesus for the children in my life, for they teach me so many things about the kingdom.

The Twentieth Week in Ordinary Time
20–26 August 2023

Something to think and pray about each day this week:

I ask myself, 'If I am to see God as Father, then who am I?' I am a son or a daughter of God – by invitation, even by adoption. This is an immense privilege. Jesus is inviting me to begin my prayer by calling to mind, not only who God is for me – Father – but also who I am for God; a son or daughter, regarded with special love and tenderness. This is what is characteristic about Christian prayer: it is about the Father and Jesus and the Holy Spirit who is the love between them.

By reflecting on the life and teaching of Jesus, I learn his attitudes; by meeting him in prayer, I absorb his attitudes. In my reflection on Jesus, I get to know about Jesus; in meeting him in prayer, I become like Jesus. I come more deeply into the space of his praying. With this word, 'Father', Jesus is telling me that I am accepted already. Prayer begins here.

Finbarr Lynch SJ,
Meeting Jesus in Prayer: Praying with Sacred Scripture

The Presence of God

Lord, help me to be fully alive to your holy presence. Enfold me in your love. Let my heart become one with yours.

My soul longs for your presence, Lord. When I turn my thoughts to you, I find peace and contentment.

Freedom

Your death on the cross has set me free. I can live joyously and freely without fear of death. Your mercy knows no bounds.

Consciousness

At this moment, Lord, I turn my thoughts to you.

I will leave aside my chores and preoccupations.

I will take rest and refreshment in your presence.

The Word

The word of God comes down to us through the Scriptures.

May the Holy Spirit enlighten my mind and my heart

to respond to the gospel teachings:

to love my neighbour as myself,

to care for my sisters and brothers in Christ.

(Please turn to the Scripture on the following pages. Inspiration points are there, should you need them. When you are ready, return here to continue.)

Conversation

Begin to talk to Jesus about the Scripture you have just read. What part of it strikes a chord in you? Perhaps the words of a friend – or some story you have heard recently – will slowly rise to the surface of your consciousness. If so, does the story throw light on what the Scripture passage may be saying to you?

Conclusion

I thank God for these moments we have spent together and for any insights I have been given concerning the text.

Sunday 20 August
Twentieth Sunday in Ordinary Time
Matthew 15:21–28

Jesus left that place and went away to the district of Tyre and Sidon. Just then a Canaanite woman from that region came out and started shouting, 'Have mercy on me, Lord, Son of David; my daughter is tormented by a demon.' But he did not answer her at all. And his disciples came and urged him, saying, 'Send her away, for she keeps shouting after us.' He answered, 'I was sent only to the lost sheep of the house of Israel.' But she came and knelt before him, saying, 'Lord, help me.' He answered, 'It is not fair to take the children's food and throw it to the dogs.' She said, 'Yes, Lord, yet even the dogs eat the crumbs that fall from their masters' table.' Then Jesus answered her, 'Woman, great is your faith! Let it be done for you as you wish.' And her daughter was healed instantly.

• Like the woman in the gospel, I come before Jesus bringing others in my prayer. As I pray for those I love, I grow in appreciation of their goodness and ask for blessings for them. I think again of how they are blessings for me and I give thanks.

Monday 21 August
Matthew 19:16–22

Then someone came to him and said, 'Teacher, what good deed must I do to have eternal life?' And he said to him, 'Why do you ask me about what is good? There is only one who is good. If you wish to enter into life, keep the commandments.' He said to him, 'Which ones?' And Jesus said, 'You shall not murder; You shall not commit adultery; You shall not steal; You shall not bear false witness; Honour your father and mother; also, You shall love your neighbour as yourself.' The young man said to him, 'I have kept all these; what do I still lack?' Jesus said to him, 'If you wish to be perfect, go, sell your possessions, and give the money to the poor, and you will have treasure in heaven; then come, follow me.' When the young man heard this word, he went away grieving, for he had many possessions.

• It might be a good exercise today for me to ask myself what would be the most difficult thing for me to give up if Jesus asked me to do so. Whatever it is, it could be coming between me and my total following of Jesus. Do the things I own really own me? I bring these things to Jesus now in this time of prayer.

Tuesday 22 August
Matthew 19:23–30

Then Jesus said to his disciples, 'Truly I tell you, it will be hard for a rich person to enter the kingdom of heaven. Again I tell you, it is easier for a camel to go through the eye of a needle than for someone who is rich to enter the kingdom of God.' When the disciples heard this, they were greatly astounded and said, 'Then who can be saved?' But Jesus looked at them and said, 'For mortals it is impossible, but for God all things are possible.'

Then Peter said in reply, 'Look, we have left everything and followed you. What then will we have?' Jesus said to them, 'Truly I tell you, at the renewal of all things, when the Son of Man is seated on the throne of his glory, you who have followed me will also sit on twelve thrones, judging the twelve tribes of Israel. And everyone who has left houses or brothers or sisters or father or mother or children or fields, for my name's sake, will receive a hundredfold, and will inherit eternal life. But many who are first will be last, and the last will be first.'

- In the world of Jesus, everyone gets because everyone gives; and because everyone gives, everyone receives. It is not a selfish world; it is a reaching out to others world.

- And when everyone reaches out, everyone is benefiting. In such a world, I do not have to worry about a roof over my head, or about brothers and sisters, or property or security. It is where love and justice meet. For too many people in our world, there is neither love nor justice. Are there areas in my life where I could give more, rather than wanting to receive?

Wednesday 23 August
Matthew 20:1–16

Jesus said to them, 'For the kingdom of heaven is like a landowner who went out early in the morning to hire labourers for his vineyard. After agreeing with the labourers for the usual daily wage, he sent them into his vineyard. When he went out about nine o'clock, he saw others standing idle in the market-place; and he said to them, "You also go into the vine-yard, and I will pay you whatever is right." So they went. When he went out again about noon and about three o'clock, he did the same. And about five o'clock he went out and found others standing around; and he said to them, "Why are you standing here idle all day?" They said to him, "Because no one has hired us." He said to them, "You also go into the vineyard." When evening came, the owner of the vineyard said to his manager, "Call the labourers and give them their pay, beginning with the last and then going to the first." When those hired about five o'clock came, each of them received the usual daily wage. Now when the first came, they thought they would receive more; but each of them also received the usual daily wage. And when they received it, they grumbled against the landowner, saying, "These last worked only one hour, and you have made them equal to us who have borne the burden of the day and the scorching heat." But he replied to one of them, "Friend, I am doing you no wrong; did you not agree with me for the usual daily wage? Take what belongs to you and go; I choose to give to this last the same as I give to you. Am I not allowed to do what I choose with what belongs to me? Or are you envious because I am generous?" So the last will be first, and the first will be last.'

- God gives his love, all of his love, to every person without exception if they open themselves to this love. It does not matter whether that happens early or late in life as this love can never be earned, only accepted. The fact that the latecomers were only employed at the last hour does not make their needs any less than those who came earlier. How big is my need for God today?

Thursday 24 August
St Bartholomew, Apostle
John 1:45–51

Philip found Nathanael and said to him, 'We have found him about whom Moses in the law and also the prophets wrote, Jesus son of Joseph from Nazareth.' Nathanael said to him, 'Can anything good come out of Nazareth?' Philip said to him, 'Come and see.' When Jesus saw Nathanael coming towards him, he said of him, 'Here is truly an Israelite in whom there is no deceit!' Nathanael asked him, 'Where did you come to know me?' Jesus answered, 'I saw you under the fig tree before Philip called you.' Nathanael replied, 'Rabbi, you are the Son of God! You are the King of Israel!' Jesus answered, 'Do you believe because I told you that I saw you under the fig tree? You will see greater things than these.' And he said to him, 'Very truly, I tell you, you will see heaven opened and the angels of God ascending and descending upon the Son of Man.'

- Being called to be one of the Twelve must have been a huge surprise and a heavy responsibility for Nathanael. Yet, after sharing Jesus' life for three years, and witnessing his passion, death, and resurrection, he was ready to commit himself to spreading the gospel to the whole world. I look with deep gratitude at this motley group of persons who turned out to be such efficacious instruments for spreading faith in Jesus. I ask for the grace to be able to introduce others to Jesus, as Philip did.

Friday 25 August
Matthew 22:34–40

When the Pharisees heard that he had silenced the Sadducees, they gathered together, and one of them, a lawyer, asked him a question to test him. 'Teacher, which commandment in the law is the greatest?' He said to him, '"You shall love the Lord your God with all your heart, and with all your soul, and with all your mind." This is the greatest and first commandment. And a second is like it: "You shall love your neighbour as yourself." On these two commandments hang all the law and the prophets.'

- I suppose we can never overestimate the importance of this saying of Jesus. For him it is absolutely clear that the greatest commandment is love. Nothing can be more important than loving God above all and loving others as oneself. I let this truth touch my mind and my heart, purify my intentions and actions, and give me a sense of real priorities in whatever I do.

Saturday 26 August
Matthew 23:1–12

Then Jesus said to the crowds and to his disciples, 'The scribes and the Pharisees sit on Moses' seat; therefore, do whatever they teach you and follow it; but do not do as they do, for they do not practise what they teach. They tie up heavy burdens, hard to bear, and lay them on the shoulders of others; but they themselves are unwilling to lift a finger to move them. They do all their deeds to be seen by others; for they make their phylacteries broad and their fringes long. They love to have the place of honour at banquets and the best seats in the synagogues, and to be greeted with respect in the market-places, and to have people call them rabbi. But you are not to be called rabbi, for you have one teacher, and you are all students. And call no one your father on earth, for you have one Father – the one in heaven. Nor are you to be called instructors, for you have one instructor, the Messiah. The greatest among you will be your servant. All who exalt themselves will be humbled, and all who humble themselves will be exalted.'

- Authority is not for power but for empowering and enabling others. Real authority is a form of service, not a way of control. We are all brothers and sisters. Jesus tells us that the greatest among us is the one who best serves the needs of those around them rather than the one who has the most impressive titles.

- Who can I serve today with love?

The Twenty-first Week in Ordinary Time
27 August–2 September 2023

Something to think and pray about each day this week:

What were you trying to get across to Moses when you said 'I am who I am'? Were you saying, 'I am simply myself; I need no explaining'? Is this what it means to be the creator – to be comfortably secure in your own existence? My existence, on the other hand, is not in my hands: it depends totally on you. I'm like a song: if you stop singing me, empty silence would follow. A great physicist surprised his students by saying that the world is made not of matter but of music: the world's continuing existence depends on you!

Years ago I dropped the image of you as the old bearded man in the clouds. Since you simply *are,* there can be no adequate image of you. You're more like a blue sky: blue symbolises heaven, serene and peaceable. A blue sky points to the divine: it is beautiful and unlimited, like you, and it encompasses everything.

Small children educate me best about you. For them, everything is a source of wonder – each person, each thing, each moment is unique and special. 'Children's faces, looking up; holding wonder like a cup.' Let me be like them, and so live even now in the kingdom of heaven.

Brian Grogan SJ,
I Am Infinitely Loved

The Presence of God

The more we call on God the more we can feel God's presence. Day by day we are drawn closer to the loving heart of God.

Freedom

I am free. When I look at these words in writing, they seem to create in me a feeling of awe. Yes, a wonderful feeling of freedom. Thank you, God.

Consciousness

Help me, Lord, become more conscious of your presence. Teach me to recognise your presence in others. Fill my heart with gratitude for the times your love has been shown to me through the care of others.

The Word

The word of God comes down to us through the Scriptures. May the Holy Spirit enlighten my mind and my heart to respond to the gospel teachings.

(Please turn to the Scripture on the following pages. Inspiration points are there, should you need them. When you are ready, return here to continue.)

Conversation

Conversation requires talking and listening.

As I talk to Jesus, may I also learn to pause and listen.

I picture the gentleness in his eyes and the love in his smile.

I can be totally honest with Jesus as I tell him my worries and cares.

I will open my heart to Jesus as I tell him my fears and doubts.

I will ask him to help me place myself fully in his care, knowing that he always desires good for me.

Conclusion

Glory be to the Father, and to the Son, and to the Holy Spirit,

As it was in the beginning, is now and ever shall be,

World without end. Amen.

Sunday 27 August
Twenty-first Sunday in Ordinary Time
Matthew 16:13–20

Now when Jesus came into the district of Caesarea Philippi, he asked his disciples, 'Who do people say that the Son of Man is?' And they said, 'Some say John the Baptist, but others Elijah, and still others Jeremiah or one of the prophets.' He said to them, 'But who do you say that I am?' Simon Peter answered, 'You are the Messiah, the Son of the living God.' And Jesus answered him, 'Blessed are you, Simon son of Jonah! For flesh and blood has not revealed this to you, but my Father in heaven. And I tell you, you are Peter, and on this rock I will build my church, and the gates of Hades will not prevail against it. I will give you the keys of the kingdom of heaven, and whatever you bind on earth will be bound in heaven, and whatever you loose on earth will be loosed in heaven.' Then he sternly ordered the disciples not to tell anyone that he was the Messiah.

- Jesus could trust Peter to be honest – he would say what was on his mind and in his heart. As Jesus asks me the same question, I answer honestly, knowing that nothing I say will alienate Jesus. If I am uncertain about what to say, I invite Jesus to look at my life and to see how I give witness.

Monday 28 August
Matthew 23:13–22

Then Jesus said to the crowds and to his disciples, 'But woe to you, scribes and Pharisees, hypocrites! For you lock people out of the kingdom of heaven. For you do not go in yourselves, and when others are going in, you stop them. Woe to you, scribes and Pharisees, hypocrites! For you cross sea and land to make a single convert, and you make the new convert twice as much a child of hell as yourselves.

'Woe to you, blind guides, who say, "Whoever swears by the sanctuary is bound by nothing, but whoever swears by the gold of the sanctuary is bound by the oath." You blind fools! For which is greater, the gold or the sanctuary that has made the gold sacred? And you say, "Whoever swears by the altar is bound by nothing, but whoever swears by the gift that is on the altar is bound by the oath." How blind you are! For which is greater, the gift or the altar that makes the gift sacred? So whoever swears by the altar, swears by it and by everything on it; and whoever swears by the sanctuary, swears by it and by the one who dwells in it; and whoever swears by heaven, swears by the throne of God and by the one who is seated upon it.'

- Jesus accuses the scribes and Pharisees of rationalising their selfishness by appealing to a higher law, even the law of God himself. I read these hard words of Jesus with humility and ask for an open and transparent heart.

Tuesday 29 August
Mark 6:17–29

For Herod himself had sent men who arrested John, bound him, and put him in prison on account of Herodias, his brother Philip's wife, because Herod had married her. For John had been telling Herod, 'It is not lawful for you to have your brother's wife.' And Herodias had a grudge against him, and wanted to kill him. But she could not, for Herod feared John, knowing that he was a righteous and holy man, and he protected him. When he heard him, he was greatly perplexed; and yet he liked to listen to him. But an opportunity came when Herod on his birthday gave a banquet for his courtiers and officers and for the leaders of Galilee. When his daughter Herodias came in and danced, she pleased Herod and his guests; and the king said to the girl, 'Ask me for whatever you wish, and I will give it.' And he solemnly swore to her, 'Whatever you ask me, I will give you, even half of my kingdom.' She went out and said to her mother, 'What should I ask for?' She replied, 'The head of John the baptiser.' Immediately she rushed back to the king and requested, 'I want you to give me at once the head of John the Baptist on a platter.' The king was deeply grieved; yet out of regard for his oaths and for the guests, he did not want to refuse her. Immediately the king sent a soldier of the guard with orders to bring John's head. He went and beheaded him in the prison, brought his head on a platter, and gave it to the girl. Then the girl gave it to her mother. When his disciples heard about it, they came and took his body, and laid it in a tomb.

- In our own times, human life is held in such little esteem, that many, like John the Baptist, are killed for the slightest reason. I look in sorrow at so much gratuitous violence in our world, and pray that the suffering of the victims may move the hearts of the perpetrators. Blessed are those who mourn, for they will be comforted.

Wednesday 30 August
Matthew 23:27–32

Jesus said, 'Woe to you, scribes and Pharisees, hypocrites! For you are like whitewashed tombs, which on the outside look beautiful, but inside they are full of the bones of the dead and of all kinds of filth. So you also on the outside look righteous to others, but inside you are full of hypocrisy and lawlessness.

'Woe to you, scribes and Pharisees, hypocrites! For you build the tombs of the prophets and decorate the graves of the righteous, and you say, "If we had lived in the days of our ancestors, we would not have taken part with them in shedding the blood of the prophets." Thus you testify against yourselves that you are descendants of those who murdered the prophets. Fill up, then, the measure of your ancestors.'

• It is so easy to condemn the mistakes of the past without realising we are still repeating them. I pray for light and freedom as we deal with such endemic sins as racism, xenophobia, imperialism and homophobia, and for those who suffer because of them. I ask for the courage to face my prejudices and to be ready to commit myself to build a better world.

Thursday 31 August
Matthew 24:42–51

Jesus said to his disciples, 'Keep awake therefore, for you do not know on what day your Lord is coming. But understand this: if the owner of the house had known in what part of the night the thief was coming, he would have stayed awake and would not have let his house be broken into. Therefore you also must be ready, for the Son of Man is coming at an unexpected hour.

'Who then is the faithful and wise slave, whom his master has put in charge of his household, to give the other slaves their allowance of food at the proper time? Blessed is that slave whom his master will find at work when he arrives. Truly I tell you, he will put that one in charge of all his possessions. But if that wicked slave says to himself, "My master is delayed", and he begins to beat his fellow-slaves, and eats and drinks with drunkards, the master of that slave will come on a day when he does not expect him and at an hour that he does not know. He will cut him in pieces and put him with the hypocrites, where there will be weeping and gnashing of teeth.'

- Our times are very sensitive to all kinds of abuse of power, yet we seem unable to eliminate it. I pray for the abused and the abusers, for politicians and judges of integrity who will enact and enforce laws that prevent abuse and bring redress. I look at my life and ask for light to see whether I am like the man in the parable.

Friday 1 September
Matthew 25:1–13

Jesus told the disciples a parable: 'Then the kingdom of heaven will be like this. Ten bridesmaids took their lamps and went to meet the bridegroom. Five of them were foolish, and five were wise. When the foolish took their lamps, they took no oil with them; but the wise took flasks of oil with their lamps. As the bridegroom was delayed, all of them became drowsy and slept. But at midnight there was a shout, "Look! Here is the bridegroom! Come out to meet him." Then all those bridesmaids got up and trimmed their lamps. The foolish said to the wise, "Give us some of your oil, for our lamps are going out." But the wise replied, "No! there will not be enough for you and for us; you had better go to the dealers and buy some for yourselves." And while they went to buy it, the bridegroom came, and those who were ready went with him into the wedding banquet; and the door was shut. Later the other bridesmaids came also, saying, "Lord, lord, open to us." But he replied, "Truly I tell you, I do not know you." Keep awake therefore, for you know neither the day nor the hour.'

- Readiness, being alert, a sense of expectancy and hope, these are all things that Jesus tries to communicate through some of his parables.
- I ask myself: Who am I in the parable? Am I willing to wait on God even when I don't know how long it will take? Can I faithfully entrust myself to the unknown with the certainty of God's goodness?

Saturday 2 September
Matthew 25:14–30

Jesus told them, 'For it is as if a man, going on a journey, summoned his slaves and entrusted his property to them; to one he gave five talents, to another two, to another one, to each according to his ability. Then he went away. The one who had received the five talents went off at once and traded with them, and made five more talents. In the same way, the one who had the two talents made two more talents. But the one who had received the one talent went off and dug a hole in the ground and hid his master's money. After a long time the master of those slaves came and settled accounts with them. Then the one who had received the five talents came forward, bringing five more talents, saying, "Master, you handed over to me five talents; see, I have made five more talents." His master said to him, "Well done, good and trustworthy slave; you have been trustworthy in a few things, I will put you in charge of many things; enter into the joy of your master." And the one with the two talents also came forward, saying, "Master, you handed over to me two talents; see, I have made two more talents." His master said to him, "Well done, good and trustworthy slave; you have been trustworthy in a few things, I will put you in charge of many things; enter into the joy of your master." Then the one who had received the one talent also came forward, saying, "Master, I knew that you were a harsh man, reaping where you did not sow, and gathering where you did not scatter seed; so I was afraid, and I went and hid your talent in the ground. Here you have what is yours." But his master replied, "You wicked and lazy slave! You knew, did you, that I reap where I did not sow, and gather where I did not scatter? Then you ought to have invested my money with the bankers, and on my return I would have received what was my own with interest. So take the talent from him, and give it to the one with the ten talents. For to all those who have, more will be given, and they will have an abundance; but from those who have nothing, even what they have will be taken away. As for this worthless slave, throw him into the outer darkness, where there will be weeping and gnashing of teeth."'

- The servant who hid his talent out of fear is branded as worthless, a harsh word indeed. Do I risk the many things and qualities I have been given for the growth of the kingdom, or I am happy with what I have, making sure I do not lose it, happy enough with a respectable existence? What will the master tell me when he calls me to account?

The Twenty-second Week in Ordinary Time
3–9 September 2023

Something to think and pray about each day this week:

The invitation of Jesus to find peace in his presence is one of the most popular of his sayings. He is contrasting his message with the burdensome law, which somehow had lost the heart of religion, over-emphasising the externals of laws and rituals. He is not devaluing laws and rituals but putting them in their place. He offers an invitation that everyone can hear; and at many times of life we really need to hear it. These may be times of illness, bereavement, anxiety, depression and worry. It is an invitation to come into his presence, which is a loving presence. It's not just an invitation to enjoy a restful time, but to rest in the presence of love.

Any notion we have of Jesus that is harsh is false: he is 'gentle and humble in heart'. This is the atmosphere he asks us all to spread. 'Once you have received the refreshment and comfort of Christ, we are called in turn to become refreshment and comfort for our brothers and sisters, with a meek and humble attitude, in imitation of the Master' (Pope Francis, July 2014).

The Church is a place of rest for the weary; the place where we find encouragement in the ordinary situations in our lives, where we are called to respond to those who suffer through poverty, homelessness and many other unjust social situations that are part of our world, near and far.

Donal Neary SJ,
Gospel Reflections for Sundays of Year A

The Presence of God

'Be still, and know that I am God!' (Psalm 46:10) Lord, your words lead us to the calmness and greatness of your presence.

Freedom

'In these days, God taught me as a schoolteacher teaches a pupil' (St Ignatius). I remind myself that there are things God has to teach me yet, and I ask for the grace to hear them and let them change me.

Consciousness

How am I really feeling? Lighthearted? Heavyhearted? I may be very much at peace, happy to be here.
Equally, I may be frustrated, worried or angry.
I acknowledge how I really am. It is the real me whom the Lord loves.

The Word

God speaks to each of us individually. I listen attentively to hear what he is saying to me. Read the text a few times, then listen.
(Please turn to the Scripture on the following pages. Inspiration points are there, should you need them. When you are ready, return here to continue.)

Conversation

Do I notice myself reacting as I pray with the word of God? Do I feel challenged, comforted, angry? Imagining Jesus sitting or standing by me, I speak out my feelings, as one trusted friend to another.

Conclusion

I thank God for these moments we have spent together and for any insights I have been given concerning the text.

Sunday 3 September
Twenty-second Sunday in Ordinary Time
Matthew 16:21–27

From that time on, Jesus began to show his disciples that he must go to Jerusalem and undergo great suffering at the hands of the elders and chief priests and scribes, and be killed, and on the third day be raised. And Peter took him aside and began to rebuke him, saying, 'God forbid it, Lord! This must never happen to you.' But he turned and said to Peter, 'Get behind me, Satan! You are a stumbling-block to me; for you are setting your mind not on divine things but on human things.'

Then Jesus told his disciples, 'If any want to become my followers, let them deny themselves and take up their cross and follow me. For those who want to save their life will lose it, and those who lose their life for my sake will find it. For what will it profit them if they gain the whole world but forfeit their life? Or what will they give in return for their life?

'For the Son of Man is to come with his angels in the glory of his Father, and then he will repay everyone for what has been done.'

• If we are to be followers of Jesus, we need to let him lead, accepting that he will not lead us away from suffering, pain or difficulty. Instead of seeking our own benefit and gain, we allow every experience – even in moments of distress – to draw us into closer relationship with Jesus, who invites us to lay our burdens on his shoulders. I pray that I may let go and grow in trust of God's love for me.

Monday 4 September
Luke 4:16–30

When he came to Nazareth, where he had been brought up, he went to the synagogue on the sabbath day, as was his custom. He stood up to read, and the scroll of the prophet Isaiah was given to him. He unrolled the scroll and found the place where it was written:

'The Spirit of the Lord is upon me,
  because he has anointed me
    to bring good news to the poor.
He has sent me to proclaim release to the captives
  and recovery of sight to the blind,

to let the oppressed go free,
  to proclaim the year of the Lord's favour.'

And he rolled up the scroll, gave it back to the attendant, and sat down. The eyes of all in the synagogue were fixed on him. Then he began to say to them, 'Today this scripture has been fulfilled in your hearing.' All spoke well of him and were amazed at the gracious words that came from his mouth. They said, 'Is not this Joseph's son?' He said to them, 'Doubtless you will quote to me this proverb, "Doctor, cure yourself!" And you will say, "Do here also in your home town the things that we have heard you did at Capernaum."' And he said, 'Truly I tell you, no prophet is accepted in the prophet's home town. But the truth is, there were many widows in Israel in the time of Elijah, when the heaven was shut up for three years and six months, and there was a severe famine over all the land; yet Elijah was sent to none of them except to a widow at Zarephath in Sidon. There were also many lepers in Israel in the time of the prophet Elisha, and none of them was cleansed except Naaman the Syrian.' When they heard this, all in the synagogue were filled with rage. They got up, drove him out of the town, and led him to the brow of the hill on which their town was built, so that they might hurl him off the cliff. But he passed through the midst of them and went on his way.

• Jesus, what if I were to stand at your shoulder as you proclaim your mandate? What is it like for me to be identified with you, seen to be on your team? Perhaps I need a moment with you, to hear your encouragement, so that I may more closely align my heart with yours.

Tuesday 5 September
Luke 4:31–37

He went down to Capernaum, a city in Galilee, and was teaching them on the sabbath. They were astounded at his teaching, because he spoke with authority. In the synagogue there was a man who had the spirit of an unclean demon, and he cried out with a loud voice, 'Let us alone! What have you to do with us, Jesus of Nazareth? Have you come to destroy us? I know who you are, the Holy One of God.' But Jesus rebuked him, saying, 'Be silent, and come out of him!' When the demon had thrown him down before them, he came out of him without having done him any harm. They were all amazed and kept saying to one another, 'What kind of utterance is this? For with authority and power he commands the unclean spirits, and out they come!' And a report about him began to reach every place in the region.

- When was the last time somebody made a deep impression on me? What did I do in consequence, how have I grown? I give thanks to God for those who have spoken or acted with authority, bringing truth or meaning to my life.

Wednesday 6 September
Luke 4:38–44

After leaving the synagogue he entered Simon's house. Now Simon's mother-in-law was suffering from a high fever, and they asked him about her. Then he stood over her and rebuked the fever, and it left her. Immediately she got up and began to serve them.

As the sun was setting, all those who had any who were sick with various kinds of diseases brought them to him; and he laid his hands on each of them and cured them. Demons also came out of many, shouting, 'You are the Son of God!' But he rebuked them and would not allow them to speak, because they knew that he was the Messiah.

At daybreak he departed and went into a deserted place. And the crowds were looking for him; and when they reached him, they wanted to prevent him from leaving them. But he said to them, 'I must proclaim the good news of the kingdom of God to the other cities also; for I was sent for this purpose.' So he continued proclaiming the message in the synagogues of Judea.

- In my quiet place, I give thanks to God for those times when my friends have brought my needs before God. I think now of those who suffer and lay them before Jesus. I open myself to his compassion and let his heart shape mine.

Thursday 7 September
Luke 5:1–11

Once while Jesus was standing beside the lake of Gennesaret, and the crowd was pressing in on him to hear the word of God, he saw two boats there at the shore of the lake; the fishermen had gone out of them and were washing their nets. He got into one of the boats, the one belonging to Simon, and asked him to put out a little way from the shore. Then he sat down and taught the crowds from the boat. When he had finished speaking, he said to Simon, 'Put out into the deep water and let down your nets for a catch.' Simon answered, 'Master, we have worked all night long but have caught nothing. Yet if you say so, I will let down the nets.' When they had done this, they caught so many fish that their nets were beginning to break. So they signalled to their partners in the other boat to come and help them. And they came and filled both boats, so that they began to sink. But when Simon Peter saw it, he fell down at Jesus' knees, saying, 'Go away from me, Lord, for I am a sinful man!' For he and all who were with him were amazed at the catch of fish that they had taken; and so also were James and John, sons of Zebedee, who were partners with Simon. Then Jesus said to Simon, 'Do not be afraid; from now on you will be catching people.' When they had brought their boats to shore, they left everything and followed him.

• The real message here is in the last few words: 'they left everything and followed him'. They left behind them their great catch, because they had been captivated instead by the person of Jesus. We too are to 'seek first the kingdom of God' – we are to live in God's world and judge the world's affairs from that vantage point.

Friday 8 September
The Nativity of the Blessed Virgin Mary
Matthew 1:1–16, 18–23

An account of the genealogy of Jesus the Messiah, the son of David, the son of Abraham.

Abraham was the father of Isaac, and Isaac the father of Jacob, and Jacob the father of Judah and his brothers, and Judah the father of Perez and Zerah by Tamar, and Perez the father of Hezron, and Hezron the father of Aram, and Aram the father of Aminadab, and Aminadab the father of Nahshon, and Nahshon the father of Salmon, and Salmon the father of Boaz by Rahab, and Boaz the father of Obed by Ruth, and Obed the father of Jesse, and Jesse the father of King David.

And David was the father of Solomon by the wife of Uriah, and Solomon the father of Rehoboam, and Rehoboam the father of Abijah, and Abijah the father of Asaph, and Asaph the father of Jehoshaphat, and Jehoshaphat the father of Joram, and Joram the father of Uzziah, and Uzziah the father of Jotham, and Jotham the father of Ahaz, and Ahaz the father of Hezekiah, and Hezekiah the father of Manasseh, and Manasseh the father of Amos, and Amos the father of Josiah, and Josiah the father of Jechoniah and his brothers, at the time of the deportation to Babylon.

And after the deportation to Babylon: Jechoniah was the father of Salathiel, and Salathiel the father of Zerubbabel, and Zerubbabel the father of Abiud, and Abiud the father of Eliakim, and Eliakim the father of Azor, and Azor the father of Zadok, and Zadok the father of Achim, and Achim the father of Eliud, and Eliud the father of Eleazar, and Eleazar the father of Matthan, and Matthan the father of Jacob, and Jacob the father of Joseph the husband of Mary, of whom Jesus was born, who is called the Messiah.

Now the birth of Jesus the Messiah took place in this way. When his mother Mary had been engaged to Joseph, but before they lived together, she was found to be with child from the Holy Spirit. Her husband Joseph, being a righteous man and unwilling to expose her to public disgrace, planned to dismiss her quietly. But just when he had resolved to do this, an angel of the Lord appeared to him in a dream and said, 'Joseph, son of David, do not be afraid to take Mary as your wife, for the child conceived in her is from the Holy Spirit. She will bear a son, and you are to name him Jesus, for he will save his people from their sins.' All this took place to fulfil what had been spoken by the Lord through the prophet:

'Look, the virgin shall conceive and bear a son,
    and they shall name him Emmanuel',
which means, 'God is with us.'

- This is more than a list of biblical names: Matthew is rattling skeletons in the cupboard of Jesus' ancestry. In addition to Mary, he adds four controversial mothers to his list of fathers. Tamar dressed as a prostitute and bore twins to her father-in-law. Rahab betrayed her city. Ruth was a Gentile. Solomon was the child of David's adulterous affair with Bathsheba. There is no airbrushing of Jesus' pedigree: he comes to us laden with all the disreputable past of his race, and shows how each birth is a fresh beginning.

- Lord, teach me to accept my humanity, my genes and my relatives, as you did.

Saturday 9 September
Luke 6:1–5

One sabbath while Jesus was going through the cornfields, his disciples plucked some heads of grain, rubbed them in their hands, and ate them. But some of the Pharisees said, 'Why are you doing what is not lawful on the sabbath?' Jesus answered, 'Have you not read what David did when he and his companions were hungry? He entered the house of God and took and ate the bread of the Presence, which it is not lawful for any but the priests to eat, and gave some to his companions?' Then he said to them, 'The Son of Man is lord of the sabbath.'

- 'The Son of Man is lord of the sabbath'! No wonder the Jews found Jesus difficult; they rightly understood he was claiming to be God himself. We sometimes reduce Jesus to his message of universal love and forgiveness, and are not ready to accept his claim that he is also our Lord and God.

The Twenty-third Week in Ordinary Time
10–16 September 2023

Something to think and pray about each day this week:

As a woman went for a prayer walk and climb one day, she became aware of two opposing forces at work. Firstly, gravity pulled at her (more so as she got higher up). Its force was drawing her downward. She couldn't see it, but my goodness could she feel it! The second force at work came from within her. It was the force of muscle, sinew and tendon. This force kept her moving onwards and upwards.

She had to work hard to battle the downward force of gravity. It would have been easy to simply give up. But she didn't. And she was rewarded with a great walk and some amazing sights of God's wonderful world all around her.

We all experience the downward drag in life in all sorts of other ways too. Maybe we are suffering anxiety, depression or worry. Maybe we are experiencing sickness or money worries or relationship difficulties.

That downward drag feels very forceful indeed but here is a second force at work – a force deep within ourselves. It is a force for good. We believe it to be the presence of the Holy Spirit dwelling within all of us, every single one of us.

Jim Deeds and Brendan McManus SJ,
Finding God in the Mess: Meditations for Mindful Living

The Presence of God
To be present is to arrive as one is and open up to the other.
At this instant, as I arrive here, God is present waiting for me.
God always arrives before me, desiring to connect with me
even more than my most intimate friend.
I take a moment and greet my loving God.

Freedom
Leave me here freely all alone. / In cell where never sunlight shone. /
Should no one ever speak to me. / This golden silence makes me free!
– Part of a poem by Bl. Titus Brandsma, written while he was a prisoner
at Dachau concentration camp

Consciousness
Where am I with God? With others?
Do I have something to be grateful for? Then I give thanks.
Is there something I am sorry for? Then I ask forgiveness.

The Word
I take my time to read the word of God slowly, a few times, allowing
myself to dwell on anything that strikes me.
*(Please turn to the Scripture on the following pages. Inspiration points are there,
should you need them. When you are ready, return here to continue.)*

Conversation
How has God's word moved me? Has it left me cold?
Has it consoled me or moved me to act in a new way?
I imagine Jesus standing or sitting beside me;
I turn and share my feelings with him.

Conclusion
Glory be to the Father, and to the Son, and to the Holy Spirit,
As it was in the beginning, is now and ever shall be,
World without end. Amen.

Sunday 10 September
Twenty-third Sunday in Ordinary Time
Matthew 18:15–20

Jesus said to his disciples, 'If another member of the church sins against you, go and point out the fault when the two of you are alone. If the member listens to you, you have regained that one. But if you are not listened to, take one or two others along with you, so that every word may be confirmed by the evidence of two or three witnesses. If the member refuses to listen to them, tell it to the church; and if the offender refuses to listen even to the church, let such a one be to you as a Gentile and a tax-collector. Truly I tell you, whatever you bind on earth will be bound in heaven, and whatever you loose on earth will be loosed in heaven. Again, truly I tell you, if two of you agree on earth about anything you ask, it will be done for you by my Father in heaven. For where two or three are gathered in my name, I am there among them.'

- Because Jesus shares his own spirit with us, the connection between the community of believers and Jesus is very close: what we bind or loose here is bound or loosed in heaven, and whatever we ask in union will be given to us by the Father. I ask for this insight and for a stronger faith in the presence of Jesus in the midst of the Church.

Monday 11 September
Luke 6:6–11

On another sabbath he entered the synagogue and taught, and there was a man there whose right hand was withered. The scribes and the Pharisees watched him to see whether he would cure on the sabbath, so that they might find an accusation against him. Even though he knew what they were thinking, he said to the man who had the withered hand, 'Come and stand here.' He got up and stood there. Then Jesus said to them, 'I ask you, is it lawful to do good or to do harm on the sabbath, to save life or to destroy it?' After looking around at all of them, he said to him, 'Stretch out your hand.' He did so, and his hand was restored. But they were filled with fury and discussed with one another what they might do to Jesus.

- Jesus rebuked the scribes and the Pharisees for their narrow-mindedness and adherence to the rule of the Law. Their practice of religion lacked compassion and love, key principles of the gospel message.

- What lesson do I draw from this incident? I ask the Lord to enlighten me about the Pharisees. What were their bad points? What good was in them?

Tuesday 12 September
Luke 6:12–19

Now during those days he went out to the mountain to pray; and he spent the night in prayer to God. And when day came, he called his disciples and chose twelve of them, whom he also named apostles: Simon, whom he named Peter, and his brother Andrew, and James, and John, and Philip, and Bartholomew, and Matthew, and Thomas, and James son of Alphaeus, and Simon, who was called the Zealot, and Judas son of James, and Judas Iscariot, who became a traitor.

He came down with them and stood on a level place, with a great crowd of his disciples and a great multitude of people from all Judea, Jerusalem, and the coast of Tyre and Sidon. They had come to hear him and to be healed of their diseases; and those who were troubled with unclean spirits were cured. And all in the crowd were trying to touch him, for power came out from him and healed all of them.

- What is it like for me to put my name among those of the apostles? What holds me back? What is it about my company that Jesus most enjoys? As he calls me, what growth does he hope for in me?

Wednesday 13 September
Luke 6:20–26

Then he looked up at his disciples and said:

'Blessed are you who are poor,
   for yours is the kingdom of God.
'Blessed are you who are hungry now,
   for you will be filled.
'Blessed are you who weep now,
   for you will laugh.

> 'Blessed are you when people hate you, and when they exclude you,
> revile you, and defame you on account of the Son of Man.
> Rejoice on that day and leap for joy, for surely your reward
> is great in heaven; for that is what their ancestors did to the
> prophets.
> 'But woe to you who are rich,
> for you have received your consolation.
> 'Woe to you who are full now,
> for you will be hungry.
> 'Woe to you who are laughing now,
> for you will mourn and weep.
> 'Woe to you when all speak well of you, for that is what their
> ancestors did to the false prophets.'

- I try to see which beatitude touches me today, whether because it helps me rejoice in God's gifts to me or because I feel a resistance in my heart. I pray for a listening heart.

Thursday 14 September
The Exaltation of the Holy Cross
John 3:13–17

Jesus said, 'No one has ascended into heaven except the one who descended from heaven, the Son of Man. And just as Moses lifted up the serpent in the wilderness, so must the Son of Man be lifted up, that whoever believes in him may have eternal life.

'For God so loved the world that he gave his only Son, so that everyone who believes in him may not perish but may have eternal life.

'Indeed, God did not send the Son into the world to condemn the world, but in order that the world might be saved through him.'

- On Good Friday we are caught up with the suffering and death of Jesus and the cost to him of losing his life in such a painful way. Today, the Feast of The Exaltation of the Holy Cross, we celebrate his great love for us as shown in that act of suffering, and praise him in thanksgiving for thinking of us in this way. No one can have greater love than this – it is the ultimate of the expression of love.

Friday 15 September
Luke 2:33–35

And the child's father and mother were amazed at what was being said about him. Then Simeon blessed them and said to his mother Mary, 'This child is destined for the falling and the rising of many in Israel, and to be a sign that will be opposed so that the inner thoughts of many will be revealed – and a sword will pierce your own soul too.'

• The reference to 'piercing your own soul too' must have revealed to Mary how she would be involved in this sacrifice of her Son. As we stand in spirit beside the 'tree of new life' on Calvary we are invited to go to Jesus, through Mary.

Saturday 16 September
Luke 6:43–49

Jesus said to his disciples, 'No good tree bears bad fruit, nor again does a bad tree bear good fruit; for each tree is known by its own fruit. Figs are not gathered from thorns, nor are grapes picked from a bramble bush. The good person out of the good treasure of the heart produces good, and the evil person out of evil treasure produces evil; for it is out of the abundance of the heart that the mouth speaks.

'Why do you call me "Lord, Lord", and do not do what I tell you? I will show you what someone is like who comes to me, hears my words, and acts on them. That one is like a man building a house, who dug deeply and laid the foundation on rock; when a flood arose, the river burst against that house but could not shake it, because it had been well built. But the one who hears and does not act is like a man who built a house on the ground without a foundation. When the river burst against it, immediately it fell, and great was the ruin of that house.'

• In our deeply relativistic times, Jesus' words on building our lives on his words sound like a real challenge. I ask to understand what it means in my own life, to see where my life is built on sand and where it is built on solid rock.

The Twenty-fourth Week in Ordinary Time
17–23 September 2023

Something to think and pray about each day this week:

'Love your enemies!' This is the most shocking command of Jesus. God forgives all 'enemies' and tries to win them over by love. This is God's fundamental response to evil, and it is to be ours too. If evil is like poison gas, forgiveness draws off its poison and enables the world to breathe freely. But when we experience ourselves as innocent victims of another's evil, forgiveness can seem too much to demand of our poor hearts. Yet if I do not at least try to forgive those who hurt me, I block the flow of the forgiving love of God to them in their need and I remain trapped by the evil they have done me. In this way I obstruct the divine resolution of the problem of evil. This is indeed a strange and unwanted power to have! So it is good to be reminded – over and over until we get the point – that in being forgiven by God for all our personal wrongdoing, we are commissioned to move out to share God's mercy with our own 'enemies'.

Brian Grogan SJ,
God, You're Breaking my Heart

The Presence of God

What is present to me is what has a hold on my becoming.
I reflect on the presence of God always there in love,
amidst the many things that have a hold on me.
I pause and pray that I may let God
affect my becoming in this precise moment.

Freedom

By God's grace I was born to live in freedom. Free to enjoy the pleasures
he created for me. Dear Lord, grant that I may live as you intended, with
complete confidence in your loving care.

Consciousness

To be conscious about something is to be aware of it.
Dear Lord, help me to remember that you gave me life.
Thank you for the gift of life.
Teach me to slow down, to be still and enjoy the pleasures created for me.
To be aware of the beauty that surrounds me: the marvel of mountains,
the calmness of lakes, the fragility of a flower petal. I need to remember
that all these things come from you.

The Word

God speaks to each of us individually. I listen attentively to hear what he
is saying to me. Read the text a few times, then listen.
*(Please turn to the Scripture on the following pages. Inspiration points are there,
should you need them. When you are ready, return here to continue.)*

Conversation

I begin to talk with Jesus about the Scripture I have just read. What part
of it strikes a chord in me? Perhaps the words of a friend – or some story
I have heard recently – will rise to the surface in my consciousness. If so,
does the story throw light on what the Scripture passage may be saying
to me?

Conclusion

Glory be to the Father, and to the Son, and to the Holy Spirit,
As it was in the beginning, is now and ever shall be,
World without end. Amen.

Sunday 17 September
Twenty-fourth Sunday in Ordinary Time
Matthew 18:21–35

Then Peter came and said to him, 'Lord, if another member of the church sins against me, how often should I forgive? As many as seven times?' Jesus said to him, 'Not seven times, but, I tell you, seventy-seven times.

'For this reason the kingdom of heaven may be compared to a king who wished to settle accounts with his slaves. When he began the reckoning, one who owed him ten thousand talents was brought to him; and, as he could not pay, his lord ordered him to be sold, together with his wife and children and all his possessions, and payment to be made. So the slave fell on his knees before him, saying, "Have patience with me, and I will pay you everything." And out of pity for him, the lord of that slave released him and forgave him the debt. But that same slave, as he went out, came upon one of his fellow-slaves who owed him a hundred denarii; and seizing him by the throat, he said, "Pay what you owe." Then his fellow-slave fell down and pleaded with him, "Have patience with me, and I will pay you." But he refused; then he went and threw him into prison until he should pay the debt. When his fellow-slaves saw what had happened, they were greatly distressed, and they went and reported to their lord all that had taken place. Then his lord summoned him and said to him, "You wicked slave! I forgave you all that debt because you pleaded with me. Should you not have had mercy on your fellow-slave, as I had mercy on you?" And in anger his lord handed him over to be tortured until he should pay his entire debt. So my heavenly Father will also do to every one of you, if you do not forgive your brother or sister from your heart.'

- Forgiveness can be very hard. C. S. Lewis wrote: 'Everyone says forgiveness is a lovely idea, until they have something to forgive.' But when I fail to forgive, I am shackled to the evil that has been done to me. I cannot move forward. How free am I, or am I tied to resentments?

Monday 18 September
Luke 7:1–10

After Jesus had finished all his sayings in the hearing of the people, he entered Capernaum. A centurion there had a slave whom he valued highly, and who was ill and close to death. When he heard about Jesus, he sent some Jewish elders to him, asking him to come and heal his slave. When they came to Jesus, they appealed to him earnestly, saying, 'He is worthy of having you do this for him, for he loves our people, and it is he who built our synagogue for us.' And Jesus went with them, but when he was not far from the house, the centurion sent friends to say to him, 'Lord, do not trouble yourself, for I am not worthy to have you come under my roof; therefore I did not presume to come to you. But only speak the word, and let my servant be healed. For I also am a man set under authority, with soldiers under me; and I say to one, "Go", and he goes, and to another, "Come", and he comes, and to my slave, "Do this", and the slave does it.' When Jesus heard this he was amazed at him, and turning to the crowd that followed him, he said, 'I tell you, not even in Israel have I found such faith.' When those who had been sent returned to the house, they found the slave in good health.

- Jesus was profoundly impressed by the quality of the life of this man and his genuine concern for his slave. He was not an Israelite yet he put his faith and trust in Jesus whom he called 'Lord' on the basis of his experience during his time of duty among the Israelites. Like the centurion we don't need to see Jesus with our eyes to know that he is alive and active in our lives.

Tuesday 19 September
Luke 7:11–17

Soon afterwards he went to a town called Nain, and his disciples and a large crowd went with him. As he approached the gate of the town, a man who had died was being carried out. He was his mother's only son, and she was a widow; and with her was a large crowd from the town. When the Lord saw her, he had compassion for her and said to her, 'Do not weep.' Then he came forward and touched the bier, and the bearers stood still. And he said, 'Young man, I say to you, rise!' The dead man sat up and began to speak, and Jesus gave him to his mother. Fear seized all of them; and they glorified God, saying, 'A great prophet has risen among us!' and 'God has looked favourably on his people!' This word about him spread throughout Judea and all the surrounding country.

- This short episode is a valuable one to remember when things seem very bleak in our lives. The pall-bearers are bringing the widow's son out for burial prematurely. He can still be restored to life through the power of Jesus' compassion. Just when the widow thought she had lost everything, everything was restored to her.

- In times of darkness, let us remember that Jesus, the great prophet hailed by the mourners, is still with us – yesterday, today and forever.

Wednesday 20 September
Luke 7:31–35

Jesus said to his disciples, 'To what then will I compare the people of this generation, and what are they like? They are like children sitting in the market-place and calling to one another,

"We played the flute for you, and you did not dance;
  we wailed, and you did not weep."

For John the Baptist has come eating no bread and drinking no wine, and you say, "He has a demon"; the Son of Man has come eating and drinking, and you say, "Look, a glutton and a drunkard, a friend of tax-collectors and sinners!" Nevertheless, wisdom is vindicated by all her children.'

- Much of the social commentary of our age is like the children shouting in the marketplace – transitory, inescapable, momentarily engaging but shallow. Being here, now, is my way of connecting with a lasting, truer message. I take the time I need to let the surface chatter go and to listen for God, who speaks in the depth of my heart.

Thursday 21 September
St Matthew, Apostle
Matthew 9:9–13

As Jesus was walking along, he saw a man called Matthew sitting at the tax booth; and he said to him, 'Follow me.' And he got up and followed him.

And as he sat at dinner in the house, many tax-collectors and sinners came and were sitting with him and his disciples. When the Pharisees saw this, they said to his disciples, 'Why does your teacher eat with tax-collectors and sinners?' But when he heard this, he said, 'Those who are well have no need of a physician, but those who are sick. Go and learn what this means, "I desire mercy, not sacrifice." For I have come to call not the righteous but sinners.'

- As I move through this day, I quietly consider how Jesus wants to call all those around me. If I do not understand why, it is because I do not see what Jesus sees.

Friday 22 September
Luke 8:1–3

Soon afterwards he went on through cities and villages, proclaiming and bringing the good news of the kingdom of God. The twelve were with him, as well as some women who had been cured of evil spirits and infirmities: Mary, called Magdalene, from whom seven demons had gone out, and Joanna, the wife of Herod's steward Chuza, and Susanna, and many others, who provided for them out of their resources.

- Jesus always understood his mission as something to be carried out with others, never on his own. I look at the ones he chose, who seem to be quite an unlikely group, and I ask myself what he wants to tell us through this choice.

Saturday 23 September
Luke 8:4–15

When a great crowd gathered and people from town after town came to him, he said in a parable: 'A sower went out to sow his seed; and as he sowed, some fell on the path and was trampled on, and the birds of the air ate it up. Some fell on the rock; and as it grew up, it withered for lack of moisture. Some fell among thorns, and the thorns grew with it and choked it. Some fell into good soil, and when it grew, it produced a hundredfold.' As he said this, he called out, 'Let anyone with ears to hear listen!'

Then his disciples asked him what this parable meant. He said, 'To you it has been given to know the secrets of the kingdom of God; but to others I speak in parables, so that

"looking they may not perceive,
    and listening they may not understand."

'Now the parable is this: The seed is the word of God. The ones on the path are those who have heard; then the devil comes and takes away the word from their hearts, so that they may not believe and be saved. The ones on the rock are those who, when they hear the word, receive it with joy. But these have no root; they believe only for a while and in a time of testing fall away. As for what fell among the thorns, these are the ones who hear; but as they go on their way, they are choked by the cares and riches and pleasures of life, and their fruit does not mature. But as for that in the good soil, these are the ones who, when they hear the word, hold it fast in an honest and good heart, and bear fruit with patient endurance.'

- Perhaps we might think of the pathway in this way – the rocky soil and the thorn-strewn patches are different areas of each of our hearts, rather than different categories of persons. Let us ask the Lord to extend the positive areas of good and productive soil in our lives, something that only he can do. In this way we will be able to 'hold it fast in an honest and good heart, and bear fruit with patient endurance'.

24–30 September 2023

Something to think and pray about each day this week:

How can we meet the challenge to eco-conversion? For a moment sit back and ask yourself, '*What is precious to me?*' Think of something or someone that perhaps means a lot to you, and which, if it were endangered, you would rush to save: a baby, a friend, a love-letter, an heirloom, a home, a tree, a new car, a work of art. If it were injured, trashed or destroyed, how would you feel?

Now consider that Creation, down to its least speck, is precious to God. Ask God, '*Why do you risk entrusting this treasure to us humans?*' Must God not feel dismayed when we destroy the forests, ravage the earth, pollute the oceans and treat billions of tons of Creation as trash? Do we bring grief to God, as to an artist who sees their handiwork being destroyed? We are told that we can grieve the Holy Spirit (Ephesians 4:30), and we know that Jesus wept over Jerusalem. The real God is a God of infinite care, whose Creation is a precious gift to be treasured and tended, and Earth is Common Home not only to us but to God as well, since Jesus pitched his tent among us. Ours is to be a civilisation of care.

Laudato Si' states that everything we see is a letter in the magnificent Book of Creation. It is for us to connect up the letters and to realise that God is manifested in all that exists. God, it has been said, is materialised in a robin, a sunset, a stone, a leaf. So close is God that everything is, so to speak, a caress of God, a revelation of the divine.

Brian Grogan SJ,
Creation Walk: The Amazing Story of a Small Blue Planet

The Presence of God
'Be still, and know that I am God!' (Psalm 46:10) Lord, your words lead us to the calmness and greatness of your presence.

Freedom
Everything has the potential to draw forth from me a fuller love and life. Yet my desires are often fixed, caught, on illusions of fulfilment. I ask that God, through my freedom, may orchestrate my desires in a vibrant loving melody rich in harmony.

Consciousness
I exist in a web of relationships: links to nature, people, God.
I trace out these links, giving thanks for the life that flows through them. Some links are twisted or broken; I may feel regret, anger, disappointment. I pray for the gift of acceptance and forgiveness.

The Word
I read the word of God slowly, a few times over, and I listen to what God is saying to me.
(Please turn to the Scripture on the following pages. Inspiration points are there, should you need them. When you are ready, return here to continue.)

Conversation
Jesus, you speak to me through the words of the Gospels. May I respond to your call today. Teach me to recognise your hand at work in my daily living.

Conclusion
I thank God for these moments we have spent together and for any insights I have been given concerning the text.

Sunday 24 September
Twenty-fifth Sunday in Ordinary Time
Matthew 20:1–16

Jesus told them, 'For the kingdom of heaven is like a landowner who went out early in the morning to hire labourers for his vineyard. After agreeing with the labourers for the usual daily wage, he sent them into his vineyard. When he went out about nine o'clock, he saw others standing idle in the market-place; and he said to them, "You also go into the vineyard, and I will pay you whatever is right." So they went. When he went out again about noon and about three o'clock, he did the same. And about five o'clock he went out and found others standing around; and he said to them, "Why are you standing here idle all day?" They said to him, "Because no one has hired us." He said to them, "You also go into the vineyard." When evening came, the owner of the vineyard said to his manager, "Call the labourers and give them their pay, beginning with the last and then going to the first." When those hired about five o'clock came, each of them received the usual daily wage. Now when the first came, they thought they would receive more; but each of them also received the usual daily wage. And when they received it, they grumbled against the landowner, saying, "These last worked only one hour, and you have made them equal to us who have borne the burden of the day and the scorching heat." But he replied to one of them, "Friend, I am doing you no wrong; did you not agree with me for the usual daily wage? Take what belongs to you and go; I choose to give to this last the same as I give to you. Am I not allowed to do what I choose with what belongs to me? Or are you envious because I am generous?" So the last will be first, and the first will be last.'

- Lord, you console me with this story, about your call going out to people at different stages of the day, that is, of their lives. You can always surprise me, both with your challenge to youth, middle age or old age, and with your rewards. Your ways are so far above my ways that I cannot grasp the whole pattern. I can simply be grateful that you have said to me now: 'You also go into the vineyard.' Please keep me on your payroll.

Monday 25 September
Luke 8:16–18

Jesus said to his disciples, 'No one after lighting a lamp hides it under a jar, or puts it under a bed, but puts it on a lampstand, so that those who enter may see the light. For nothing is hidden that will not be disclosed, nor is anything secret that will not become known and come to light. Then pay attention to how you listen; for to those who have, more will be given; and from those who do not have, even what they seem to have will be taken away.'

- Jesus asks me to pay attention to how I listen, to notice how I notice. If my prayer is full of distraction or if my mind is always racing, I need to do as Jesus asks and pay attention. If I see only deficiency I will lose everything; if I am able to recognise, appreciate and receive blessing, I can trust in God's goodness and love.

Tuesday 26 September
Luke 8:19–21

Then his mother and his brothers came to him, but they could not reach him because of the crowd. And he was told, 'Your mother and your brothers are standing outside, wanting to see you.' But he said to them, 'My mother and my brothers are those who hear the word of God and do it.'

- Hearing the word and doing it: for Jesus these two verbs go together. Once he said that those who do so are building their life on rock rather than on sand so that they can be strong in the midst of difficulties.

- Here he goes even further, identifying those who hear the word of God and do it with his own innermost circle, with his own mother and brothers. I thank Jesus for this great compliment, and ask for the grace to be able to put into practice the word of God in my life, not as an obligation but as a privilege.

Wednesday 27 September
Luke 9:1–6

Then Jesus called the twelve together and gave them power and authority over all demons and to cure diseases, and he sent them out to proclaim the kingdom of God and to heal. He said to them, 'Take nothing for your journey, no staff, nor bag, nor bread, nor money – not even an extra tunic. Whatever house you enter, stay there, and leave from there. Wherever they do not welcome you, as you are leaving that town shake the dust off your feet as a testimony against them.' They departed and went through the villages, bringing the good news and curing diseases everywhere.

• What is the dust I need to shake off? What is it that tarnishes me and dulls my shine? I pray that I may keep my focus on the good news and not allow myself to be slowed down by attention to other messages, no matter how compelling.

Thursday 28 September
Luke 9:7–9

Now Herod the ruler heard about all that had taken place, and he was perplexed, because it was said by some that John had been raised from the dead, by some that Elijah had appeared, and by others that one of the ancient prophets had arisen. Herod said, 'John I beheaded; but who is this about whom I hear such things?' And he tried to see him.

• Herod tried to see Jesus, and he managed to do so only during his trial. There he showed he was not really interested in having a personal encounter with Jesus, but rather in meeting a celebrity. Jesus once thanked the Father for showing the little ones who he really was, and hiding it from the wise and the proud. I pray to be small enough to desire a personal encounter with Jesus.

Friday 29 September
Ss Michael, Gabriel and Raphael, Archangels
John 1:47–51

When Jesus saw Nathanael coming towards him, he said of him, 'Here is truly an Israelite in whom there is no deceit!' Nathanael asked him, 'Where did you come to know me?' Jesus answered, 'I saw you under the fig tree before Philip called you.' Nathanael replied, 'Rabbi, you are the Son of God! You are the King of Israel!' Jesus answered, 'Do you believe because I told you that I saw you under the fig tree? You will see greater things than these.' And he said to him, 'Very truly, I tell you, you will see heaven opened and the angels of God ascending and descending upon the Son of Man.'

- Jesus lifts Nathanael's eyes from the everyday and prompts him to think of heaven; I might consider my hoped-for destination and see how my daily concerns are enlightened and brought into another perspective.

Saturday 30 September
Luke 9:43b–45

While everyone was amazed at all that he was doing, he said to his disciples, 'Let these words sink into your ears: The Son of Man is going to be betrayed into human hands.' But they did not understand this saying; its meaning was concealed from them, so that they could not perceive it. And they were afraid to ask him about this saying.

- See how Jesus emphasises his words; he knows that the disciples will find them difficult to accept. It is still the case. Sometimes it is easier for me to accept that I might betray Jesus than it is for me to receive his assurance of continuing love and presence. I ask, now, that I might listen to Jesus' words and not be preoccupied with my own hesitation.

The Twenty-sixth Week in Ordinary Time
1–7 October 2023

Something to think and pray about each day this week:

It is extraordinary to think that some people thought Jesus' power to heal and make whole was not from God but from the devil. They were saying that far from being of God, Jesus was of the devil. How could someone who revealed the goodness of God be associated with the prince of devils? The tendency to demonise has reared its head throughout human history. One group demonises another. An individual is demonised without foundation. Once someone or some group is demonised, it gives those doing the demonising a licence to do terrible things to them. Declaring Jesus to be in league with Satan is the most extreme example of such irrational demonising. In response to this perception of him, Jesus declares that it is the finger of God that is revealed in all he does and that it is the kingdom of God that is breaking out through him. We are encouraged to look for the signs of the finger of God in the lives of those we might be tempted to demonise in whatever way.

Martin Hogan,
The Word of God Is Living and Active:
Reflections on the Weekday Readings

The Presence of God

'Come to me, all you who are weary and are carrying heavy burdens, and I will give you rest' (Matthew 11:28). Here I am, Lord. I come to seek your presence. I long for your healing power.

Freedom

God is not foreign to my freedom. The Spirit breathes life into my most intimate desires, gently nudging me towards all that is good. I ask for the grace to let myself be enfolded by the Spirit.

Consciousness

I remind myself that I am in the presence of the Lord. I will take refuge in his loving heart. He is my strength in times of weakness. He is my comforter in times of sorrow.

The Word

I take my time to read the word of God slowly, a few times, allowing myself to dwell on anything that strikes me.

(Please turn to the Scripture on the following pages. Inspiration points are there, should you need them. When you are ready, return here to continue.)

Conversation

Jesus, you always welcomed little children when you walked on this earth. Teach me to have a childlike trust in you. Teach me to live in the knowledge that you will never abandon me.

Conclusion

Glory be to the Father, and to the Son, and to the Holy Spirit,
As it was in the beginning, is now and ever shall be,
World without end. Amen.

Sunday 1 October
Twenty-sixth Sunday in Ordinary Time
Matthew 21:28–32

Jesus said to his disciples, 'What do you think? A man had two sons; he went to the first and said, "Son, go and work in the vineyard today." He answered, "I will not"; but later he changed his mind and went. The father went to the second and said the same; and he answered, "I go, sir"; but he did not go. Which of the two did the will of his father?' They said, 'The first.' Jesus said to them, 'Truly I tell you, the tax-collectors and the prostitutes are going into the kingdom of God ahead of you. For John came to you in the way of righteousness and you did not believe him, but the tax-collectors and the prostitutes believed him; and even after you saw it, you did not change your minds and believe him.'

• There are different responses to the Lord in my own life. I pray to be more aware of my need for the Lord and to let that need open me to the gift. My emptiness can become space for the Lord. Does my frailty turn me to the Lord or to myself? I desire freedom and pray to see the Lord more clearly for who he is so that I may love him more dearly.

Monday 2 October
Matthew 18:1–5, 10

At that time the disciples came to Jesus and asked, 'Who is the greatest in the kingdom of heaven?' He called a child, whom he put among them, and said, 'Truly I tell you, unless you change and become like children, you will never enter the kingdom of heaven. Whoever becomes humble like this child is the greatest in the kingdom of heaven. Whoever welcomes one such child in my name welcomes me.

'Take care that you do not despise one of these little ones; for, I tell you, in heaven their angels continually see the face of my Father in heaven.'

• Am I free to challenge my friends, my family or my work colleagues with a childlike fearlessness when my heart tells me that something is not right?

• I might pause in silence to reflect on the true greatness to be found in a child, and pray for those who have children in their care.

Tuesday 3 October
Luke 9:51–56

When the days drew near for him to be taken up, he set his face to go to Jerusalem. And he sent messengers ahead of him. On their way they entered a village of the Samaritans to make ready for him; but they did not receive him, because his face was set towards Jerusalem. When his disciples James and John saw it, they said, 'Lord, do you want us to command fire to come down from heaven and consume them?' But he turned and rebuked them. Then they went on to another village.

- The disciples thought, 'If only everybody were like us', as they asked Jesus to teach a lesson to the obstinate Samaritans. Even as he had set his face to Jerusalem, Jesus recognised how his followers did not understand his heart. Help me, Jesus, to follow you in humility, to seek your way. Let the logic of my head be tempered by the compassion of your heart.

Wednesday 4 October
Luke 9:57–62

As they were going along the road, someone said to him, 'I will follow you wherever you go.' And Jesus said to him, 'Foxes have holes, and birds of the air have nests; but the Son of Man has nowhere to lay his head.' To another he said, 'Follow me.' But he said, 'Lord, first let me go and bury my father.' But Jesus said to him, 'Let the dead bury their own dead; but as for you, go and proclaim the kingdom of God.' Another said, 'I will follow you, Lord; but let me first say farewell to those at my home.' Jesus said to him, 'No one who puts a hand to the plough and looks back is fit for the kingdom of God.'

- Enthusiasm and good desires are important, but not enough. Decision and implementation must follow. Am I someone who starts well, but if the going gets rough do I drop off? Is my following of Jesus conditional on things going smoothly? Jesus says that this will not do.

- I rightly say, 'Lord, I will follow you wherever you go.' This is a beautiful and loving promise. But left to myself I do not have the inner strength to keep it. I must ask Jesus for his strength day by day, and I start now.

Thursday 5 October
Luke 10:1–12

After this the Lord appointed seventy others and sent them on ahead of him in pairs to every town and place where he himself intended to go. He said to them, 'The harvest is plentiful, but the labourers are few; therefore ask the Lord of the harvest to send out labourers into his harvest. Go on your way. See, I am sending you out like lambs into the midst of wolves. Carry no purse, no bag, no sandals; and greet no one on the road. Whatever house you enter, first say, "Peace to this house!" And if anyone is there who shares in peace, your peace will rest on that person; but if not, it will return to you. Remain in the same house, eating and drinking whatever they provide, for the labourer deserves to be paid. Do not move about from house to house. Whenever you enter a town and its people welcome you, eat what is set before you; cure the sick who are there, and say to them, "The kingdom of God has come near to you." But whenever you enter a town and they do not welcome you, go out into its streets and say, "Even the dust of your town that clings to our feet, we wipe off in protest against you. Yet know this: the kingdom of God has come near." I tell you, on that day it will be more tolerable for Sodom than for that town.'

- In instructing the disciples to travel light, Jesus is encouraging them to depend on him for all that they need to accomplish their mission. What heavy baggage am I carrying that slows me down on my spiritual journey?

Friday 6 October
Luke 10:13–16

Jesus said to his disciples, 'Woe to you, Chorazin! Woe to you, Bethsaida! For if the deeds of power done in you had been done in Tyre and Sidon, they would have repented long ago, sitting in sackcloth and ashes. But at the judgement it will be more tolerable for Tyre and Sidon than for you. And you, Capernaum,

> will you be exalted to heaven?
> No, you will be brought down to Hades.

'Whoever listens to you listens to me, and whoever rejects you rejects me, and whoever rejects me rejects the one who sent me.'

- It is striking that Jesus' ministry took place outside of the big cities of the region, in the villages and small towns of Galilee. He had decided that the cities – except for Jerusalem – were not the places where he was to preach. He moved instead among communities of subsistence farmers and day labourers, working for one day's sustenance at a time. Yet it is among them that God works his 'deeds of power'.

- And what about me? Do I look for this power in places of prestige? Or can I walk with Jesus among the vulnerable?

Saturday 7 October
Luke 10:17–24

The seventy returned with joy, saying, 'Lord, in your name even the demons submit to us!' He said to them, 'I watched Satan fall from heaven like a flash of lightning. See, I have given you authority to tread on snakes and scorpions, and over all the power of the enemy; and nothing will hurt you. Nevertheless, do not rejoice at this, that the spirits submit to you, but rejoice that your names are written in heaven.'

At that same hour Jesus rejoiced in the Holy Spirit and said, 'I thank you, Father, Lord of heaven and earth, because you have hidden these things from the wise and the intelligent and have revealed them to infants; yes, Father, for such was your gracious will. All things have been handed over to me by my Father; and no one knows who the Son is except the Father, or who the Father is except the Son and anyone to whom the Son chooses to reveal him.'

Then turning to the disciples, Jesus said to them privately, 'Blessed are the eyes that see what you see! For I tell you that many prophets and kings desired to see what you see, but did not see it, and to hear what you hear, but did not hear it.'

- We remember that Jesus sent out the seventy to prepare the way for him. He is to follow in their footsteps, he will build on their preparatory work. You can feel that Jesus is excited at this prospect of the next stage of the mission.

- Does it help me to think of my own mission as a Christian in these terms? That through my words and deeds of witness I am preparing the way for Jesus, so that those who have yet to encounter him effectively will do so?

The Twenty-seventh Week in Ordinary Time
8–14 October 2023

Something to think and pray about each day this week:

Pope Francis begins his apostolic exhortation, *Evangelii Gaudium*, by drawing attention to the source of freedom when he declares, 'The joy of the gospel fills the hearts and lives of all who encounter Jesus. Those who accept his offer of salvation are set free from sin, sorrow, inner emptiness and loneliness. With Christ joy is constantly born anew' (EG, 1). It is important to note that freedom for him has two aspects. Firstly, it is a freedom to relate with and 'encounter' Christ at a deeply personal level. This brings fundamental changes, he says. Most notably people experience joy. Secondly, it is freedom from, in that it heals sin and selfishness, and assures a divine help and presence in times of 'sorrow, inner emptiness and loneliness'.

Scholastic teaching had already distinguished between 'freedom for' and 'freedom from'. The first identifies the purpose of freedom as the capacity for self-giving and surrender to love, generosity, altruism, moral codes and service. For the Christian, this path engages, through surrender, with the Father's love, and embraces his joy. The second challenges the perception of freedom as thinking and acting without restraints and moral inhibitions, and doing whatever one wishes. Such a path sets limits to our human potential and runs the risk of defining persons, events and possessions in terms of their usefulness and as means to personal comfort and peace, and with God seen as absent.

Michael Hurley,
Inspiring Faith Communities

The Presence of God

'I am standing at the door, knocking' (Revelation 3:20), says the Lord. What a wonderful privilege that the Lord of all creation desires to come to me. I welcome his presence.

Freedom

I will ask God's help
to be free from my own preoccupations,
to be open to God in this time of prayer,
to come to know, love and serve God more.

Consciousness

In God's loving presence I unwind the past day,
starting from now and looking back, moment by moment.
I gather in all the goodness and light, in gratitude.
I attend to the shadows and what they say to me,
seeking healing, courage, forgiveness.

The Word

Now I turn to the Scripture set out for me this day. I read slowly over the words and see if any sentence or sentiment appeals to me.
(Please turn to the Scripture on the following pages. Inspiration points are there, should you need them. When you are ready, return here to continue.)

Conversation

Sometimes I wonder what I might say if I were to meet you in person, Lord. I think I might say, 'Thank you' because you are always there for me.

Conclusion

I thank God for these moments we have spent together and for any insights I have been given concerning the text.

Sunday 8 October
Twenty-seventh Sunday in Ordinary Time
Matthew 21:33–43

Jesus said to his disciples, 'Listen to another parable. There was a land-owner who planted a vineyard, put a fence around it, dug a wine press in it, and built a watch-tower. Then he leased it to tenants and went to another country. When the harvest time had come, he sent his slaves to the tenants to collect his produce. But the tenants seized his slaves and beat one, killed another, and stoned another. Again he sent other slaves, more than the first; and they treated them in the same way. Finally he sent his son to them, saying, "They will respect my son." But when the tenants saw the son, they said to themselves, "This is the heir; come, let us kill him and get his inheritance." So they seized him, threw him out of the vineyard, and killed him. Now when the owner of the vineyard comes, what will he do to those tenants?' They said to him, 'He will put those wretches to a miserable death, and lease the vineyard to other tenants who will give him the produce at the harvest time.'

Jesus said to them, 'Have you never read in the scriptures:

"The stone that the builders rejected
    has become the cornerstone;
this was the Lord's doing,
    and it is amazing in our eyes"?

Therefore I tell you, the kingdom of God will be taken away from you and given to a people that produces the fruits of the kingdom.'

• Jesus speaks about the landlord whose absence causes the tenants to forget themselves. I pray for all those who overlook signs of God's care and imagine God's absence; may my prayer for them and my action this day witness to God's presence and love.

Monday 9 October
Luke 10:25–37

Just then a lawyer stood up to test Jesus. 'Teacher,' he said, 'what must I do to inherit eternal life?' He said to him, 'What is written in the law? What do you read there?' He answered, 'You shall love the Lord your God with all your heart, and with all your soul, and with all your strength, and with all your mind; and your neighbour as yourself.' And he said to him, 'You have given the right answer; do this, and you will live.'

But wanting to justify himself, he asked Jesus, 'And who is my neighbour?' Jesus replied, 'A man was going down from Jerusalem to Jericho, and fell into the hands of robbers, who stripped him, beat him, and went away, leaving him half dead. Now by chance a priest was going down that road; and when he saw him, he passed by on the other side. So likewise a Levite, when he came to the place and saw him, passed by on the other side. But a Samaritan while travelling came near him; and when he saw him, he was moved with pity. He went to him and bandaged his wounds, having poured oil and wine on them. Then he put him on his own animal, brought him to an inn, and took care of him. The next day he took out two denarii, gave them to the innkeeper, and said, "Take care of him; and when I come back, I will repay you whatever more you spend." Which of these three, do you think, was a neighbour to the man who fell into the hands of the robbers?' He said, 'The one who showed him mercy.' Jesus said to him, 'Go and do likewise.'

- Pope Francis, preaching on this reading, said: 'The priest and the Levite see but ignore; they look but they do not offer to help. Yet there is no true worship if it is not translated into service to neighbour. Let us never forget this: before the suffering of so many people exhausted by hunger, violence and injustice, we cannot remain spectators.'

- Lord, as I make my way through this and every day, give me eyes to see my marginalised and suffering brothers and sisters. Give me a heart that will love you present in the faces of others. Give me hands that help as well as lips that pray.

Tuesday 10 October
Luke 10:38–42

Now as they went on their way, he entered a certain village, where a woman named Martha welcomed him into her home. She had a sister named Mary, who sat at the Lord's feet and listened to what he was saying. But Martha was distracted by her many tasks; so she came to him and asked, 'Lord, do you not care that my sister has left me to do all the work by myself? Tell her then to help me.' But the Lord answered her, 'Martha, Martha, you are worried and distracted by many things; there is need of only one thing. Mary has chosen the better part, which will not be taken away from her.'

- In the traditional interpretation of this gospel, prayer and action are pitted against each other. Or, we could see it as food versus the communion of spirits. We can afford to do with less food or to go without food for a time. We can never afford to be unaware of the deeper mysteries. Sometimes we go the opposite way. We don't miss a meal but we do forget to stop for a few moments to dip into the depths of being quiet and totally present.

Wednesday 11 October
Luke 11:1–4

He was praying in a certain place, and after he had finished, one of his disciples said to him, 'Lord, teach us to pray, as John taught his disciples.' He said to them, 'When you pray, say:

Father, hallowed be your name.
　　Your kingdom come.
　　Give us each day our daily bread.
　　And forgive us our sins,
　　　　for we ourselves forgive everyone indebted to us.
　　And do not bring us to the time of trial.'

- The disciples were looking outwards at John and his disciples, at Jesus in prayer. Jesus suggests to them that their prayer might begin by looking in, by starting with our most important relationships. To call God 'Father' is to recognise where my life comes from and establishes me in relation to others. If I focus on my needs, it is so that I might grow in trust as I recognise who is ready to answer them.

Thursday 12 October
Luke 11:5–13

And he said to them, 'Suppose one of you has a friend, and you go to him at midnight and say to him, "Friend, lend me three loaves of bread; for a friend of mine has arrived, and I have nothing to set before him." And he answers from within, "Do not bother me; the door has already been locked, and my children are with me in bed; I cannot get up and give you anything." I tell you, even though he will not get up and give him anything because he is his friend, at least because of his persistence he will get up and give him whatever he needs.

'So I say to you, Ask, and it will be given to you; search, and you will find; knock, and the door will be opened for you. For everyone who asks receives, and everyone who searches finds, and for everyone who knocks, the door will be opened. Is there anyone among you who, if your child asks for a fish, will give a snake instead of a fish? Or if the child asks for an egg, will give a scorpion? If you then, who are evil, know how to give good gifts to your children, how much more will the heavenly Father give the Holy Spirit to those who ask him!'

- An Australian Lutheran pastor put it like this: 'Prayer is not humans taking the initiative and trying to reach up to God attempting to speak in his ear. The picture that comes to mind here is one of a small child who wants to tell his dad something really important. The dad bends down, lovingly puts his arm around the child and lets the child whisper in his ear. In this sense then prayer is not so much us reaching up to God with special words or techniques, but it is God reaching down to us.'

Friday 13 October
Luke 11:15–26

But some of them said, 'He casts out demons by Beelzebul, the ruler of the demons.' Others, to test him, kept demanding from him a sign from heaven. But he knew what they were thinking and said to them, 'Every kingdom divided against itself becomes a desert, and house falls on house. If Satan also is divided against himself, how will his kingdom stand? —for you say that I cast out the demons by Beelzebul. Now if I cast out the demons by Beelzebul, by whom do your exorcists cast them out? Therefore they will be your judges. But if it is by the finger of God that I cast out the demons, then the kingdom of God has come to you. When a strong man, fully armed, guards his castle, his property is safe. But when one stronger than he attacks him and overpowers him, he takes away his armour in which he trusted and divides his plunder. Whoever is not with me is against me, and whoever does not gather with me scatters.

'When the unclean spirit has gone out of a person, it wanders through waterless regions looking for a resting-place, but not finding any, it says, "I will return to my house from which I came." When it comes, it finds it swept and put in order. Then it goes and brings seven other spirits more evil than itself, and they enter and live there; and the last state of that person is worse than the first.'

- How could anyone say that Jesus was casting out demons through the power of the prince of demons? The hardness of heart, so evident all around us, and within us, remains a great mystery: how can we resist the truth, goodness, justice, finding empty excuses to justify our hardness of heart? How can so much human suffering, so much ecological degradation, leave us unmoved? I ask the Lord for an open heart, and for light to see the hardness in me.

Saturday 14 October
Luke 11:27–28

While he was saying this, a woman in the crowd raised her voice and said to him, 'Blessed is the womb that bore you and the breasts that nursed you!' But he said, 'Blessed rather are those who hear the word of God and obey it!'

- I spend time rejoicing with Mary, the mother of Jesus, the one who was closest to him, and the greatest influence on his life.

- I ask her to help me grow in trust and freedom of heart, so that I too, like her, can hear the word of God and keep it.

15–21 October 2023

Something to think and pray about each day this week:

Anger is a gift from God. This can sound surprising, shocking even, as so many people struggle with anger and frustration, often feeling they live under a heavy cloud of resentment. We need only look at Jesus clearing the Temple (John 2:13–22) to realise how he uses anger effectively and appropriately to correct a wrong (trading and selling) that had crept into this sacred place.

Anger is a volatile and fiery emotion; it can flare quickly, easily dominate our thinking and take over our minds and actions to the point where it comes out as harsh, ugly and damaging. The problem is that incorrectly used it is hijacked by our emotions, not used for God's plan.

If the purpose of anger is to right a wrong, then we have to be careful to use it appropriately and to direct it at the problem. Many people end up carrying enormous amounts of unexpressed anger because of real or perceived hurts, or end up letting fly at anyone or anything that gets in the way (I see red and let go so all around me feel the anger).

Asking 'How would God want me to express this?' can help turn down the emotional heat so that another person can hear the words and choose how to act. It is the difference between aggression and assertion; Jesus knew how to combine love and criticism in a powerful way. Sometimes we come to a point where we don't need to express our anger; we can move beyond it. So we can ask ourselves, am I able to let it go and let God?

Brendan McManus SJ and Jim Deeds,
Deeper into the Mess: Praying Through Tough Times

The Presence of God
'Be still, and know that I am God!' (Psalm 46:10) Lord, your words lead us to the calmness and greatness of your presence.

Freedom
If God were trying to tell me something, would I know?
If God were reassuring me or challenging me, would I notice?
I ask for the grace to be free of my own preoccupations
and open to what God may be saying to me.

Consciousness
In the presence of my loving Creator, I look honestly at my feelings over the past day: the highs, the lows and the level ground. Can I see where the Lord has been present?

The Word
In this expectant state of mind, please turn to the text for the day with confidence. Believe that the Holy Spirit is present and may reveal whatever the passage has to say to you. Read reflectively, listening with a third ear to what may be going on in your heart.
(Please turn to the Scripture on the following pages. Inspiration points are there, should you need them. When you are ready, return here to continue.)

Conversation
Remembering that I am still in God's presence,
I imagine Jesus standing or sitting beside me,
and I say whatever is on my mind, whatever is in my heart,
speaking as one friend to another.

Conclusion
Glory be to the Father, and to the Son, and to the Holy Spirit,
As it was in the beginning, is now and ever shall be,
World without end. Amen.

Sunday 15 October
Twenty-eighth Sunday in Ordinary Time
Matthew 22:1–14

Once more Jesus spoke to them in parables, saying: 'The kingdom of heaven may be compared to a king who gave a wedding banquet for his son. He sent his slaves to call those who had been invited to the wedding banquet, but they would not come. Again he sent other slaves, saying, "Tell those who have been invited: Look, I have prepared my dinner, my oxen and my fat calves have been slaughtered, and everything is ready; come to the wedding banquet." But they made light of it and went away, one to his farm, another to his business, while the rest seized his slaves, maltreated them, and killed them. The king was enraged. He sent his troops, destroyed those murderers, and burned their city. Then he said to his slaves, "The wedding is ready, but those invited were not worthy. Go therefore into the main streets, and invite everyone you find to the wedding banquet." Those slaves went out into the streets and gathered all whom they found, both good and bad; so the wedding hall was filled with guests.

'But when the king came in to see the guests, he noticed a man there who was not wearing a wedding robe, and he said to him, "Friend, how did you get in here without a wedding robe?" And he was speechless. Then the king said to the attendants, "Bind him hand and foot, and throw him into the outer darkness, where there will be weeping and gnashing of teeth." For many are called, but few are chosen.'

- This parable tells a very strange story: all those who received the invitation to the king's banquet not only refused to attend but treated the messengers very badly. The king was not to be stopped: he sent his servants to the crossroads and they gathered 'all whom they found, both good and bad'. The hall was full. God's invitation to partake of his great banquet is not restricted to the Jews, his kingdom is now open to all, without any distinction, even to those who seem unworthy. I stand and wonder at God's goodness and mercy towards all. I ask to be like the Father in his mercy and generosity.

Monday 16 October
Luke 11:29–32

When the crowds were increasing, he began to say, 'This generation is an evil generation; it asks for a sign, but no sign will be given to it except the sign of Jonah. For just as Jonah became a sign to the people of Nineveh, so the Son of Man will be to this generation. The queen of the South will rise at the judgement with the people of this generation and condemn them, because she came from the ends of the earth to listen to the wisdom of Solomon, and see, something greater than Solomon is here! The people of Nineveh will rise up at the judgement with this generation and condemn it, because they repented at the proclamation of Jonah, and see, something greater than Jonah is here!'

• Jonah is the sign of God's care for all. His call was to go to a far country who did not know him or his God. He is also a sign of God's care for us individually – his care was for Jonah's safety. Jonah's strength was in his trust in God. Prayer is a time of allowing trust in God to grow and become a central part of our being.

Tuesday 17 October
Luke 11:37–41

While he was speaking, a Pharisee invited him to dine with him; so he went in and took his place at the table. The Pharisee was amazed to see that he did not first wash before dinner. Then the Lord said to him, 'Now you Pharisees clean the outside of the cup and of the dish, but inside you are full of greed and wickedness. You fools! Did not the one who made the outside make the inside also? So give for alms those things that are within; and see, everything will be clean for you.'

• The Pharisees seem to have been the only group of people who really upset Jesus. They were good people, keen to observe the law as perfectly as possible, but this often made them blind to more important things. Can I see a Pharisee in my heart, big or small? I pray for light and for integrity in all that I do. And I ask pardon for being so inconsistent.

Wednesday 18 October
St Luke, Evangelist
Luke 10:1–9

After this the Lord appointed seventy others and sent them on ahead of him in pairs to every town and place where he himself intended to go. He said to them, 'The harvest is plentiful, but the labourers are few; therefore ask the Lord of the harvest to send out labourers into his harvest. Go on your way. See, I am sending you out like lambs into the midst of wolves. Carry no purse, no bag, no sandals; and greet no one on the road. Whatever house you enter, first say, "Peace to this house!" And if anyone is there who shares in peace, your peace will rest on that person; but if not, it will return to you. Remain in the same house, eating and drinking whatever they provide, for the labourer deserves to be paid. Do not move about from house to house. Whenever you enter a town and its people welcome you, eat what is set before you; cure the sick who are there, and say to them, "The kingdom of God has come near to you."'

- 'Greet no one on the road.' The single-minded urgency of the gospel requires a suspension of social norms, even of basic travellers' courtesy. What does my own spiritual 'journey' look like? Does it have something of the same intensity and focus that makes people take notice of something unusual? Do I come across as someone on a mission?

Thursday 19 October
Luke 11:47–54

And Jesus said to the Pharisees, 'Woe to you! For you build the tombs of the prophets whom your ancestors killed. So you are witnesses and approve of the deeds of your ancestors; for they killed them, and you build their tombs. Therefore also the Wisdom of God said, "I will send them prophets and apostles, some of whom they will kill and persecute", so that this generation may be charged with the blood of all the prophets shed since the foundation of the world, from the blood of Abel to the blood of Zechariah, who perished between the altar and the sanctuary. Yes, I tell you, it will be charged against this generation. Woe to you lawyers! For you have taken away the key of knowledge; you did not enter yourselves, and you hindered those who were entering.'

When he went outside, the scribes and the Pharisees began to be very hostile towards him and to cross-examine him about many things, lying in wait for him to catch him in something he might say.

- Reflecting on the last twenty-four hours, is there any time that I acted in a way contrary to what I believe? Or pretended to be something that I am not? How might I avoid this in the day ahead?

Friday 20 October
Luke 12:1–7

Meanwhile, when the crowd gathered in thousands, so that they trampled on one another, he began to speak first to his disciples, 'Beware of the yeast of the Pharisees, that is, their hypocrisy. Nothing is covered up that will not be uncovered, and nothing secret that will not become known. Therefore whatever you have said in the dark will be heard in the light, and what you have whispered behind closed doors will be proclaimed from the housetops.

'I tell you, my friends, do not fear those who kill the body, and after that can do nothing more. But I will warn you whom to fear: fear him who, after he has killed, has authority to cast into hell. Yes, I tell you, fear him! Are not five sparrows sold for two pennies? Yet not one of them is forgotten in God's sight. But even the hairs of your head are all counted. Do not be afraid; you are of more value than many sparrows.'

- People who are suffering or are on the fringes of society may not know that they are 'of more value than many sparrows'. Trusting that the millions of people who suffer terrible trials of injustice here on earth will find consolation in the life after death is a huge leap of faith. Even the most ordinary life has its trials and needs the leap of faith that hopes for life after death. The message is, do not fear. Every little bird is cared for by God. Even the hairs of our heads are counted.

Saturday 21 October
Luke 12:8–12

And Jesus said, 'And I tell you, everyone who acknowledges me before others, the Son of Man also will acknowledge before the angels of God; but whoever denies me before others will be denied before the angels of God. And everyone who speaks a word against the Son of Man will be forgiven; but whoever blasphemes against the Holy Spirit will not be forgiven. When they bring you before the synagogues, the rulers, and the authorities, do not worry about how you are to defend yourselves or what you are to say; for the Holy Spirit will teach you at that very hour what you ought to say.'

- It is not always easy to declare oneself openly for Jesus in the presence of others. Sometimes because we deem it counterproductive, but at other times because we are fearful of what the others might think about us. Today I ask for the gift of light and for fortitude, to be able to live in integrity before Jesus and before others.

The Twenty-ninth Week in Ordinary Time
22–28 October 2023

Something to think and pray about each day this week:

We are called to forgive; and that can be really difficult. You have been defrauded by the banks of your life's savings – can you forgive? You were abused as a child – can you forgive? You were done out of a job because another lied to get it – can you forgive? The answer is maybe 'no'. What then does God want? He asks us to open our hearts to the other so that we may forgive. Forgiveness is the deepest of God's desires on our behalf, and he hopes that we can forgive each other.

Our hurts and burdens are heavy to carry through life. To forgive can release some of that weight. The person who hurt us may be dead, or may not even know (or care) that we are hurting. When we desire to forgive but don't know how, one way of looking for this strength is to pray for it. We often pray, *'Lord, make my heart like yours'*. When we pray that we are praying to be forgiving people!

Another way is to pray for the person. When we realise that as God loves me, he also loves everyone, we may find a spark or light of forgiveness in our souls.

Out of this we may find the will to meet the other and talk to him or her, and find the grace of forgiveness between us.

Forgiveness sometimes comes slowly. When God sees us wanting to be on the road to forgiveness, he gives us the graces we need to unburden ourselves and be able to love like him.

Donal Neary SJ,
Gospel Reflections for Sundays of Year A

The Presence of God

As I sit here, the beating of my heart,
the ebb and flow of my breathing, the movements of my mind
are all signs of God's ongoing creation of me.

Freedom

It is so easy to get caught up
with the trappings of wealth in this life.
Grant, O Lord, that I may be free
from greed and selfishness.
Remind me that the best things in life are free:
Love, laughter, caring and sharing.

Consciousness

Knowing that God loves me unconditionally, I can afford to be honest
about how I am.
How has the day been, and how do I feel now? I share my feelings openly
with the Lord.

The Word

Lord Jesus, you became human to communicate with me.
You walked and worked on this earth.
You endured the heat and struggled with the cold.
All your time on this earth was spent in caring for humanity.
You healed the sick, you raised the dead.
Most important of all, you saved me from death.
(Please turn to the Scripture on the following pages. Inspiration points are there, should you need them. When you are ready, return here to continue.)

Conversation

Sometimes I wonder what I might say if I were to meet you in person, Lord. I think I might say, 'Thank you', because you are always there for me.

Conclusion

I thank God for these moments we have spent together and for any insights I have been given concerning the text.

Sunday 22 October
Twenty-ninth Sunday in Ordinary Time
Matthew 22:15–21

Then the Pharisees went and plotted to entrap him in what he said. So they sent their disciples to him, along with the Herodians, saying, 'Teacher, we know that you are sincere, and teach the way of God in accordance with truth, and show deference to no one; for you do not regard people with partiality. Tell us, then, what you think. Is it lawful to pay taxes to the emperor, or not?' But Jesus, aware of their malice, said, 'Why are you putting me to the test, you hypocrites? Show me the coin used for the tax.' And they brought him a denarius. Then he said to them, 'Whose head is this, and whose title?' They answered, 'The emperor's.' Then he said to them, 'Give therefore to the emperor the things that are the emperor's, and to God the things that are God's.'

- To be a good citizen and to serve God are not in contradiction, since God works through all human systems and institutions to build the final community of love. God needs me to help build good relationships wherever I find myself.

Monday 23 October
Luke 12:13–21

Someone in the crowd said to him, 'Teacher, tell my brother to divide the family inheritance with me.' But he said to him, 'Friend, who set me to be a judge or arbitrator over you?' And he said to them, 'Take care! Be on your guard against all kinds of greed; for one's life does not consist in the abundance of possessions.' Then he told them a parable: 'The land of a rich man produced abundantly. And he thought to himself, "What should I do, for I have no place to store my crops?" Then he said, "I will do this: I will pull down my barns and build larger ones, and there I will store all my grain and my goods. And I will say to my soul, Soul, you have ample goods laid up for many years; relax, eat, drink, be merry." But God said to him, "You fool! This very night your life is being demanded of you. And the things you have prepared, whose will they be?" So it is with those who store up treasures for themselves but are not rich towards God.'

- This is the parable for our times, where most of us seem obsessed with the idea of accumulating more and more possessions, as if the value of our life depends on how much we possess. I might not be the greedy person who is ready to trample over others to get more things, but I need to ask myself to what extent I place my security in material things. I ask for light and for more inner freedom.

Tuesday 24 October
Luke 12:35–38

Jesus said to his disciples, 'Be dressed for action and have your lamps lit; be like those who are waiting for their master to return from the wedding banquet, so that they may open the door for him as soon as he comes and knocks. Blessed are those slaves whom the master finds alert when he comes; truly I tell you, he will fasten his belt and have them sit down to eat, and he will come and serve them. If he comes during the middle of the night, or near dawn, and finds them so, blessed are those slaves.'

- There is a condition called acedia. It is a listlessness of the soul which the ancient monks called 'the noonday devil' – a demonic force intent on breaking the monks' spiritual resolve. When life seems overwhelming, and I am paralysed by fear, fatigue and inertia, can I look forward to the end of the day when Jesus brings me to a laden table, sits down beside me and talks with me about what I have been through?

Wednesday 25 October
Luke 12:39–48

Jesus said to his disciples, 'But know this: if the owner of the house had known at what hour the thief was coming, he would not have let his house be broken into. You also must be ready, for the Son of Man is coming at an unexpected hour.'

Peter said, 'Lord, are you telling this parable for us or for everyone?' And the Lord said, 'Who then is the faithful and prudent manager whom his master will put in charge of his slaves, to give them their allowance of food at the proper time? Blessed is that slave whom his master will find at work when he arrives. Truly I tell you, he will put that one in charge of all his possessions. But if that slave says to himself, "My master is delayed in coming", and if he begins to beat the other slaves, men and women, and to eat and drink and get drunk, the master of that slave will come on a day when he does not expect him and at an hour that he does not know, and will cut him in pieces, and put him with the unfaithful. That slave who knew what his master wanted, but did not prepare himself or do what was wanted, will receive a severe beating. But one who did not know and did what deserved a beating will receive a light beating. From everyone to whom much has been given, much will be required; and from one to whom much has been entrusted, even more will be demanded.'

• Lord, grant that I may live in such a way that your coming at the close of my earthly life will not be something to be feared, but to be looked forward to with the most joyful anticipation.

Thursday 26 October
Luke 12:49–53

Jesus said, 'I came to bring fire to the earth, and how I wish it were already kindled! I have a baptism with which to be baptised, and what stress I am under until it is completed! Do you think that I have come to bring peace to the earth? No, I tell you, but rather division! From now on, five in one household will be divided, three against two and two against three; they will be divided:

> father against son
>   and son against father,
> mother against daughter
>   and daughter against mother,
> mother-in-law against her daughter-in-law
>   and daughter-in-law against mother-in-law.'

• He came to bring division, and we know what this means: following Jesus can bring us into confrontation with others, even with our closest and dearest. I ask for wisdom and fortitude to know how best to deal with situations when my beliefs lead to differences with those around me.

Friday 27 October
Luke 12:54–59

He also said to the crowds, 'When you see a cloud rising in the west, you immediately say, "It is going to rain"; and so it happens. And when you see the south wind blowing, you say, "There will be scorching heat"; and it happens. You hypocrites! You know how to interpret the appearance of earth and sky, but why do you not know how to interpret the present time?

'And why do you not judge for yourselves what is right? Thus, when you go with your accuser before a magistrate, on the way make an effort to settle the case, or you may be dragged before the judge, and the judge hand you over to the officer, and the officer throw you in prison. I tell you, you will never get out until you have paid the very last penny.'

- The second part of the reading may seem unconnected to the first. However, this is not the case. Jesus is asking us to put things right while there is still time. What do I need to put right in my life?

Saturday 28 October
Ss Simon and Jude, Apostles
Luke 6:12–16

Now during those days he went out to the mountain to pray; and he spent the night in prayer to God. And when day came, he called his disciples and chose twelve of them, whom he also named apostles: Simon, whom he named Peter, and his brother Andrew, and James, and John, and Philip, and Bartholomew, and Matthew, and Thomas, and James son of Alphaeus, and Simon, who was called the Zealot, and Judas son of James, and Judas Iscariot, who became a traitor.

- Jesus spent the night in prayer before choosing his apostles. Do I pray before making an important decision?

29 October–4 November 2023

Something to think and pray about each day this week:

Gardens offer endless scope for budding mystics! They are safe places, places of life, abounding in beauty. Where there is a garden, there will be water and living things with their varied beauty. Charles Darwin, although remembered as the great proponent of evolution, saw himself primarily as a beholder of the natural world. He spent much of his life contemplating the simplest things, and he ends his great work, *The Origin of Species,* by noting: 'It is interesting to contemplate an entangled bank … '. This humble bank he studied is clothed with many plants, with birds singing, insects flitting about and worms crawling through the damp earth. It leads him to reflect that 'these elaborately constructed forms, so different from each other and dependent on each other … have all been produced by laws acting around us.'

So, find your entangled bank, contemplate it, muse on its long history and reflect on what it is trying to say to you. Let this be your holy place where you fall in love with the natural world and with its maker. Let the tapestry of life come alive under your gaze. Perhaps you may exclaim, like Darwin, 'It has been for me a glorious day, like giving to a blind man eyes.'

Brian Grogan SJ,
Creation Walk: The Amazing Story of a Small Blue Planet

The Presence of God
At any time of the day or night we can call on Jesus.
He is always waiting, listening for our call.
What a wonderful blessing.
No phone needed, no e-mails, just a whisper.

Freedom
Lord, grant me the grace to have freedom of the spirit. Cleanse my heart
and soul so that I may live joyously in your love.

Consciousness
Knowing that God loves me unconditionally, I look honestly over the
past day, its events, and my feelings. Do I have something to be grateful
for? Then I give thanks. Is there something I am sorry for? Then I ask
forgiveness.

The Word
The word of God comes down to us through the Scriptures.
May the Holy Spirit enlighten my mind and my heart
to respond to the gospel teachings:
to love my neighbour as myself,
to care for my sisters and brothers in Christ.
*(Please turn to the Scripture on the following pages. Inspiration points are there,
should you need them. When you are ready, return here to continue.)*

Conversation
I know with certainty that there were times when you carried me, Lord.
There were times when it was through your strength that I got through
the dark times in my life.

Conclusion
Glory be to the Father, and to the Son, and to the Holy Spirit,
As it was in the beginning, is now and ever shall be,
World without end. Amen.

Sunday 29 October
Thirtieth Sunday in Ordinary Time
Matthew 22:34–40

When the Pharisees heard that he had silenced the Sadducees, they gathered together, and one of them, a lawyer, asked him a question to test him. 'Teacher, which commandment in the law is the greatest?' He said to him, '"You shall love the Lord your God with all your heart, and with all your soul, and with all your mind." This is the greatest and first commandment. And a second is like it: "You shall love your neighbour as yourself." On these two commandments hang all the law and the prophets.'

- I recall what St Paul once said, that whatever I do without love is absolutely worthless. I look at the quality of my love, and ask for a truly loving heart.

Monday 30 October
Luke 13:10–17

Now he was teaching in one of the synagogues on the sabbath. And just then there appeared a woman with a spirit that had crippled her for eighteen years. She was bent over and was quite unable to stand up straight. When Jesus saw her, he called her over and said, 'Woman, you are set free from your ailment.' When he laid his hands on her, immediately she stood up straight and began praising God. But the leader of the synagogue, indignant because Jesus had cured on the sabbath, kept saying to the crowd, 'There are six days on which work ought to be done; come on those days and be cured, and not on the sabbath day.' But the Lord answered him and said, 'You hypocrites! Does not each of you on the sabbath untie his ox or his donkey from the manger, and lead it away to give it water? And ought not this woman, a daughter of Abraham whom Satan bound for eighteen long years, be set free from this bondage on the sabbath day?' When he said this, all his opponents were put to shame; and the entire crowd was rejoicing at all the wonderful things that he was doing.

- For Jesus mercy and compassion are paramount. I ask for a heart that is like the heart of Jesus, always compassionate and ready to defend the poor and suffering.

Tuesday 31 October
Luke 13:18–21

He said therefore, 'What is the kingdom of God like? And to what should I compare it? It is like a mustard seed that someone took and sowed in the garden; it grew and became a tree, and the birds of the air made nests in its branches.'

And again he said, 'To what should I compare the kingdom of God? It is like yeast that a woman took and mixed in with three measures of flour until all of it was leavened.'

- To have an effect on the dough the leaven does not need to be added in large quanitites, it just needs to form part of the whole mix, indistinguishable from it. So also the kingdom, if it is really embedded in the world, will make its presence felt and transform the world. A presence that is strong but separate from the world, or even opposed to it, will not have any effect. I pray for courage to enter the struggle to change the world through my loving presence.

Wednesday 1 November
The Solemnity of All Saints
Matthew 5:1–12

When Jesus saw the crowds, he went up the mountain; and after he sat down, his disciples came to him. Then he began to speak, and taught them, saying:

'Blessed are the poor in spirit, for theirs is the kingdom of heaven.

'Blessed are those who mourn, for they will be comforted.

'Blessed are the meek, for they will inherit the earth.

'Blessed are those who hunger and thirst for righteousness,
    for they will be filled.

'Blessed are the merciful, for they will receive mercy.

'Blessed are the pure in heart, for they will see God.

'Blessed are the peacemakers, for they will be called children of
    God.

'Blessed are those who are persecuted for righteousness' sake, for
    theirs is the kingdom of heaven.

'Blessed are you when people revile you and persecute you and utter
    all kinds of evil against you falsely on my account. Rejoice and

be glad, for your reward is great in heaven, for in the same way they persecuted the prophets who were before you.'

- We have no portrait of you, Lord, but in the Beatitudes you show us your interior landscape, the source of your joy. This is not a set of regulations, but a vision of where true happiness lies. Let me taste it, phrase by phrase.

- I might choose two of these beatitudes to be a backdrop to my prayer and reflection today: one that affirms me and one that calls me further.

Thursday 2 November
The Commemoration of All the Faithful Departed (All Souls)
John 6:37–40

And Jesus said to them, 'Everything that the Father gives me will come to me, and anyone who comes to me I will never drive away; for I have come down from heaven, not to do my own will, but the will of him who sent me. And this is the will of him who sent me, that I should lose nothing of all that he has given me, but raise it up on the last day. This is indeed the will of my Father, that all who see the Son and believe in him may have eternal life; and I will raise them up on the last day.'

- I may choose to reflect before God on my own death, whether I feel it near or not. It is the greatest demand on my inner freedom, an invitation to welcome the small deaths that daily life, especially my relationships, demand of me. I ask to grow in the freedom to live life fully: even my own life, so limited and vulnerable, and including death at some point, is called to live with God for eternity, it is already life eternal.

Friday 3 November
Luke 14:1–6

On one occasion when Jesus was going to the house of a leader of the Pharisees to eat a meal on the sabbath, they were watching him closely. Just then, in front of him, there was a man who had dropsy. And Jesus asked the lawyers and Pharisees, 'Is it lawful to cure people on the sabbath, or not?' But they were silent. So Jesus took him and healed him, and sent him away. Then he said to them, 'If one of you has a child or an ox that has fallen into a well, will you not immediately pull it out on a sabbath day?' And they could not reply to this.

• The Pharisees would have the dropsical man wait for his healing until the sabbath was over. Do I ever enter prayer while leaving unaddressed the need of someone who relies on me?

Saturday 4 November
Luke 14:1, 7–11

On one occasion when Jesus was going to the house of a leader of the Pharisees to eat a meal on the sabbath, they were watching him closely.

When he noticed how the guests chose the places of honour, he told them a parable. 'When you are invited by someone to a wedding banquet, do not sit down at the place of honour, in case someone more distinguished than you has been invited by your host; and the host who invited both of you may come and say to you, "Give this person your place", and then in disgrace you would start to take the lowest place. But when you are invited, go and sit down at the lowest place, so that when your host comes, he may say to you, "Friend, move up higher"; then you will be honoured in the presence of all who sit at the table with you. For all who exalt themselves will be humbled, and those who humble themselves will be exalted.'

• Is Jesus being petty, or is he reminding us that we would do well to look at how we behave even in small everyday things to discover what really lies in our hearts? I ask him to give me light and freedom in my everyday dealings with others, especially in my competitive world.

The Thirty-first Week in Ordinary Time
5–11 November 2023

Something to think and pray about each day this week:

Our lives are often shrouded in mystery. Events happen (or don't happen) and we feel confused, bemused, amazed or anxious. What does it all mean? Is there a purpose to anything at all? We can have so many questions. Some seek certainty in the face of mystery. We seek it in science. We seek it in rules. We seek it in religion. We seek it in a combination of all of these. And yet, mystery still exists. Just when we feel certain about this or that, something happens to us or to the world around us to cause uncertainty to return and the mystery to continue.

We are faced with: illness, grief, natural disaster, terrorism, political upheaval, untimely death, poverty, cruelty, and we wonder: what is this all about?

Equally we are faced with or experience extreme self-sacrifice, generosity beyond belief, selfless love, wisdom, leadership, and we wonder: where did that come from?

Life itself is a mystery. And a glorious one at that! How did we get here? What is life all about? Wonderful mysteries!

Perhaps in the face of these mysteries, we could simply – just for a wee while – rest in the mystery.

Jim Deeds and Brendan McManus SJ,
Finding God in the Mess: Meditations for Mindful Living

The Presence of God

Dear Jesus, as I call on you today, I realise that often I come asking for favours. Today I'd like just to be in your presence. Draw my heart in response to your love.

Freedom

God my creator, you gave me life and the gift of freedom. Through your love I exist in this world. May I never take the gift of life for granted. May I always respect others' right to life.

Consciousness

Dear Lord, help me to remember that you gave me life. Teach me to slow down, to be still and enjoy the pleasures created for me. To be aware of the beauty that surrounds me: the marvel of mountains, the calmness of lakes, the fragility of a flower petal. I need to remember that all these things come from you.

The Word

The word of God comes down to us through the Scriptures. May the Holy Spirit enlighten my mind and my heart to respond to the gospel teachings.

(Please turn to the Scripture on the following pages. Inspiration points are there, should you need them. When you are ready, return here to continue.)

Conversation

What feelings are rising in me as I pray and reflect on God's word? I imagine Jesus himself sitting or standing near me, and I open my heart to him.

Conclusion

I thank God for these moments we have spent together and for any insights I have been given concerning the text.

Sunday 5 November
Thirty-first Sunday in Ordinary Time
Matthew 23:1–12

Then Jesus said to the crowds and to his disciples, 'The scribes and the Pharisees sit on Moses' seat; therefore, do whatever they teach you and follow it; but do not do as they do, for they do not practise what they teach. They tie up heavy burdens, hard to bear, and lay them on the shoulders of others; but they themselves are unwilling to lift a finger to move them. They do all their deeds to be seen by others; for they make their phylacteries broad and their fringes long. They love to have the place of honour at banquets and the best seats in the synagogues, and to be greeted with respect in the market-places, and to have people call them rabbi. But you are not to be called rabbi, for you have one teacher, and you are all students. And call no one your father on earth, for you have one Father – the one in heaven. Nor are you to be called instructors, for you have one instructor, the Messiah. The greatest among you will be your servant. All who exalt themselves will be humbled, and all who humble themselves will be exalted.'

• What's it like to stand before Jesus today, with all my failures and my giftedness, and to be loved without conditions, without any reservations? Are there elements of 'control' in the way I love others? I talk to Jesus about this and how he sees and loves me.

Monday 6 November
Luke 14:12–14

He said also to the one who had invited him, 'When you give a luncheon or a dinner, do not invite your friends or your brothers or your relatives or rich neighbours, in case they may invite you in return, and you would be repaid. But when you give a banquet, invite the poor, the crippled, the lame, and the blind. And you will be blessed, because they cannot repay you, for you will be repaid at the resurrection of the righteous.'

• The writers of the first centuries of Christianity used to say that it will be the poor who will welcome us at the doors of heaven. Will they know me well enough to let me in, do they have an important place in my heart?

Tuesday 7 November
Luke 14:15–24

One of the dinner guests, on hearing this, said to him, 'Blessed is anyone who will eat bread in the kingdom of God!' Then Jesus said to him, 'Someone gave a great dinner and invited many. At the time for the dinner he sent his slave to say to those who had been invited, "Come; for everything is ready now." But they all alike began to make excuses. The first said to him, "I have bought a piece of land, and I must go out and see it; please accept my apologies." Another said, "I have bought five yoke of oxen, and I am going to try them out; please accept my apologies." Another said, "I have just been married, and therefore I cannot come." So the slave returned and reported this to his master. Then the owner of the house became angry and said to his slave, "Go out at once into the streets and lanes of the town and bring in the poor, the crippled, the blind, and the lame." And the slave said, "Sir, what you ordered has been done, and there is still room." Then the master said to the slave, "Go out into the roads and lanes, and compel people to come in, so that my house may be filled. For I tell you, none of those who were invited will taste my dinner."'

• How would I feel if I were invited to a dinner at which Jesus was going to be present? Would I care if I knew none of the other guests? Would I, instead, feel a common bond with all who were invited with me, each rejoicing at the other's inclusion in the feast?

• Lord, let me hear you calling me, gently but insistently, out of my comfort zone.

Wednesday 8 November
Luke 14:25–33

Now large crowds were travelling with him; and he turned and said to them, 'Whoever comes to me and does not hate father and mother, wife and children, brothers and sisters, yes, and even life itself, cannot be my disciple. Whoever does not carry the cross and follow me cannot be my disciple. For which of you, intending to build a tower, does not first sit down and estimate the cost, to see whether he has enough to complete it? Otherwise, when he has laid a foundation and is not able to finish, all who see it will begin to ridicule him, saying, "This fellow began to build and was not able to finish." Or what king, going out to wage war against another king, will not sit down first and consider whether he is able with ten thousand to oppose the one who comes against him with twenty thousand? If he cannot, then, while the other is still far away, he sends a delegation and asks for the terms of peace. So therefore, none of you can become my disciple if you do not give up all your possessions.'

- Jesus wants us to know the scale of the task ahead of us; when it seems too much for us, what are we to do? To whom can we turn for help? I ask God to keep me in mind of my own need, that I may have the humility and trust always to seek help.

Thursday 9 November
The Dedication of the Lateran Basilica
John 2:13–22

The Passover of the Jews was near, and Jesus went up to Jerusalem. In the temple he found people selling cattle, sheep, and doves, and the money-changers seated at their tables. Making a whip of cords, he drove all of them out of the temple, both the sheep and the cattle. He also poured out the coins of the money-changers and overturned their tables. He told those who were selling the doves, 'Take these things out of here! Stop making my Father's house a market-place!' His disciples remembered that it was written, 'Zeal for your house will consume me.' The Jews then said to him, 'What sign can you show us for doing this?' Jesus answered them, 'Destroy this temple, and in three days I will raise it up.' The Jews then said, 'This temple has been under construction for forty-six years, and will you raise it up in three days?' But he was speaking of the temple of his body. After he was raised from the dead, his disciples remembered that he had said this; and they believed the scripture and the word that Jesus had spoken.

- Jesus cautions us against being careless or blasé. I think again about what I need to take him seriously, reviewing my life with the help of the Holy Spirit so I may recognise how I honour what is really important.

Friday 10 November
Luke 16:1–8

Then Jesus said to the disciples, 'There was a rich man who had a manager, and charges were brought to him that this man was squandering his property. So he summoned him and said to him, "What is this that I hear about you? Give me an account of your management, because you cannot be my manager any longer." Then the manager said to himself, "What will I do, now that my master is taking the position away from me? I am not strong enough to dig, and I am ashamed to beg. I have decided what to do so that, when I am dismissed as manager, people may welcome me into their homes." So, summoning his master's debtors one by one, he asked the first, "How much do you owe my master?" He answered, "A hundred jugs of olive oil." He said to him, "Take your bill, sit down quickly, and make it fifty." Then he asked another, "And how much do you owe?" He replied, "A hundred containers of wheat." He said to him, "Take your bill and make it eighty." And his master commended the dishonest manager because he had acted shrewdly; for the children of this age are more shrewd in dealing with their own generation than are the children of light.'

- Jesus calls me to take care of the resources that are available to me. I consider the benefits that I have – such as intelligence, opportunities and time – and ask God how I might best use them for God's glory, for the service of others and for my own growth.

Saturday 11 November
Luke 16:9–15

Jesus said to them, 'And I tell you, make friends for yourselves by means of dishonest wealth so that when it is gone, they may welcome you into the eternal homes.

'Whoever is faithful in a very little is faithful also in much; and whoever is dishonest in a very little is dishonest also in much. If then you have not been faithful with the dishonest wealth, who will entrust to you the true riches? And if you have not been faithful with what belongs to another, who will give you what is your own? No slave can serve two masters; for a slave will either hate the one and love the other, or be devoted to the one and despise the other. You cannot serve God and wealth.'

The Pharisees, who were lovers of money, heard all this, and they ridiculed him. So he said to them, 'You are those who justify yourselves in the sight of others; but God knows your hearts; for what is prized by human beings is an abomination in the sight of God.'

- What is my relationship with money? How much of my time and energy does it take up? Has it become my master? What do I think Jesus is inviting me to in relation to my possessions? I talk to him honestly about it.

12–18 November 2023

Something to think and pray about each day this week:

I have a friend who, at sixteen, started taking drugs. By age twenty-two his life seemed to be completely destroyed. He had no home, no family and almost no possessions, except the clothes he stood up in. He had tried to kill himself three times. When he went to church, it was not to pray, but to beg from the people there. He found that Christians are most generous just after Mass.

One Sunday, the Gospel of the Transfiguration was read. The priest said in his sermon: 'the meaning of the Transfiguration is that God does not make junk. God created the world, and he is not a bad workman. God sent his only-begotten Son into the world to die and rise again for our salvation.'

At the end of the homily the priest made everyone stand up and say: 'God made me. God doesn't make junk.' He made them say it out loud three times. Along with everyone else my friend had to stand up and say three times aloud, 'God made me. God doesn't make junk.'

For days, those words burned into his heart: 'God doesn't make junk.' It became his prayer; it became his faith; it became his life. With that courage behind him he gave up drugs, found a wife and found a life. Not in a moment, but over several months, he was transfigured.

Let us promise God that when we are tempted to despair we may be given the grace to know that the true meaning of the Resurrection is not how much I love God – it is how much God loves me. Try it for yourself some time today, when you are quiet and alone. Say to yourself, 'God made me. God doesn't make junk.'

Paul O'Reilly SJ,
Hope in All Things

The Presence of God

Dear Jesus, I come to you today longing for your presence. I desire to love you as you love me. May nothing ever separate me from you.

Freedom

Lord, grant me the grace to be free from the excesses of this life. Let me not get caught up with the desire for wealth. Keep my heart and mind free to love and serve you.

Consciousness

Where do I sense hope, encouragement and growth in my life? By looking back over the past few months, I may be able to see which activities and occasions have produced rich fruit. If I do notice such areas, I will determine to give those areas both time and space in the future.

The Word

God speaks to each of us individually. I listen attentively, to hear what he is saying to me. Read the text a few times, then listen.

(Please turn to the Scripture on the following pages. Inspiration points are there should you need them. When you are ready, return here to continue.)

Conversation

What is stirring in me as I pray? Am I consoled, troubled, left cold? I imagine Jesus standing or sitting at my side, and I share my feelings with him.

Conclusion

Glory be to the Father, and to the Son, and to the Holy Spirit,
As it was in the beginning, is now and ever shall be,
World without end. Amen.

Sunday 12 November
Thirty-second Sunday in Ordinary Time
Matthew 25:1–13

And Jesus said to them, 'Then the kingdom of heaven will be like this. Ten bridesmaids took their lamps and went to meet the bridegroom. Five of them were foolish, and five were wise. When the foolish took their lamps, they took no oil with them; but the wise took flasks of oil with their lamps. As the bridegroom was delayed, all of them became drowsy and slept. But at midnight there was a shout, "Look! Here is the bridegroom! Come out to meet him." Then all those bridesmaids got up and trimmed their lamps. The foolish said to the wise, "Give us some of your oil, for our lamps are going out." But the wise replied, "No! there will not be enough for you and for us; you had better go to the dealers and buy some for yourselves." And while they went to buy it, the bridegroom came, and those who were ready went with him into the wedding banquet; and the door was shut. Later the other bridesmaids came also, saying, "Lord, lord, open to us." But he replied, "Truly I tell you, I do not know you." Keep awake therefore, for you know neither the day nor the hour.'

• This gospel helps us to focus on the here and now. It helps us to learn to live totally in the present, to seek and find God there. If we can do that, then all the rest will take care of itself. Whether the Groom arrives early or late, it will not matter as he has been constantly part of my everyday life.

Monday 13 November
Luke 17:1–6

Jesus said to his disciples, 'Occasions for stumbling are bound to come, but woe to anyone by whom they come! It would be better for you if a millstone were hung around your neck and you were thrown into the sea than for you to cause one of these little ones to stumble. Be on your guard! If another disciple sins, you must rebuke the offender, and if there is repentance, you must forgive. And if the same person sins against you seven times a day, and turns back to you seven times and says, "I repent", you must forgive.'

The apostles said to the Lord, 'Increase our faith!' The Lord replied, 'If you had faith the size of a mustard seed, you could say to this mulberry tree, "Be uprooted and planted in the sea", and it would obey you.'

- Jesus reminds us to be aware of our words, attitudes and actions. Today I have the potential to be a positive or negative influence on others. What will I choose?

Tuesday 14 November
Luke 17:7–10

Jesus said to them, 'Who among you would say to your slave who has just come in from ploughing or tending sheep in the field, "Come here at once and take your place at the table"? Would you not rather say to him, "Prepare supper for me, put on your apron and serve me while I eat and drink; later you may eat and drink"? Do you thank the slave for doing what was commanded? So you also, when you have done all that you were ordered to do, say, "We are worthless slaves; we have done only what we ought to have done!"'

- I reflect on Jesus' teaching. How do I find it? Does it resonate with me or do I find it hard to apply? When I am serving others do I seek rewards? I ask Jesus to teach me how to serve.

Wednesday 15 November
Luke 17:11–19

On the way to Jerusalem Jesus was going through the region between Samaria and Galilee. As he entered a village, ten lepers approached him. Keeping their distance, they called out, saying, 'Jesus, Master, have mercy on us!' When he saw them, he said to them, 'Go and show yourselves to the priests.' And as they went, they were made clean. Then one of them, when he saw that he was healed, turned back, praising God with a loud voice. He prostrated himself at Jesus' feet and thanked him. And he was a Samaritan. Then Jesus asked, 'Were not ten made clean? But the other nine, where are they? Was none of them found to return and give praise to God except this foreigner?' Then he said to him, 'Get up and go on your way; your faith has made you well.'

- Jesus recognised the faith of the leper who saw the source of the goodness he had enjoyed. I see that sometimes my faith is demonstrated in how ready I am to see God at work and to attribute blessings to their source.

Thursday 16 November
Luke 17:20–25

Once Jesus was asked by the Pharisees when the kingdom of God was coming, and he answered, 'The kingdom of God is not coming with things that can be observed; nor will they say, "Look, here it is!" or "There it is!" For, in fact, the kingdom of God is among you.'

Then he said to the disciples, 'The days are coming when you will long to see one of the days of the Son of Man, and you will not see it. They will say to you, "Look there!" or "Look here!" Do not go, do not set off in pursuit. For as the lightning flashes and lights up the sky from one side to the other, so will the Son of Man be in his day. But first he must endure much suffering and be rejected by this generation.'

- The disciples eagerly await the coming of the kingdom. For us, the death and resurrection of Jesus mean that the kingdom is already within our reach: 'Behold, the kingdom of God is among you.' It is already present through the teaching and healing ministry of Jesus.

Friday 17 November
Luke 17:26–37

Then Jesus said, 'Just as it was in the days of Noah, so too it will be in the days of the Son of Man. They were eating and drinking, and marrying and being given in marriage, until the day Noah entered the ark, and the flood came and destroyed all of them. Likewise, just as it was in the days of Lot: they were eating and drinking, buying and selling, planting and building, but on the day that Lot left Sodom, it rained fire and sulphur from heaven and destroyed all of them—it will be like that on the day that the Son of Man is revealed. On that day, anyone on the housetop who has belongings in the house must not come down to take them away; and likewise anyone in the field must not turn back. Remember Lot's wife. Those who try to make their life secure will lose it, but those who lose their life will keep it. I tell you, on that night there will be two in one bed; one will be taken and the other left. There will be two women grinding meal together; one will be taken and the other left.' Then they asked him, 'Where, Lord?' He said to them, 'Where the corpse is, there the vultures will gather.'

- How do I feel about Jesus' words? What things give me security? I spend some time in silence and listen to what Jesus might want to say to me, remembering that I am loved and cherished by God.

Saturday 18 November
Luke 18:1–8

Then Jesus told them a parable about their need to pray always and not to lose heart. He said, 'In a certain city there was a judge who neither feared God nor had respect for people. In that city there was a widow who kept coming to him and saying, "Grant me justice against my opponent." For a while he refused; but later he said to himself, "Though I have no fear of God and no respect for anyone, yet because this widow keeps bothering me, I will grant her justice, so that she may not wear me out by continually coming."' And the Lord said, 'Listen to what the unjust judge says. And will not God grant justice to his chosen ones who cry to him day and night? Will he delay long in helping them? I tell you, he will quickly grant justice to them. And yet, when the Son of Man comes, will he find faith on earth?'

- I think about the difficulties I might be facing at this time. Have I lost hope that God will hear me? Can I bring them to God now, knowing that he is attentive to what I have to share? Do I feel I can trust him?

The Thirty-third Week in Ordinary Time
19–25 November

Something to think and pray about each day this week:

The Prayer of the Frog is a book title that caught my attention. It's a collection of stories, messages and jokes from different religious traditions. The title story is about Brother Bruno and the bullfrog that disturbed him one night when he was at prayer. He tried to ignore the croaking, but he couldn't. So he shouted out the window, 'Quiet, I'm trying to pray!'

Since Bruno was a saint, the frog and every other living creature within earshot instantly held their peace. But then Bruno heard an inner voice telling him that maybe God liked the frog's croaking as much as his prayers. 'Nonsense,' said the saint, 'how could God like that sound?'

'Then why do you think,' asked the voice, 'that God invented it?'

This unsettled Bruno, so he thought he'd do some research. He called out once again from his window but this time he shouted 'sing!' The bullfrog started croaking at once, with all the frogs in the vicinity as a backing group. But as Bruno listened this time, he discovered, so the story tells us, that if he stopped resisting them, they helped to enrich the silence of the night. The story ends with the words, 'for the first time in his life he understood what it meant to pray'.

The message that I get is that prayer is more than the practice of chanting or reciting words, however profound the words may be. It is about paying attention to the world we're living in and everything it contains, paying attention to the presence and power of creation in all kinds of sights and sounds.

Denis Tuohy,
Streets and Secret Places: Reflections of a News Reporter

The Presence of God

'Come to me, all you who are weary and are carrying heavy burdens, and I will give you rest' (Matthew 11:28). Here I am, Lord. I come to seek your presence. I long for your healing power.

Freedom

God is not foreign to my freedom. The Spirit breathes life into my most intimate desires, gently nudging me towards all that is good. I ask for the grace to let myself be enfolded by the Spirit.

Consciousness

I remind myself that I am in the presence of the Lord. I will take refuge in his loving heart. He is my strength in times of weakness. He is my comforter in times of sorrow.

The Word

I take my time to read the word of God slowly, a few times, allowing myself to dwell on anything that strikes me.

(Please turn to the Scripture on the following pages. Inspiration points are there, should you need them. When you are ready, return here to continue.)

Conversation

Jesus, you always welcomed little children when you walked on this earth. Teach me to have a childlike trust in you. Teach me to live in the knowledge that you will never abandon me.

Conclusion

Glory be to the Father, and to the Son, and to the Holy Spirit,
As it was in the beginning, is now and ever shall be,
World without end. Amen.

Sunday 19 November
Thirty-third Sunday in Ordinary Time
Matthew 25:14–30

Jesus said, 'For it is as if a man, going on a journey, summoned his slaves and entrusted his property to them; to one he gave five talents, to another two, to another one, to each according to his ability. Then he went away. The one who had received the five talents went off at once and traded with them, and made five more talents. In the same way, the one who had the two talents made two more talents. But the one who had received the one talent went off and dug a hole in the ground and hid his master's money. After a long time the master of those slaves came and settled accounts with them. Then the one who had received the five talents came forward, bringing five more talents, saying, "Master, you handed over to me five talents; see, I have made five more talents." His master said to him, "Well done, good and trustworthy slave; you have been trustworthy in a few things, I will put you in charge of many things; enter into the joy of your master." And the one with the two talents also came forward, saying, "Master, you handed over to me two talents; see, I have made two more talents." His master said to him, "Well done, good and trustworthy slave; you have been trustworthy in a few things, I will put you in charge of many things; enter into the joy of your master." Then the one who had received the one talent also came forward, saying, "Master, I knew that you were a harsh man, reaping where you did not sow, and gathering where you did not scatter seed; so I was afraid, and I went and hid your talent in the ground. Here you have what is yours." But his master replied, "You wicked and lazy slave! You knew, did you, that I reap where I did not sow, and gather where I did not scatter? Then you ought to have invested my money with the bankers, and on my return I would have received what was my own with interest. So take the talent from him, and give it to the one with the ten talents. For to all those who have, more will be given, and they will have an abundance; but from those who have nothing, even what they have will be taken away. As for this worthless slave, throw him into the outer darkness, where there will be weeping and gnashing of teeth."'

- Do I risk the many things and qualities I have been given for the growth of the kingdom, or I am happy with what I have, making sure

I do not lose it, happy enough with a respectable existence? What will the master tell me when he calls me to account?

Monday 20 November
Luke 18:35–43

As he approached Jericho, a blind man was sitting by the roadside begging. When he heard a crowd going by, he asked what was happening. They told him, 'Jesus of Nazareth is passing by.' Then he shouted, 'Jesus, Son of David, have mercy on me!' Those who were in front sternly ordered him to be quiet; but he shouted even more loudly, 'Son of David, have mercy on me!' Jesus stood still and ordered the man to be brought to him; and when he came near, he asked him, 'What do you want me to do for you?' He said, 'Lord, let me see again.' Jesus said to him, 'Receive your sight; your faith has saved you.' Immediately he regained his sight and followed him, glorifying God; and all the people, when they saw it, praised God.

• If the man had not kept calling out, Jesus might not have heard him and might have passed for ever out of his life. How often does that happen to me? Is there something I need to call out to Jesus for today?

Tuesday 21 November
Luke 19:1–10

He entered Jericho and was passing through it. A man was there named Zacchaeus; he was a chief tax-collector and was rich. He was trying to see who Jesus was, but on account of the crowd he could not, because he was short in stature. So he ran ahead and climbed a sycamore tree to see him, because he was going to pass that way. When Jesus came to the place, he looked up and said to him, 'Zacchaeus, hurry and come down; for I must stay at your house today.' So he hurried down and was happy to welcome him. All who saw it began to grumble and said, 'He has gone to be the guest of one who is a sinner.' Zacchaeus stood there and said to the Lord, 'Look, half of my possessions, Lord, I will give to the poor; and if I have defrauded anyone of anything, I will pay back four times as much.' Then Jesus said to him, 'Today salvation has come to this house, because he too is a son of Abraham. For the Son of Man came to seek out and to save the lost.'

- Lord, like Zacchaeus, I hear you calling me by name and I gladly welcome you to my house today. Help me become more aware that I am, at all times and in all places, in your loving presence. Help me to realise that the divine is in me and in every person that I meet, and this includes those whom I may find difficult.

Wednesday 22 November
Luke 19:11–28

As they were listening to this, he went on to tell a parable, because he was near Jerusalem, and because they supposed that the kingdom of God was to appear immediately. So he said, 'A nobleman went to a distant country to get royal power for himself and then return. He summoned ten of his slaves, and gave them ten pounds, and said to them, "Do business with these until I come back." But the citizens of his country hated him and sent a delegation after him, saying, "We do not want this man to rule over us." When he returned, having received royal power, he ordered these slaves, to whom he had given the money, to be summoned so that he might find out what they had gained by trading. The first came forward and said, "Lord, your pound has made ten more pounds." He said to him, "Well done, good slave! Because you have been trustworthy in a very small thing, take charge of ten cities." Then the second came, saying, "Lord, your pound has made five pounds." He said to him, "And you, rule over five cities." Then the other came, saying, "Lord, here is your pound. I wrapped it up in a piece of cloth, for I was afraid of you, because you are a harsh man; you take what you did not deposit, and reap what you did not sow." He said to him, "I will judge you by your own words, you wicked slave! You knew, did you, that I was a harsh man, taking what I did not deposit and reaping what I did not sow? Why then did you not put my money into the bank? Then when I returned, I could have collected it with interest." He said to the bystanders, "Take the pound from him and give it to the one who has ten pounds." (And they said to him, "Lord, he has ten pounds!") "I tell you, to all those who have, more will be given; but from those who have nothing, even what they have will be taken away. But as for these enemies of mine who did not want me to be king over them – bring them here and slaughter them in my presence."'

- The third slave in the story was paralysed by his fear; if I can recognise anything of his hesitation in myself, I ask God for the courage I need.

Thursday 23 November
Luke 19:41–44

As he came near and saw the city, he wept over it, saying, 'If you, even you, had only recognised on this day the things that make for peace! But now they are hidden from your eyes. Indeed, the days will come upon you, when your enemies will set up ramparts around you and surround you, and hem you in on every side. They will crush you to the ground, you and your children within you, and they will not leave within you one stone upon another; because you did not recognise the time of your visitation from God.'

- Images of threat and destruction can haunt and immobilise us if we neglect to see that there is always an alternative, an offer of life. If these words of Jesus appear to be grim, I listen again to notice what he is longing for.

Friday 24 November
Luke 19:45–48

Then he entered the temple and began to drive out those who were selling things there; and he said, 'It is written,

> "My house shall be a house of prayer";
>   but you have made it a den of robbers.'

Every day he was teaching in the temple. The chief priests, the scribes, and the leaders of the people kept looking for a way to kill him; but they did not find anything they could do, for all the people were spellbound by what they heard.

- How could people who were dedicated to the observance of God's law get it so wrong? Our Church is a church of sinners, for sinners and by sinners. And we are greatly, greatly loved by the Abba God!

Saturday 25 November
Luke 20:27–40

Some Sadducees, those who say there is no resurrection, came to him and asked him a question, 'Teacher, Moses wrote for us that if a man's brother dies, leaving a wife but no children, the man shall marry the widow and raise up children for his brother. Now there were seven brothers; the first married, and died childless; then the second and the third married her, and so in the same way all seven died childless. Finally the woman also died. In the resurrection, therefore, whose wife will the woman be? For the seven had married her.'

Jesus said to them, 'Those who belong to this age marry and are given in marriage; but those who are considered worthy of a place in that age and in the resurrection from the dead neither marry nor are given in marriage. Indeed they cannot die any more, because they are like angels and are children of God, being children of the resurrection. And the fact that the dead are raised Moses himself showed, in the story about the bush, where he speaks of the Lord as the God of Abraham, the God of Isaac, and the God of Jacob. Now he is God not of the dead, but of the living; for to him all of them are alive.' Then some of the scribes answered, 'Teacher, you have spoken well.' For they no longer dared to ask him another question.

- Do I see the people in my life, and those with whom I am in relationship, as equals? And that they are all equally loved by God? Do I treat them as such?

The Thirty-fourth Week in Ordinary Time
26 November–2 December 2023

Something to think and pray about each day this week:

Jesus had a dream. His dream was God's dream. He dreamt that all people would live together as one family, God's family. Jesus dreamt of a world where no one would be hungry and have nothing to eat, where no one would be thirsty and have nothing to drink, where no one would be naked and have nothing to wear, where no one would be sick and have no one to visit them, where no one would be in prison and rejected by their community (Matthew 25). Jesus dreamt that all people would love each other, care for each other, share with each other and respect each other. What unites us as Christians is that we share this dream of Jesus.

To follow Jesus is to announce to the world that we have committed our lives to building this dream for all of us to live together as God's precious people.

God's dream, God's hope for our world, then, is that we might love one another as God has loved us, by reaching out to those who suffer: the poor, the homeless, the lonely, the sick, the rejected and the unwanted. Jesus came to make God's dream for our world a reality. To transform our world from where it is today to where God would like it to be tomorrow requires a revolution. That revolution is the community of Christians, which Jesus called the Kingdom of God.

John Scally,
Waiting in Joy

The Presence of God

I pause for a moment and think of the love and the grace that God showers on me. I am created in the image and likeness of God; I am God's dwelling place.

Freedom

Lord, you granted me the great gift of freedom. In these times, O Lord, grant that I may be free from any form of racism or intolerance. Remind me that we are all equal in your loving eyes.

Consciousness

Knowing that God loves me unconditionally, I can afford to be honest about how I am. How has the day been, and how do I feel now? I share my feelings openly with the Lord.

The Word

I take my time to read the word of God slowly, a few times, allowing myself to dwell on anything that strikes me.

(Please turn to the Scripture on the following pages. Inspiration points are there, should you need them. When you are ready, return here to continue.)

Conversation

Sometimes I wonder what I might say if I were to meet you in person, Lord. I think I might say, 'Thank you' because you are always there for me.

Conclusion

I thank God for these moments we have spent together and for any insights I have been given concerning the text.

Sunday 26 November
Our Lord Jesus Christ, King of the Universe
Matthew 25:31–46

Jesus said to them, 'When the Son of Man comes in his glory, and all the angels with him, then he will sit on the throne of his glory. All the nations will be gathered before him, and he will separate people one from another as a shepherd separates the sheep from the goats, and he will put the sheep at his right hand and the goats at the left. Then the king will say to those at his right hand, "Come, you that are blessed by my Father, inherit the kingdom prepared for you from the foundation of the world; for I was hungry and you gave me food, I was thirsty and you gave me something to drink, I was a stranger and you welcomed me, I was naked and you gave me clothing, I was sick and you took care of me, I was in prison and you visited me." Then the righteous will answer him, "Lord, when was it that we saw you hungry and gave you food, or thirsty and gave you something to drink? And when was it that we saw you a stranger and welcomed you, or naked and gave you clothing? And when was it that we saw you sick or in prison and visited you?" And the king will answer them, "Truly I tell you, just as you did it to one of the least of these who are members of my family, you did it to me." Then he will say to those at his left hand, "You that are accursed, depart from me into the eternal fire prepared for the devil and his angels; for I was hungry and you gave me no food, I was thirsty and you gave me nothing to drink, I was a stranger and you did not welcome me, naked and you did not give me clothing, sick and in prison and you did not visit me." Then they also will answer, "Lord, when was it that we saw you hungry or thirsty or a stranger or naked or sick or in prison, and did not take care of you?" Then he will answer them, "Truly I tell you, just as you did not do it to one of the least of these, you did not do it to me." And these will go away into eternal punishment, but the righteous into eternal life.'

- Jesus is very clear about the criteria for knowing whether I am a sheep or a goat – how have I loved, how have I cared for others, especially the poor, the needy and the marginalised? Looking back over the last day or week, I recall times when I have acted as Jesus asked, and give thanks.

Monday 27 November
Luke 21:1–4

He looked up and saw rich people putting their gifts into the treasury; he also saw a poor widow put in two small copper coins. He said, 'Truly I tell you, this poor widow has put in more than all of them; for all of them have contributed out of their abundance, but she out of her poverty has put in all she had to live on.'

- Preaching on this, Pope Francis said: 'Faced with the needs of others, we are called to deprive ourselves of essential things, not only the superfluous; we are called to give the necessary time, not only what remains extra; we are called to give immediately and unconditionally some of our talent, not after using it for our own purposes or our own group.'

Tuesday 28 November
Luke 21:5–11

When some were speaking about the temple, how it was adorned with beautiful stones and gifts dedicated to God, he said, 'As for these things that you see, the days will come when not one stone will be left upon another; all will be thrown down.'

They asked him, 'Teacher, when will this be, and what will be the sign that this is about to take place?' And he said, 'Beware that you are not led astray; for many will come in my name and say, "I am he!" and, "The time is near!" Do not go after them.

'When you hear of wars and insurrections, do not be terrified; for these things must take place first, but the end will not follow immediately.' Then he said to them, 'Nation will rise against nation, and kingdom against kingdom; there will be great earthquakes, and in various places famines and plagues; and there will be dreadful portents and great signs from heaven.'

- In our times, the destruction of the environment brings us suffering. Does this give birth only to desolation, or to compassion and a practical response? And do we believe that nature can be remade by the God who first created it?

Wednesday 29 November
Luke 21:12–19

Jesus said to his disciples, 'But before all this occurs, they will arrest you and persecute you; they will hand you over to synagogues and prisons, and you will be brought before kings and governors because of my name. This will give you an opportunity to testify. So make up your minds not to prepare your defence in advance; for I will give you words and a wisdom that none of your opponents will be able to withstand or contradict. You will be betrayed even by parents and brothers, by relatives and friends; and they will put some of you to death. You will be hated by all because of my name. But not a hair of your head will perish. By your endurance you will gain your souls.'

• 'You will be betrayed', even by those close to you. When relationships fail, I know the truth of this warning. But do I believe that God is very close to me then, watching over 'the hair of my head'? Does this help me to retain my equilibrium and integrity?

Thursday 30 November
St Andrew, Apostle
Matthew 4:18–22

As he walked by the Sea of Galilee, he saw two brothers, Simon, who is called Peter, and Andrew his brother, casting a net into the lake – for they were fishermen. And he said to them, 'Follow me, and I will make you fish for people.' Immediately they left their nets and followed him. As he went from there, he saw two other brothers, James son of Zebedee and his brother John, in the boat with their father Zebedee, mending their nets, and he called them. Immediately they left the boat and their father, and followed him.

• This is Matthew's account of the calling of the first four disciples. 'Come follow me and I will make you fishers of people,' Jesus says, and they drop everything and go after him. They leave behind all their security and means of livelihood and even their family. They follow Jesus in complete trust, unaware of where he is going or what will happen to them. Following Jesus is a liberating experience.

Friday 1 December
Luke 21:29–33

Then he told them a parable: 'Look at the fig tree and all the trees; as soon as they sprout leaves you can see for yourselves and know that summer is already near. So also, when you see these things taking place, you know that the kingdom of God is near. Truly I tell you, this generation will not pass away until all things have taken place. Heaven and earth will pass away, but my words will not pass away.'

- What are the signs of life and of hope that I see around me? How often do I take time out to see and savour these signs of hope in my life? What words of Jesus give me life and give me hope?
- I ask Jesus to help me focus on these life signs, these hope signs.

Saturday 2 December
Luke 21:34–36

Jesus said to his disciples, 'Be on guard so that your hearts are not weighed down with dissipation and drunkenness and the worries of this life, and that day does not catch you unexpectedly, like a trap. For it will come upon all who live on the face of the whole earth. Be alert at all times, praying that you may have the strength to escape all these things that will take place, and to stand before the Son of Man.'

- Today is the last day of the liturgical year – tomorrow being the first Sunday of Advent. And the cycle of the liturgical year begins again. In this text Jesus reminds us of the passing aspect of life. In this way he urges us not to be caught unawares and to pay attention to fulfilling our desires for good.

Books on Ignatian Spirituality

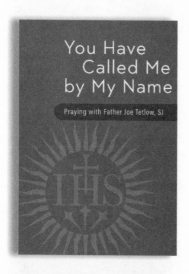

YOU HAVE CALLED ME BY MY NAME
Praying with Father Joe Tetlow, SJ

FATHER JOE TETLOW, SJ

St. Ignatius encouraged people to nurture their relationship with the Creator to the point of speaking "as one friend to another." In *You Have Called Me by My Name*, Father Joe Tetlow shares original prayers that have emerged from his decades-long friendship with God.

PB | 978-0-8294-5270-9

HEARTS ON FIRE
Praying with Jesuits

MICHAEL HARTER, SJ

Discover the rich tradition of Ignatian prayer in *Hearts on Fire: Praying with Jesuits*, compiled by Michael Harter, SJ. The book includes hundreds of prayers, many written by the most illustrious Jesuits, giving eloquent voice to Ignatian spirituality.

PB | 978-0-8294-2120-0

Books on Ignatian Spirituality

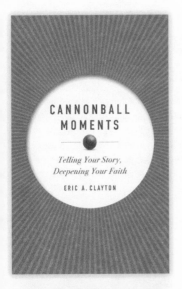

CANNONBALL MOMENTS
Telling Your Story, Deepening Your Faith

ERIC A. CLAYTON

By applying Ignatian principles of inner work and self-reflection to storytelling, Eric Clayton offers guidance on how to recognize the opportunities our "cannonball moments" offer, notice details in our daily lives, to develop an attitude of healthy indifference in matters great and small, and respond to feelings of restlessness with clarity and focus.

PB | 978-0-8294-5436-9

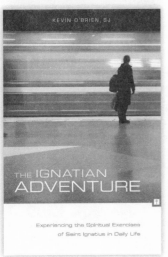

THE IGNATIAN ADVENTURE
Embracing the Spiritual Exercises of Saint Ignatius in Daily Life

KEVIN O'BRIEN, SJ

There is no better guide than St. Ignatius Loyola if one desires to discover how faith and everyday life can thrive together. In *The Ignatian Adventure*, Kevin O'Brien, SJ, follows St. Ignatius's lead and offers today's time-strapped individual a unique way of "making" the Spiritual Exercises in daily life.

PB | 978-0-8294-3577-1

Available in English and in Spanish.

To Order:
Call **800.621.1008,** visit **store.loyolapress.com,** or visit your local bookseller.

LOYOLAPRESS.
A JESUIT MINISTRY

Books by Julianne Stanz

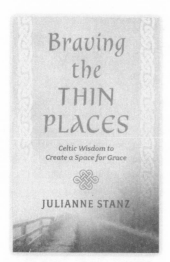

BRAVING THE THIN PLACES
Celtic Wisdom to Create a Space for Grace

JULIANNE STANZ

In *Braving the Thin Places*, author Julianne Stanz draws on her Irish-Celtic heritage, helping us explore times and holy places of transformation. Inspired by faith and guided by spiritual practices, we can experience each thin place as a point of departure on a sacred journey to a truer understanding of who we are meant to be.

PB | 978-0-8294-4886-3

START WITH JESUS
How Everyday Disciples Will Renew the Church

JULIANNE STANZ

Start with Jesus is an essential resource for parish decision-makers and thought-leaders, but its true strength lies in its value for the countless Catholics longing for peace, healing, and hope in the context of our parish communities.

PB | 978-0-8294-4884-9

Books by Becky Eldredge

THE INNER CHAPEL
Embracing the Promises of God

BECKY ELDREDGE

In *The Inner Chapel*, Becky Eldredge offers readers down-to-earth stories, prayer experiences to try, and enthusiastic encouragement for spiritual growth and a deeper friendship with God. The Inner Chapel will inspire individuals but also provide excellent material for small groups and people going on retreat.

PB | 978-0-8294-4933-4

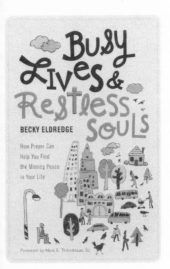

BUSY LIVES & RESTLESS SOULS
How Prayer Can Help You Find the Missing Peace in Your Life

BECKY ELDREDGE

In *Busy Lives & Restless Souls*, author and spiritual director Becky Eldredge interprets principles of Ignatian spirituality in a fresh way to equip us with prayer tools that are accessible and practical within the relentless realities of our daily routines.

PB | 978-0-8294-4495-7

To Order:
Call **800.621.1008,** visit **store.loyolapress.com,**
or visit your local bookseller.

LOYOLAPRESS.
A JESUIT MINISTRY